ADAPTING *THE WIZARD OF OZ*

ADAPTING
THE WIZARD OF OZ

Musical Versions from Baum
to MGM and Beyond

Edited by Danielle Birkett
and
Dominic McHugh

OXFORD
UNIVERSITY PRESS

Oxford University Press is a department of the University of Oxford. It furthers
the University's objective of excellence in research, scholarship, and education
by publishing worldwide. Oxford is a registered trade mark of Oxford University
Press in the UK and certain other countries.

Published in the United States of America by Oxford University Press
198 Madison Avenue, New York, NY 10016, United States of America.

Library of Congress Cataloging-in-Publication Data
Names: Birkett, Danielle, 1989– | McHugh, Dominic.
Title: Adapting the Wizard of Oz : musical versions from Baum to MGM and
beyond / edited by Danielle Birkett and Dominic McHugh.
Description: New York, NY : Oxford University Press, [2019] | Includes
bibliographical references and index.
Identifiers: LCCN 2018013226 | ISBN 9780190663179 (hardcover) |
ISBN 9780190663186 (pbk.) | ISBN 9780190663216 (companion website)
Subjects: LCSH: Oz (Imaginary place)—Songs and music—History and criticism. |
Musicals—United States—History and criticism. |
Musical films—United States—History and criticism. |
Motion picture music—United States—History and criticism. |
Baum, L. Frank (Lyman Frank), 1856–1919. Wizard of Oz. |
Wizard of Oz (Motion picture : 1939)
Classification: LCC ML1711.9 .A33 2018 | DDC 782.1/4—dc23
LC record available at https://lccn.loc.gov/2018013226

9 8 7 6 5 4 3 2 1

Paperback printed by Webcom, Inc., Canada
Hardback printed by Bridgeport National Bindery, Inc., United States of America

CONTENTS

ACKNOWLEDGMENTS

The Wizard of Oz has always been one of our favorite movie musicals. Several years ago we began to discuss the possibility of writing a new volume that celebrated our shared interest in this iconic film and offered a new academic discourse. We quickly agreed that gathering a range of writers from different perspectives would be the most effective strategy to produce a volume that considered early adaptations of Baum's novel, the MGM film, and its more recent reinterpretations. Producing such a broad volume would therefore not have been possible without the expertise of nine contributors: Jonas Westover, Benjamin Sears, Laura Lynn Broadhurst, Nathan Platte, Claudia Funder, Hannah Robbins, Ryan Bunch, Paul Laird, and Walter Frisch. We are extremely grateful for their commitment to the volume and their enthusiasm to collaborate with us: their hard work has made the editing process a delight.

We also owe a great debt of gratitude to Norm Hirschy at Oxford University Press, who has been tremendously supportive of the project from the beginning; his choice of several anonymous reviewers has also been significant in transforming the volume. Subsequently, particular thanks must go to these individuals: their detailed comments and guidance have made an important difference to the book and we are very grateful for their sound advice. Lauralee Yeary at OUP must also be thanked for her diligence in making this book a reality.

Finally, we also extend warmest thanks to colleagues, friends, and family who have given precious feedback and are a continual source of encouragement. Particular thanks go to Phil Birkett and Lawrence Broomfield for their daily patience and support, and to our parents Geoff and Merlyn Brown and Gilly and Larry McHugh for nurturing our love of music from an early age. We are so grateful for their ongoing support.

CONTRIBUTORS

Danielle Birkett, Lecturer in Music, Northern Regional College

Laura Lynn Broadhurst, PhD Candidate in Musicology, Rutgers University

Ryan Bunch, Artist Associate, Rutgers University-Camden

Walter Frisch, H. Harold Gumm/Harry and Albert von Tilzer Professor of Music, Columbia University

Claudia Funder, Director, Swing Patrol

Paul R. Laird, Professor of Musicology, University of Kansas

Dominic McHugh, Senior Lecturer in Musicology and Director of Performance, University of Sheffield

Nathan Platte, Associate Professor of Musicology, University of Iowa

Hannah Robbins, Frederick Loewe Research Associate, University of Sheffield

Benjamin Sears, Professional Singer and Independent Scholar

Jonas Westover, University of Minnesota

INTRODUCTION—RAINBOW REFLECTIONS

THE WIZARD OF OZ AS A MUSICAL

Danielle Birkett and Dominic McHugh

More than a century after its first publication, L. Frank Baum's *The Wonderful Wizard of Oz* has proved to be one of America's most enduring literary masterpieces. Although it is framed as a children's novel, the book is widely acknowledged to have transcended such a modest status. It has been called "America's greatest and best-loved fairy tale,"[1] pulling away from its European counterparts with its series of unusual landscapes and magical characters. Yet it also has wider implications as a philosophical text for all ages, with allegorical references to American society at the time of writing. Jack Zipes, among other scholars, explains how the book depicts a "socialist utopia" through Munchkinland.[2] Nobody wants for anything; everyone has his or her role, to provide food or services; everyone has somewhere to live; and there is broad equality. This vision for a place where society shares its riches is presented in stark relief to the Emerald City. Through the Wizard's apparent powers, almost anything can happen there; yet it transpires that everything is fake in the Emerald City. It is not even truly green: the Wizard forces visitors to don emerald-tinted spectacles upon their entrance and these are fixed to their faces so that he can control everyone's view of his world. Domination, currency, and manipulation define the Wizard's domain, and the possibility of obtaining happiness through financial transaction (money is visible in Oz, unlike in Munchkinland) seems empty after the gentle beneficence of the Munchkins. The role of technology in the maintenance of the Wizard's realm represents the threat of capitalism to the Munchkins' socialist paradise.

Baum's pro-socialist message is perhaps ironic, given his own entrepreneurial predilections: for his many innovations and businesses, he is closely associated with the character of the Wizard. In the next two decades, he wrote a series of further books about the Land of Oz, expanding the characters and their experiences. Yet as important as the original novel remains, it is arguably as a musical that the story has achieved the greatest cultural resonance, with adaptations ranging from Baum's own early stage version to the celebrated 1939 MGM film starring Judy Garland in an iconic performance, and from the African American reinterpretation *The Wiz* to the more recent blockbuster *Wicked*. The musical genre's capacity to shape identity and heighten experience and emotion through song has repeatedly emerged as the perfect lens through which to view Baum's story. This phenomenon is the focus of the present volume.

In the opening chapter, Jonas Westover addresses the earliest stage adaptation of Baum's book. The first musical comedy in 1902–1903 generated huge excitement and inspired Baum to continue with his second novel in 1904. The following two decades were full of interchange between novels, stage productions, and films, with each iteration fueling interest in the world of Oz and its fantastic characters. Westover's chapter examines Baum's first production, focusing in particular on the relationship between the stars chosen for the roles and the talents (dancing, singing, comedy, drama) they brought to the version they starred in. For example, Montgomery and Stone, a comedy duo popular in vaudeville and on Broadway, were the stars of the show, thus the Tin Woodsman and the Scarecrow were the focus. Westover proves that the key to putting the novel on the stage with success was by finding clever ways to allow star players to shine and showcase their talents while maintaining some element of the narrative.

It is this formula that would, in part, lead directly to the powerful impact of the 1939 film musical. Taking over this theme, Ben Sears's chapter (Chapter 2) offers insights into the adaptation of the original novel to a full-length feature film, addressing the issues of changing medium from stage to screen. It looks at alterations made to the story, including the deletion of episodes in the book for the film, and changes in (and deletions of) characters. Comparing the novel to the final screenplay, as well as exploring the stages of collaborative screenwriting that brought about the version seen in the film, Sears identifies the differences and similarities between the novel and the film by which the story is best known today.

The film itself provides the focus for the next few chapters, as befits its status as one of the greatest movies of all time. Three case studies address elements of the film that have not previously received much attention: the songs, the underscore, and the choreography. Laura Lynn Broadhurst's contribution (Chapter 3) describes the assembly-line process by which film musical scores were created during the studio era, shedding light on the culture in which Harold Arlen and E. Y. Harburg wrote their extraordinary songs. Attention then shifts to the specifics of the creation of the musical numbers, using primary sources to consider the evolution of each song from conception through orchestration. This central section of the chapter therefore provides both extensive information on the collaborative method of Arlen and Harburg and also a commentary on their musical contribution to *The Wizard of Oz*. Finally, the discussion briefly considers post-orchestration developments, including how the songs were prerecorded and then shot to playback, and edited or cut for the final film.

Complementing Broadhurst's work, Nathan Platte offers an in-depth exploration of the film's underscore (Chapter 4). Contemporary discourse on the musical soundtrack emphasized its role in underscoring—literally and figuratively—the film's extraordinary content, often stressing its "special" and "effect"-like qualities. Studio publicists plugged the score's idiosyncratic length and complexity, and composer Herbert Stothart also drew connections between music and elaborate illusions, stating: "Music and sound must be highly imaginative, unreal while super-realistic. Here sounds must stir the fantasy. . . . The difficulty is to blend music and the special sound effects." Elsewhere Stothart averred that the striking hues of Technicolor warranted special musical treatment. Drawing on studio records, contemporary newspaper accounts, the conductor's score, and the film itself, Platte contemplates musical gestures in the underscore that work *as* and *in tandem with* special effects.

For her part, Claudia Funder delves into one of the film's most overlooked elements: the choreography (Chapter 5). As she reveals, the film's two most significant dance moments were cut before release, namely, the Scarecrow's dance to "If I Only Had a Brain" and the production number "The Jitterbug." Funder offers insights into these two dances and why they were cut, but she also explores the culture of the Hollywood musical at the time, where—despite the popularity of the Astaire-Rogers and Busby Berkeley films—it was common for the choreographer not to be credited, and choreography had little formal status. She also looks at other dance aspects of the film, such as Dorothy's skipping down the Yellow Brick Road, reminding us of how integral movement is to the film even after the deletion of the main dance moments.

After these case studies, the volume shifts attention to the legacy of the film. Danielle Birkett's chapter (Chapter 6) underlines the fact that the movie was made for prestige rather than to make money and that on its initial release it achieved neither a profit nor uniform popularity. Birkett examines the studio's approach to marketing the film and points to key topics in its critical reception, such as attitudes to casting and technology. A rave review in the *New York Times* recognized the film's special qualities, but many other reviewers were less enthusiastic, including Noel Langley, one of the credited screenwriters, who hated the movie when he saw it. It was only in the mid-1950s, when Garland's career was fully established and the film was rereleased, that it started to be acknowledged as a landmark in the movie musical genre. Its debut on television in 1956, introduced by Bert Lahr and Liza Minnelli, reached a reported 45 million viewers, and *Oz* started to achieve wider cultural momentum.

Hannah Robbins homes in on a particular manifestation of the story's cultural importance in her chapter on the film's queer reception (Chapter 7). Using insights from personal discourses and queer theory, she appraises how *The Wizard of Oz* facilitates individual assimilation and celebrates nonnormative identities for generations of audiences. Associations between "Over the Rainbow," Judy Garland's star persona, the phrase "friends of Dorothy," and the Rainbow Flag have made the film important to the queer community; this has often been intensified by a perceived "queer aesthetic" in the making of the film. Both in and beyond the movie, *Oz* has come to represent a site of hope, friendship, and equality for many queer audiences.

After the film, the story has frequently been seen on stage in a variety of guises. Dominic McHugh's chapter (Chapter 8) focuses on three key adaptations of the MGM movie, each of which had its innovations and problems. The 1942 version presented by the St. Louis Municipal Opera used the movie's score (including the cut number "The Jitterbug") but provided an entirely new script that reduced the piece almost to a pantomime. In 1987, the Royal Shakespeare Company returned to the movie for inspiration, adopting most of the screenplay, songs, and even the underscore; but the physical production was firmly rooted in the 1980s and did little to acknowledge the movie. More recently, Andrew Lloyd Webber reunited with his most famous collaborator, Tim Rice, to provide several songs for a new adaptation of the movie, blending new and familiar material. Arguably, none of these adaptations quite resolved how to put the movie on stage, but they demonstrate the continuing appeal of the story to new generations.

While the Muny version was still popular, in the 1970s a fresh take on the story was presented in the form of *The Wiz*. Ryan Bunch's chapter (Chapter 9) analyzes this revolutionary African American adaptation, which rejects the whiteness of *Oz* as an American myth. Exploring both the 1975 stage production and the 1978 film adaptation of *The Wiz,* Bunch outlines how the *Wizard of Oz* story is reinvented as an urban, contemporary narrative of mobility informed by the African American and pan-African histories of diaspora and migration. At the same time, by examining the musical's production history, content, and reception, Bunch also shows *The Wiz* to be adaptable in its ability to speak to multiple, fluid, and intersectional identities. Promoted as the "Super Soul Musical" version of *The Wizard of Oz, The Wiz* engaged with authenticating images and discourses of African American representation that were current in the 1970s, but it sustained broad appeal beyond a single demographic, resulting in an intriguing performance and reception history.

Almost forty years after *The Wiz*'s triumphant debut on Broadway, Stephen Schwartz struck gold with a new *Oz* musical. *Wicked* was adapted from Gregory Maguire's novel of the same name and retold the story of *The Wizard of Oz* from the perspective of the Wicked Witch. But despite their new interpretation of the familiar tale, the show's creators wanted to include as many resonances as possible from the famed MGM film, a crusade that took them into difficult legal waters resulting in unwelcome changes to the show, courtesy of lawyers at Universal Pictures, the show's principal producer. Paul Laird's chapter (Chapter 10) considers how Stephen Schwartz and Winnie Holzman, the writers of *Wicked*, appropriated narrative and musical aspects of Baum's original book and the 1939 film, where they ran into problems in doing so, and how some of those problems were solved.

In the final chapter (Chapter 11), Walter Frisch reflects on how the songs from the MGM movie have resonated in different performances, times, and places. Of particular importance is the use of "Over the Rainbow"—a song that was almost cut from the film before its release—at times of emotional vulnerability, such as Ariana Grande's performance after the Manchester bombings in 2017, released as a charity single. More controversially, sales of "Ding-Dong! The Witch Is Dead" in the United Kingdom rose sharply after the death of Margaret Thatcher in 2013. Frisch explores how the songs generally, and "Rainbow" in particular, have gone beyond their original dramatic context to form new meanings and associations.

In January 2015, a study at Northwestern University declared *The Wizard of Oz* to be the most culturally significant film in history, due to the number of times it is referenced in other films (565; the original *Star Wars* film came second with 297 references).[3] It is the most-viewed film in television history and was voted favorite film of the twentieth century in a *People* magazine poll.[4] In 2014, the seventy-fifth anniversary of the movie was marked by the international release of a new 3D rendering. The story has also been reinterpreted by The Muppets (2005) and Tom and Jerry (2011), and in a Japanese animated version (1982); more recently, Disney's *Oz the Great and Powerful* (2015) offered another retelling. Yet its cultural power has always been at its greatest in musical versions, from MGM to *Wicked*. Delving into archives, trawling through newspaper articles, and exploiting cultural theory, the eleven contributors to this book examine and celebrate that magical legacy, taking readers, like Dorothy before them, over the rainbow and into the Land of Oz.

Notes

1. Frank J. Evina, *The Wizard of Oz: An American Fairy Tale*, Library of Congress exhibition website (2000), www.loc.gov/exhibits/oz/. accessed October 10, 2017.
2. Jack Zipes, "Introduction" to *The Wizard of Oz and Other Wonderful Books of Oz*, Penguin Classics Deluxe Edition (New York: Penguin, 2012).
3. Max Wasserman, Xiao Han T. Zeng, and Luís A. N. Amaral, "Cross-evaluation of Metrics to Estimate the Significance of Creative Works," *Proceedings of the National Academy of Sciences of the United States of America* 112, no. 5 (2015): 1281–1286.
4. Evina, *The Wizard of Oz*, https://www.loc.gov/exhibits/oz/ozsect2.html, accessed October 11, 2017.

1

"STARRING MONTGOMERY AND STONE!"

THE WIZARD OF OZ MUSICAL EXTRAVAGANZA (1902) AND THE BIRTH OF A BRAND

Jonas Westover

For many fans of *The Wizard of Oz*, the story begins with the 1939 movie. Its immense popularity was due in part to its excellent music and lyrics, the visual sepia and Technicolor display, and, of course, the impressive performances. And among the leading players, it would be difficult to draw attention away from Judy Garland's portrayal of young Dorothy Gale and her adventures. Her performance of "Over the Rainbow" has become one of the most iconic moments in film history, simultaneously displaying Dorothy's longing, vulnerability, and hope for the future. In the twenty-first century, however, it is difficult to imagine anyone other than Dorothy at the center of the story; Garland was already a major Hollywood star when she made the movie, and her character's journey is the central element of the narrative. In this way, the film's audience experienced the same plot as the readers of the original 1900 book by L. Frank Baum, which although still a favorite for fairy-tale enthusiasts is less commonly known than the movie.[1]

Some devoted followers know, however, that Dorothy was not the central protagonist in many of the sequels written by Baum himself. The author penned fourteen novels in total (or fifteen, depending on how one counts), featuring either new characters, such as Princess Ozma, or older supporting characters, such as Glinda the Good Witch.[2] With Baum's death in 1919, Ruth Plumly Thompson continued the Oz stories, adding nineteen titles to the collection. Numerous additional tales have been added by illustrator John Neill and others. Even the book enthusiasts might not know it, but the explosion of novels that built the Oz franchise was connected to a single event—the stage musical. *The Wizard of Oz* (1902, Chicago; 1903, New York) was adapted by Baum himself, with music by Paul Tietjens. Instead of focusing on Dorothy, the musical became a star-making device for the vaudeville team of Montgomery and Stone, whose turns as the Tin Woodman and Scarecrow, respectively, were wildly popular. Baum realized there was a strong demand for more stories, musical productions, films, and novelties, and he quickly responded. Known for his business acumen, Baum wrote the follow-up story to the first tale and made the two star characters the central protagonists, capitalizing on the buzz created by the musical extravaganza. Baum's legacy, then, is not only as a literary luminary but also as one of the first brand ambassadors, building a multimedia franchise that relied on the interconnected popularity of his two theatrical stars and the extravaganza in which they starred.

Those familiar with this stage production are aware of its impact on the Oz universe, but there remain a number of unexplored questions. The first of these centers on just what, exactly, the stage show was. The songs changed over time, which was common for musical productions at the turn of the century, but what is interesting is that the story changed, too. There was a script, but it was regularly reworked, and this constant adaptation created difficulty in charting changes that took place over the course of the original show in Chicago, the various touring versions, and the multiyear run on Broadway. Examining descriptions of the show from these versions helps to give a sense of just what *The Wizard of Oz* was like on stage, and part of the answer lies with the term "extravaganza," which was an attempt to identify its genre at the time. Related to this is a consideration of Montgomery and Stone's early career and their magical transformation from vaudeville routine to international superstars. Their onstage antics were, like the story itself, considered "modern," indicative of the possibilities of the new century while simultaneously employing the best theatrical techniques from the past. Their relationship to their co-stars, especially Dorothy and the Wizard, will also be discussed. And finally, once the show became a smash hit, Baum embraced his role as businessman and "the Royal Historian of Oz," telling the stories of a real place, as told to him by the characters themselves. The combined success of the show, the stars, and the stories kept the Land of Oz vibrant and colorful in the popular consciousness for decades, laying the groundwork for the movie that has cemented Oz's place as the first and most enduring of twentieth-century fairy tales.

Baum's Interest in Theater

For those who knew Baum personally, the notion that he would combine his artistic aspirations with his business sense would have come as no surprise. His ventures during his youth often conflated the two interests, most notably his childhood obsession with the theater—a love that never faltered. His father, Benjamin, a prosperous merchant in Syracuse, New York, recognized his son's drive for theatrical success, both as a performer and an owner.[3] Frank had joined an acting troupe in 1878 under the stage name of Louis F. Baum, and in 1880, Benjamin helped his career when he made Frank the manager of several small venues he himself owned. Shortly afterward, Frank was made the owner of these theaters. Thus, he set about writing several plays (referred to by one contemporary as "Irish dramas"), many of which are now lost due to a fire, ironically, during a performance of Baum's play, *Matches*.[4] The most successful of his plays was *The Maid of Arran* (1882), a melodrama that employed incidental music, songs, and scenic stage effects.[5] Journalism, raising chickens, and running a store all followed as vocations for Baum, but it was not until he moved to Chicago in 1891 and rethought his vision of selling goods that Baum found his greatest success to that point.

Baum became a national sensation as a designer and business "guru" for store window displays.[6] It was the perfect choice for someone who had written pieces for the theater that included visually enticing stage machinery. The move to the Windy City just before the tremendous World's Fair there in 1893 allowed for some new ventures. Using his combined interests in business and art, Baum began to look past buying goods on a need-based system and instead focused on a means of moving inventory by sparking the desires of the consumer. There was a magic in wanting, Baum suggested, and this could be most effectively tapped by creating magnificent displays in the windows of stores, triggering new sales. William Leach, in his pioneering study on the rise of American consumerism, states that Baum did this by "lift[ing] taboos on the expression of desire," transforming the experience of purchase from a utilitarian exercise into a carnival of pleasure.[7] Baum achieved this through his work designing store windows, and he took to journalism, one of his former vocations, to entice merchants to follow his advice. He started a magazine called *The Show Window* in 1878, and within only "a few short months, its circulation was in the tens of thousands."[8] Baum realized that it was the visual splendor of design that captured consumer attention, and he was correct, given that this device is still a central part of American merchandising.

Making a Musical

Given this powerful awareness of mercantile entertainment, when Baum published *The Wonderful Wizard of Oz* (1900), he capitalized on the theatrical possibilities inherent in his modern fairy tale. Mark Evan Swartz's book, *Oz before the Rainbow*, is the definitive study of the pre-MGM film Oz productions; the author recounts several versions of the genesis of the musical but found the most reliable source for these early days to be the diaries of Paul Tietjens, the composer.[9] Tietjens and Baum had been working together on other projects when the composer suggested using Oz as the basis for a project, and Baum eventually agreed. One wonders why mounting the story on stage would have made the author hesitate, given his love of the theater and his remarkable imagination, but by the summer of 1901, the two men began work in earnest on the undertaking. William Wallace Denslow, the book's illustrator, joined the group as a designer of costumes and sets, and by September, the contracts between the three were signed.[10] Two figures in Chicago's theatrical community were soon attached to the project: Fred Hamlin, a young and inexperienced producer, and Julian Mitchell, a seasoned director who could be trusted to transform the project into a reality. Swartz's examination of the materials includes early drafts of the script and traces the path to the stage, including several changes that were made over time.[11]

These alterations and deletions from the novel and from the early script eventually set up the relationships that would come to define this version of Oz and would lead directly to the expanding Oz universe that continues today. In the book, it is the emotional connection to Dorothy and her journey that creates the primary narrative thrust. Her connection to Toto, her developing friendships along the way, her conflict with the Wicked Witch of the West, and her return to Kansas all seem essential elements to fans now. But in the version of the musical that was produced in Chicago in the summer of 1902, Dorothy's journey is merely an overarching skeleton that frames the musical rather than making it the focus of the story. Instead, a multitude of subplots was introduced, involving a barrage of new characters and concerns. The most prominent of these was about the deposed King of Oz, Pastoria, and his quest to get rid of the Wizard, who had stolen the throne from him years before. In the process, a number of other elements are deleted to make room for these new components. One of the biggest surprises is that Toto is replaced by a dancing cow named Imogene. Another is that the Wicked Witch is entirely expunged, along with any real threat to Dorothy's path to the Wizard. The silver (or ruby) slippers are replaced by an ineffective magic ring, and finally, many sequences from the book, such as the encounter with the Field Mice and the attack of the Kalidahs, were removed because they were considered impossible to stage.[12] Conversely, there are also some scenes that would be familiar to the modern audience member, including the opening cyclone/tornado sequence, the reception of Dorothy by the Munchkins, and the sleep-inducing poppy field that halted Dorothy's progress. This last was presented as a transformation scene, with the flowers wilting and dying after the Good

Witch calls down a freezing snowstorm to punish them for causing Dorothy and her group to sleep.

Swartz explains that many of the alterations were made at the behest of Mitchell, who worked closely with Baum and Tietjens during rehearsals to turn the plot-based book into a loose-knit collection of moments that only intermittently returned to the main plot.[13] One of the reasons for the sweeping changes was that the production team based *The Wizard of Oz* on a variety of genres; Hamlin told the *Chicago Daily Tribune* that the show "combines the elements of comic opera, spectacle, [English] pantomime, and extravaganza in a unique degree."[14] This would have surprised theatergoers at the time because the American musical was still finding its shape during the turn of the century, and it was not uncommon for shows to adhere to the comic opera formula exemplified by Gilbert and Sullivan. The pantomime was seen mainly as a children's genre, and both spectacle and extravaganza were considered relics, more akin to the 1860s or '70s than the modern era. One of these was *Evangeline* (1874), an important landmark of American musical theater, which was marketed as an extravaganza. Just what an extravaganza *was* or *is* remains a matter of debate and had been such even in the nineteenth century; many modern authors avoid trying to give any official definition, and others identify components of the shows bearing the title that tie them together.[15] Cecil Smith identifies the term as a means of including comic elements of burlesque while distancing itself from the racy opéra-bouffe.[16] Larry Stempel goes further, emphasizing the importance of visual splendor through two means: the "sheer spectacle and scenic effects" as well as the visual display of the female form.[17] For Mitchell, who was directing *Oz*, the storyline was only a means to an end, creating an excuse for an array of sumptuousness, be it songs, dance, or scenic wonders. He told one reporter that scripts were "rather tiresome," and the press was quick to point out this weakness in the show, with most agreeing that it did not harm the overall experience for the audience.[18]

An Extravaganza!

Critics in both Chicago and New York resorted to elaborate descriptions to explain what they had seen, often stating that this extravaganza was not necessarily held together by a plot. Amy Leslie, the drama expert for the *Chicago Daily News*, wrote that the "book does not amount to much," but dismisses this as unimportant given the "modern amazements" with "gorgeous panoramas of mystic scenes and fairy incantations, jovial processions of funny men and bright, sweet girls and such indescribable achievements of light, movement, and color."[19] When the show went on tour, similar comments were made; a critic in Milwaukee said, "Spectacular extravaganza is not so common a form of entertainment as it was ten or fifteen years ago when 'Evangeline' and 'The Black Crook' were in their prime. . . . It might be said that nonsense stories and light music framed in magnificent scenery and costumes are a thing of the past. But 'The Wizard of Oz' . . . proves extravaganza is still in the lists." As the show prepared to open in New York, a pamphlet advertising the new piece declared "There Is Something New Under the Sun" and featured a drawing of the Tin Woodman and Scarecrow on the cover. It called the show "a new development of the field of extravaganza . . . a [*sic*] agreeable relief from the bombardment of inane musical comedies which have held the boards in recent seasons."[20] Finally, when the show opened, it was the first production in the New Majestic Theatre, and the hype surrounding its first night brought a sold-out crowd as well as the usual bevy of critics. Alan Dale wrote in the *New York Journal* that "it purports to be a 'musical extravaganza.' . . . And perhaps it is one. It may be that and it may be anything. Whatever you call it, nobody can possibly dispute your word. For 'The Wizard of Oz' is . . . anything. . . . The piece itself is absolutely inexplicable."[21] These reviews provide insight into the complicated world of musical theater at this time—one that relied not on genre conventions but on finding inventive new ways to entertain, something that *The Wizard of Oz* accomplished admirably.

The hodge-podge of terms used as descriptors for the show also points to a very important development in theatrical categories that was just beginning to take shape. Although the extravaganza had held an important place in the nineteenth century, it was not a driving force in the following era. Instead, by the middle of the decade, a clear distinction was made between two major genres, and these would define musical theater until the Second World War: the "book" musical (or musical comedy) and the revue. The former relied on narrative cohesion for the basis of its dramatic thrust while the latter could unfold in a variety of ways depending on how a director shaped the production. A few revues (pieces that carried the descriptor) had already taken place in the 1890s, most notably *The Passing Show* (1894), but they would not become repeated events until Florenz Ziegfeld Jr. began his annual *Follies* series in 1907. What is surprising about Leslie's report of *The Wizard of Oz* is that it carries almost all the hallmarks of these early revues: the use of a script, but one that was not the essence of the show; visual spectacle (in terms of both stagecraft and the display of the young female form); a reliance on comedy; and—although not mentioned above—a musical fabric that made significant use of interpolations.[22] Some scholars have mentioned the connection between these large-scale nineteenth-century pieces and the revue, but none of the earlier examples provides as clear a connection as this Chicago-based show.[23] *Oz*, then, is a perfect example of a proto-revue, demonstrating conclusively that the elaborate extravaganza was the precursor to one of the central entertainments of the twentieth century.

Another vital connection between the genres is that *The Wizard of Oz* eventually became a star vehicle, allowing two vaudevillians to transition out of the rough, two-a-day bills across the country and into regular work on Broadway. Both men, Fred A. Stone and David Montgomery, experienced nearly instant stardom from their respective roles as the Scarecrow and Tin Woodman, and the theatrical flexibility they found as members of the *Oz* cast forever changed their lives. For so many entertainers, revues provided a similar path out of intermittent work on the country's many vaudeville stages and onto national fame; Ethel Merman, Al Jolson, Ed Wynn, Fanny Brice, Bob Hope, and literally hundreds of others made the jump from the revue to greater stage and screen prominence. That the team of Montgomery and Stone would pioneer this path years before by using similar techniques only makes the connection between the extravaganza and the revue more significant.

When *The Wizard of Oz* was in preparation, the initial announcements placed the strongest emphasis on one person, and it was not anyone in the cast. Instead, the name that appeared largest in print was Julian Mitchell. Since he was such a highly respected personality in Chicago, it is not surprising that Mitchell was one of the main reasons people flocked to see the show. He was known for his work as a director for the comedy team of Weber and Fields and the more elaborate spectacles of Charles Hoyt (including the hit, *A Trip to Chinatown*), who was based in Chicago.[24] Mitchell had begun as a Shakespearean actor, but his approach to being a "stage manager" or the one who "staged" productions (both terms were used interchangeably, while the term "director" was not used in programs of the day) was to "concentrate . . . on the chorus numbers, sets, and costumes."[25] The scene designer for *The Wizard of Oz*, Walter Burridge, was also featured in a number of articles praising his work, but he never overshadowed Mitchell in press releases, interviews, or reviews.[26] Leslie praised Mitchell's work repeatedly, noting his creativity as the main reason for the success of the extravaganza:

> Costumes embroidered in jewels and thrones all gold and precious metals, prancing reindeer and dancing cows, lions, beasts, wise birds and speaking flowers all help the actors. Storms, bewildering fairy groves and grottos, and lively vagaries of elfs and sprites belong to Mitchell and the painter's [Burridge's] fertile inventive genius. Mr. Mitchell has gathered all about him all the pretty girls he could find idle and given them gay dances and resplendent robes, he has selected his comedians practically and they fit the roles assigned them as if they had dropped in a groove. He has generaled the ensembles with enormous evidence of the marshalling gift so rare and his tableaux alone are worth staying in town a while to see.[27]

It is not surprising, given this impressive fanfare, that Mitchell's name in the advertisements for the Chicago run was larger than anyone else's. This was *his* production at the outset, and this was what Hamlin, a young and untried producer, was hoping would ensure an audience.

Hamlin need not have worried, though, because the cast was solid, too. John Slavin played the Wizard himself, and he was given some attention by critics; he was considered "tremendously funny" and "the only human being in the cast who can sing" with a "clear, punctual and convincing barytone [*sic*] of a buffo singer."[28] Dorothy was portrayed by Anna Laughlin, a young woman rather than a girl. Laughlin had been appearing with Dan Daly in vaudeville in Chicago before the show, and she was considered suitable, if not impressive. One critic said, "With her small face . . . her small figure, which twists its way into odd dances, and her small voice, which wavers through a half-dozen songs, she was assuredly one of the features of the production."[29] A few of the other cast members were given accolades as well, including Helen Byron (Cynthia Cynch), Aileenn May (Good Witch of the North), Bessie Wynn (Sir Dashemoff Daily), and Neil McNeil (Pastoria).[30] But above all else, the reviewers from early in the run, on tour, and in New York all identified the stars of the show as David Montgomery and Fred A. Stone.

Montgomery and Stone

The two men had been a vaudeville duo for several years by the time they were engaged by Hamlin for his new show. One of the earliest articles about the extravaganza included the two but did not identify them because, according to the producer, "as they are in the service of other managers, I am not at liberty to disclose their names."[31] He was right; not only were they otherwise engaged, but they were also not yet in the United States. They were just ending a run of performances in England as part of Robert Arthur's Sixth Liverpool Pantomime when Hamlin contacted them about the roles. Although they were well received, even performing three times for King Edward VII, the pair carried no particular distinction among their vaudeville counterparts. This was the case for them in both England and America. An article in *Leslie's Weekly* pointed out that "nobody east of Chicago, unless it were a few vaudeville devotees, knew anything at all about these two young men when they came to New York as the Scarecrow and the Tin-man . . . , but now they are stars in the ascendancy that are just beginning to gleam on the horizon of public approval. In time we may expect to see them moving upward in the welkin just as Weber and Fields, Rogers Brothers, and other 'teams' have done."[32] This rise in popularity is exactly what happened; *Oz* was, for Montgomery and Stone, their star-making moment.

In the flurry of activity that surrounded *The Wizard of Oz*, the vaudeville pair went through three stages of popularity. First, the reviews were released in Chicago, then on tour, and eventually in New York. As the critics responded to the elements of the production that worked best, the Scarecrow and the Tin Woodman (whose name was identified as Nick Chopper) were consistently pointed out as the most compelling reason to see the show. As the second stage began to unfold, interviews with the two began appearing everywhere, although more attention was given to Fred Stone than to Montgomery, largely because of the nature of the Scarecrow's part, especially the physical eccentricities the role demanded. The final phase saw the show modified over time to incorporate new skits and songs, with the duo offering some highly peculiar new material to keep the show fresh and new.

So how did two nondescript comedians become poised to make such a memorable impression on audiences across America? Much of the answer lies in their training. Although it seems improbable, Fred Stone was actually from Kansas (specifically, Wellington), and he began as an acrobat in the circus. With his father acting as manager, Fred and his younger brother, Edwin, worked their way throughout the territories doing tightrope walking and trapeze acts, dancing, and singing minstrel songs in blackface; Stone recalls that "those circus experiences through the West were terrifying to us boys. It was during the days when the cowboys were especially free with their revolvers and whenever anything in the entertainment pleased them they shot a hole through the top of the tent by way of applause."[33] Montgomery also started in the circus but then focused on singing, becoming one of the "end men" in Haverly's Minstrels, a troupe run by Billy Rice.[34] The two men had met in St. Joseph, Missouri, while part of these separate groups, but when Stone's circus disbanded unexpectedly leaving him in Galveston, Texas, they met again when the minstrel troupe came to town. Montgomery had appreciated Stone's talent, and he convinced Rice to hire his friend. The two eventually formed their own blackface act and went into vaudeville. Montgomery explained that this work prepared them for their future in an essential way:

> In the old days everyone was a good blackface minstrel, and then made his mark as a funmaker of one sort or another in whiteface. It was a hard, practical school. Boys were taught to dance in blackface minstrelsy as they have never been taught since. Dancing is after all the foundation of musical comedy funny work. The blackface work taught a youth what was funny—or at least what an audience thought was funny. It was a practical school, above all. I wish there were such a training for young men on the stage nowadays.[35]

Performing in "whiteface" meant that they continued to sing minstrel songs but without the burnt cork makeup. By the mid-1890s, tunes called "coon songs" became all the rage in Jim Crow–era America, and many performers, including the boisterous May Irwin, made a career out of performing these numbers. Coon songs were often sung in black dialect and included lyrics about stereotypical black life, and these were the main types of melodies Montgomery and Stone performed in vaudeville. Most of their touring was throughout the far West, but by the turn of the century, they had also been seen throughout the Midwest and East. A description of their act in Buffalo, New York, in 1899 predicted their reception in *Oz*: "[They] are as uproariously funny as ever, [Stone] being just as ungainly, loose-jointed, and limber as of yore, with 'rag-time' cropping out of every pore, from his giddy 'plug dice' to his musical toes."[36] As they continued to hone their act, they were noticed and engaged for Charles Frohman's production of *The Girl from Up There* (1901), which took them to London early in the year. It was during this show that they started performing in whiteface, and they developed a new act over the course of the production.[37] According to contemporary reports, this new version of their performance was a distinct improvement, and it substantially increased their popularity; their dancing was "the feature of the act" and the new makeup was "funnier than their black work" with material that was "a pleasant variant of rag time singing."[38] They again returned to England in the winter of 1901, and that was where they were officially approached by Hamlin just after the New Year. Stone claimed that he had learned about the extravaganza earlier, though, when he ran into Mitchell on the street in New York just before the transcontinental journey, and the director, who had worked with them in *The Girl from Up There*, told the actor that he had a part for him that would match his uncanny flexibility.[39] The years the pair had worked together had made Montgomery and Stone seasoned performers who had polished their eccentric dancing, well preparing them for the roles they would play.

The Scarecrow and the Tin Woodman

It did not take long for the duo to be singled out from the rest of the cast for their remarkable abilities. Early reviews make it clear that although Baum's story and Mitchell's fame were instrumental in packing the Grand Opera House, there was no question who the stars of the show were. Even with Slavin and Laughlin's past accomplishments (and thus their top billing in promotional material for the engagement), Montgomery and Stone quickly became the audience favorites. Stone's specialty included bending one leg underneath him followed by the other in a comical attempt to walk, and oversized gloves and wild movements with his arms also added to the fun. Montgomery would at times play the flute and offer huge smiles but always keeping his motions robotic, as befitted a metal man. One reviewer's take after opening night was that these two were the real stars, noting that "the honors of the evening were carried off by David Montgomery and Fred Stone, who . . . not only introduced two characters virtually new to the comic stage, but by their irresistibility funny presentment of them scored an immediate and pronounced 'hit.' Their dancing, singing, and funmaking gave the chief life to the performance and reached culmination in the 'Cockney Negro Song,' which they interpolated in the last act."[40] Other critics agreed, and although they generally found some praise for the other cast members, they gushed over Montgomery and Stone throughout the sixteen-week Chicago engagement. It was not just that they were funny but that they were inventive, and it was the freshness they brought to the roles and in their particular style that gave them a unique edge. One newspaper declared that "something absolutely new on the stage is rare. But to [these two] the *Tribune* awards the honor of pioneers in absolutely original comedy. These young men . . . landed right in the front row—and practically the head of the class—of eccentric comedians."[41] As the show developed in the first few weeks, changes were made to cut songs, shorten dialogue, and add touches to the production. For example, several ineffective songs were dropped, including "The Many Ways of Making Love," a duet between Cynthia and Dorothy. Some character changes were made, too, the most significant being Slavin's transformation of the Wizard into a "German comedy character."[42] But no matter what others did, audiences wanted as much Montgomery and Stone as they could get.

By the end of the third week, Hamlin announced that he had arranged for a five-year contract with his new stars. At least one critic was surprised at this, saying, "It is obvious that Mr. Hamlin would not engage [them] for five years in order to retain them in 'The Wizard of Oz.' It is fair to assume that these players will be utilized in another presentation next summer after a road tour in their present success."[43] There was no way to know that Montgomery and Stone would work with the producer to reshape the production repeatedly over multiple years, developing effective alternative scenes that brought repeat viewers back from season to season to see what new comedic turns the two had invented. Tweaking things over time became easier because eventually the show left its home at the Grand Opera House and went on tour throughout the upper Midwest and the East. At this point, the advertisements had changed, and instead of Julian Mitchell's name, the large type was used for Montgomery and Stone. Since the show's structure was flexible, new songs were allowed to move in and out (and sometimes back in) of *The Wizard of Oz*, and sometimes whole original scenarios were developed to place the Scarecrow and the Tin Woodman in new situations. *Oz before the Rainbow* chronicles the many transformations of the production, and almost all of the changes were made to develop more opportunities for the vaudeville duo to shine in new ways.[44] Some of the more unusual scenes included a football game between the two, a nautical section that included the smash hit "Hurrah for Baffin's Bay," and even a moment when the Scarecrow was taken apart in pieces and reassembled. The last of these changes was put in place for the New York audience when *Oz* opened at the Majestic Theatre; not only was this a new version of the extravaganza, which packed the house nightly, but this was also the first engagement for the house itself. As it had been throughout its run, *The Wizard of Oz* was again a smash success in its new home. It did well enough that even though it would close more than once, several major revivals were held within months of each other, giving the show a prolonged life that few Broadway productions could boast in this era. A late addition signals just how far from the Emerald City the show strayed: "A novel Indian specialty by Fred Stone will be introduced in this season's edition of 'The Wizard of Oz.' He appears as the famous warrior, Sitting Bull, surrounded by a chorus of Mexican vacqueros, cowboys, and Indian girls."[45]

Swartz singles out two major reasons for the show's longevity, especially in New York.[46] The first was that Montgomery and Stone were simply tremendous draws; their remarkable ability to choose material well suited to their talents and popular with crowds meant they repeatedly infused *Oz* with new life. The second was that Townsend Walsh, a publicity agent, was able to find amusing anecdotes and small tidbits about them to feed to the media throughout the run. I would add a third reason for the continued box-office draw, and that was the structural elasticity created by Mitchell that provided a continually evolving experience for theatergoers. Mitchell himself was not always responsible for changes that took place—the movement of musical interpolations was often at the behest of the performers—but it was the very nature of this proto-revue that allowed for a revolving door through which material could move smoothly in and out of circulation. One event that took place when *The Wizard of Oz* returned to Chicago in 1904 is a perfect example of what the narrative could endure when matched with the high quality of entertainers such as the famous vaudeville duo:

Miss Blanche Ring created something of a sensation at the second anniversary of "The Wizard of Oz" last Thursday night. . . . Miss Ring took the audience by surprise by walking abruptly upon the stage in the last act, while Messrs. Montgomery and Stone were holding the boards. The two comedians received her with elaborate suavity, Stone's unctuousness reaching an astonishing degree of contortionate politeness that almost tied him in a knot. He and Montgomery became rivals for the smiles of

Miss Ring and carried on the fun until the audience shouted with laughter. They did a cakewalk with her that would be worth a princely salary in vaudeville. Fred Hamlin . . . watched the performance from a stage box, and George Ade and other notables were in the audience.[47]

This event, probably agreed upon beforehand to mark the special occasion, must have been one of the most talked-about moments of the season, but it would have been less effective if the jovial interruption had intruded on a tightly knit narrative. Instead, laced with Mitchell's aesthetic, which valued *entertainment* over *plot*, the older form of the extravaganza melded with the burgeoning revue, embracing the stream-of-consciousness structure that had been so prevalent in variety and vaudeville for the three decades preceding the production. Modern audiences, inundated with praise only for the "integrated musical," might find it difficult to imagine, but the freedom celebrated in the nonsense of *The Wizard of Oz* was invigorating for those who saw the show, and it played a central part in keeping this extravaganza at the center of attention wherever it went.

Lasting Impressions

Over time, multiple road tours were arranged, and of course this required that new actors learn the parts of the Scarecrow and Tin Woodman. The stars found it hard to maintain their roles, even with the new scenes added. Swartz relates a request by Stone, who early in 1906 went so far as to publish a plea to audiences to allow him to move on from the role.[48] Two years before this breaking point, however, Stone had taken great pride in the number of times he had "become" the straw man, and he provided a vivid description of his star-making role through a series of numbers giving the reader a real sense of his experiences as the Scarecrow.

When Fred Stone began to act the part of the Scarecrow in "The Wizard of Oz" two years ago, he weighed 165 pounds. Now, he tips the beam at 148 pounds, having lost 17 pounds in the meantime. . . . Taking the width of the proscenium opening and the depth from rear wall to footlights, he gets a total of 5,300 feet, to say nothing of the walk to the dressing room, which is frequent and usually of considerable length, and the energy he expends on his complicated makeup. He has played the part more than 900 times, and at one mile a performance (his estimate), he has danced over 900 miles. There is no time during his performance that he is motionless, save the five minutes after the Scarecrow is carried on to the stage.

There is more physical energy devoted to the Scarecrow role than to any other part known to the theater. It is hustle and hard work from 7:30 until 11:45 o'clock every night, and a similar length of time on matinee days. If there were an actor's union, Mr. Stone would probably be blacklisted for working overtime.

Three times during each performance he is forced to change his clothing, and to subject himself to a "rub down" by his dresser. No pugilist training for a contest goes through such a vigorous course of physical discipline as that entailed by the Scarecrow's performance daily, and he has maintained it without cessation for 100 weeks instead of the three months usually devoted to preparation for a fistic encounter. He goes to bed regularly at 1 o'clock each night, sleeps soundly until 12 the next day, doesn't drink, nor smoke, and takes care of himself as jealously as if he were a football player in training.

Mr. Stone's statistical inclinations lead him to make interesting calculations. At the rate of three bales of straw a week he has consumed 300 tons in his makeup. He has used 500 sticks of grease paint of six inches in length each, 200 cans of powder, 100 cans of cold cream, four wigs, and 200 pairs of gloves since June 16, 1902. He is using the same hat, the same coat, and the same boot-toed shoe that he did on the first night.[49]

Montgomery and Stone would continue to invoke the Scarecrow and the Tin Woodman throughout the rest of their careers. The most obvious method was to use a similar chemistry between the roles, and they almost always played a pair. This was most evident in their two high-profile follow-up musicals to *The Wizard of Oz*, Victor Herbert and Henry Blossom's *The Red Mill* (1906) and Ivan Caryll and Anne Caldwell's *Chin Chin* (1914). In both productions, the interaction between the actors was revisited, with Stone taking the energetic role and Montgomery that of the "feeder" (the one who fed the other jokes to set up a punchline). Their costumes for *The Lady of the Slipper* (1912) were even of similar types, with a Scarecrow and a Pumpkin (named Punks and Spooks) reminding audiences of the former roles. Sometimes, though, they waxed nostalgic while not on the stage. Stone was an avid sportsman, and articles about him hunting, swimming, playing football (which he had done professionally for a brief time), and more were common into the 1930s. At a baseball game in which Stone, A. R. Erlanger, and other theatrical notables played, Stone wore a version of his original costume on the field.[50] Sadly, Montgomery died after falling unconscious while in Chicago in 1917, and Stone refused to replace him. The former Scarecrow performed in *Jack O'Lantern* beginning in 1917, and the following year he went to Hollywood, where he was in numerous films, including *Johnny Get Your Gun* (1919) and *Broadway after Dark* (1924). He continued to appear both on stage and in movies throughout the rest of his career, which ended in the mid-1940s. *Oz* offered Stone more than just a starring role, though. He also met his wife, Allene Crater (who replaced Byron as Cynthia Cynch), in the cast, and it is not a surprise that they named their first child Dorothy. The reflexive impact *Oz* and the vaudeville team had on each other was profound, and the long-term effects went further than anyone in the show could have foreseen.

As stated earlier, the show became the catalyst for everything Oz, and Baum knew almost immediately that his extravaganza was a hit; the author's son claims that his father knew by the end of the second act on opening night that the show was going to thrive.[51] It did not take long for Baum to realize that many people wanted to hear more about the Land of Oz, and within a year after the show opened in New York, Baum released the second book in what would grow to be a series. In the message to the reader for *The Marvelous Land of Oz* (1904), he stated that many children had written to him "'wanting [him] to write more' about the Scarecrow and the Tin Woodman" (not, interestingly, about Dorothy). And, on the following page, he included a dedication to Montgomery and Stone (see Figure 1.1). Photos of the two actors are even incorporated in the illustration on the front and back covers of the first edition.

After the release of the second book, a third followed in 1907 and fourth a year later. Soon, Baum was writing a book a year. He also capitalized on other possible means of profiting from his creation. Puzzles, games, and dolls were sold within the first two decades, and Baum spearheaded more stage works (*The Woggle-Bug*, 1905, and *The Tik-Tok Man of Oz*, 1913) and films. The world of Oz became a recognized brand that expanded steadily up until the 1939 movie and continues unabated since then.

Stone was a small part of the prerelease publicity for the MGM movie, too. He appeared alongside Judy Garland, Ray Bolger, Burt Lahr, Frank Morgan, and Harold Arlen on the radio show, *Good News of 1939*. Hosted by Robert Young, the broadcast was the first time any of the songs from the movie were heard by audiences, including "Over the Rainbow." It also featured an imagined party where some of the new cast members got to meet Stone. One was Ray Bolger, who expressed his admiration for the man, and the other was Frank Morgan, who humorously claimed that he was the star of the old Broadway production.

BOLGER: Mr. Stone, I've always considered you to be the greatest eccentric dancer who's ever lived.

STONE: Thank you, Ray. I sincerely consider you the finest eccentric dancer of the present time . . .

FIGURE 1.1. Dedication to *The Marvelous Land of Oz*.

BOLGER: I remember when you came to Boston at the Colonial Theater with your great show, *Jack O' Lantern*, which by the way was the first show that I was ever allowed to see. And your wonderful performance in that show gave me my inspiration to become an actor.[52]

This exchange sounds well rehearsed on the radio program, and there is no doubt the dialogue was written for the actors. One might suggest that this was mere publicity fantasy, but forty years later, in 1976, Bolger repeated the comment in an interview for his part in the television movie of John Osborne's play, *The Entertainer*.[53] "I never danced a step until I was 16," Bolger said, "Then I went to see Fred Stone, the original scarecrow." The performance genealogy that connects the two Scarecrows only enhances the powerful momentum of *The Wizard of Oz*'s legendary status, offering up an official "passing of the torch" between the two actors and, though they may not have realized it at the time, between the versions of Oz that were foremost in the public's eye.

Notes

1. Many of the well-known *Oz* tropes, such as the Ruby Slippers and the Emerald City being green, come from the movie, as discussed in Chapter 2.
2. A collection of short stories by Baum, titled *Little Wizard Stories of Oz*, was published in 1913 by Reilley and Britton and is considered by some fans to bring the total to fifteen.
3. Katharine M. Rogers, *L. Frank Baum, Creator of Oz: A Biography* (New York: St. Martin's Press, 2002), 8.
4. "Puts His Book on the Stage," *Chicago Daily Tribune*, June 7, 1902, p. 18.
5. Rogers, *L. Frank Baum*, 9–10.
6. William Leach, *Land of Desire: Merchants, Power, and the Rise of a New American Culture* (New York: Vintage Books, 1993), 56–61.
7. Leach, *Land of Desire*, 56–57.
8. Leach, *Land of Desire*, 60.
9. Mark Evan Swartz, *Oz before the Rainbow: L. Frank Baum's* The Wonderful Wizard of Oz *on Stage and Screen to 1939* (Baltimore: Johns Hopkins University Press, 2000), 29.
10. Swartz, *Oz before the Rainbow*, 30.
11. Swartz, *Oz before the Rainbow*, 30–38.
12. Baum discussed the difficulties of adapting the book in an interview; see *Chicago Record-Herald*, June 10, 1902, n.p., from Townsend Walsh Scrapbook, MWEZ n.c. 4543, New York Public Library for the Performing Arts, Billy Rose Theater Collection. Swartz covers the changes from the book extensively in *Oz before the Rainbow*.
13. Swartz, *Oz before the Rainbow*, 38.
14. "News of the Theaters," *Chicago Daily Tribune*, February 6, 1902, p. 13.
15. It is notable that Gerald Bordman, an authoritative author on the history of the American musical, does not even try to define the genre. See Gerald Bordman, *American Musical Theatre: A Chronicle*, 3rd ed. (Oxford: Oxford University Press, 2001).
16. Cecil Smith and Glenn Litton, *Musical Comedy in America*, 2nd ed. (New York: Theatre Arts Books, 1981), 21.
17. Larry Stempel, *Showtime: A History of the Broadway Musical Theater* (New York: W. W. Norton, 2010), 79. Stempel explains that the burlesque and the extravaganza

are difficult to distinguish but that the elements mentioned here are important components of both.

18. Swartz, *Oz before the Rainbow*, 36.

19. Amy Leslie, "For 'Wizard of Oz,'" *Chicago Daily News*, n.d., n.p., from Townsend Walsh Scrapbook, MWEZ n.c. 4543, New York Public Library for the Performing Arts, Billy Rose Theater Collection.

20. Pamphlet, Montgomery and Stone Programs, MWEZ n.c. 5120, New York Public Library for the Performing Arts, Billy Rose Theater Collection.

21. Alan Dale, "New Majestic Theatre Is a Model of Beauty and Comfort," *New York Journal*, n.d., n.p., from Townsend Walsh Scrapbook, MWEZ n.c. 4543, New York Public Library for the Performing Arts, Billy Rose Theater Collection.

22. My study of the annual *Passing Show* series covers each of these topics in detail. See Jonas Westover, *The Shuberts and Their Passing Shows: The Untold Tale of Ziegfeld's Rivals* (Oxford: Oxford University Press, 2016).

23. See Gerald Bordman, *American Musical Revue from the Passing Show to Sugar Babies* (Oxford: Oxford University Press, 1985) and Lee Davis, *Scandals and Follies: The Rise and Fall of the Great Broadway Revue* (New York: Limelight, 2000).

24. "The New Plays," clipping from Townsend Walsh Scrapbook, MWEZ n.c. 4543, New York Public Library for the Performing Arts, Billy Rose Theater Collection.

25. See Armond Fields and L. Mark Fields, *From the Bowery to Broadway: Lew Fields and the Roots of American Popular Theater* (Oxford: Oxford University Press, 1993), 134. The middle years of Mitchell's career are explored in this source, but Mitchell is one of many stage personages of this period who deserve significant attention from scholars. His Broadway credits only illuminate a small portion of his exceptional career, and a biography would be a welcome addition to the story of American theater.

26. The Townsend Walsh Scrapbook includes dozens of these items, and one can easily see Mitchell's prominence throughout the collection. See MWEZ n.c. 4543, New York Public Library for the Performing Arts, Billy Rose Theater Collection.

27. See Amy Leslie, "For 'Wizard of Oz,'" *Chicago Daily News*, n.d., n.p., from Townsend Walsh Scrapbook, MWEZ n.c. 4543, New York Public Library for the Performing Arts, Billy Rose Theater Collection.

28. "Music and the Drama," n.d., n.p., from Townsend Walsh Scrapbook, MWEZ n.c. 4543, New York Public Library for the Performing Arts, Billy Rose Theater Collection.

29. Untitled clipping from Townsend Walsh Scrapbook, MWEZ n.c. 4543, New York Public Library for the Performing Arts, Billy Rose Theater Collection.

30. See Swartz, *Oz before the Rainbow*, chap. 3, for more reviewer commentary on each character, including many not mentioned here.

31. "News of the Theaters," *Chicago Daily Tribune*, February 6, 1902, p. 13.

32. Eleanor Franklin, "How Two Western Comedians Won Their Way into Public Favor," *Leslie's Weekly*, October 8, 1903, pp. 340–344.

33. "Life of a Stage Scarecrow and Its Queer Features," n.s., July 13, 1902, n.p. from Townsend Walsh Scrapbook, MWEZ n.c. 4543, New York Public Library for the Performing Arts, Billy Rose Theater Collection.

34. "From Tan Bark to Stage," *Chicago Tribune*, June 2, 1902, p. 12.

35. "Making a Comedian: Dave Montgomery Tells How He Graduated from the Circus Ring: Burnt Cork School," *New York Telegraph*, September 26, 1909, n.p.

36. "First-Rate Vaudeville," *Buffalo Evening News*, August 29, 1899, p. 8.

37. An early mention of their whiteface act in the United States can be found in Just and Fair, "The Brooklyn Stage," *New York Dramatic Mirror*, November 9, 1901, p. 13.

38. Chicot (Epes Winthrop Sargent), "Fletcher's Mimicry Improves with Time and Hard Work," *New York Morning Telegraph*, September 12, 1901, p. 8.

39. Fred Stone, *Rolling Stone* (New York: McGraw-Hill, 1945), 129–132. Swartz recounts the challenges of finding the right part for Montgomery in *Oz before the Rainbow*, 83.

40. "Wizard of Oz," *Chicago Tribune*, June 17, 1902, n.p. The song was performed using black dialect as text but was sung with a cockney accent, and it was one of the biggest successes for the pair in England, so it was used for this show.

41. "'The Scarecrow' and the 'Tin Woodman,'" *Chicago Tribune*, June 18, 1902, n.p., from Townsend Walsh Scrapbook, MWEZ n.c. 4543, New York Public Library for the Performing Arts, Billy Rose Theater Collection.

42. "Music and Drama," *Chicago Daily Tribune*, June 24, 1902, p. 13.

43. "Music and Drama," from Townsend Walsh Scrapbook, MWEZ n.c. 4543, New York Public Library for the Performing Arts, Billy Rose Theater Collection.

44. Swartz, *Oz before the Rainbow*, chaps. 4 and 5.

45. "Something New," unidentified source, November 25, 1905, n.p., from Locke Collection, #1509, New York Public Library for the Performing Arts, Billy Rose Theater Collection.

46. Swartz, *Oz before the Rainbow*, 125–128.

47. "Stage Notes," *Brooklyn Daily Eagle*, July 3, 1904, p. 6.

48. Swartz, *Oz before the Rainbow*, 146.

49. "Scarecrow Statistics," *Chicago Daily Tribune*, May 29, 1904, p. 21.

50. See photo in *Saturday Evening Post*, November 6, 1909, n.p. Montgomery and Stone Clippings File, New York Public Library for the Performing Arts, Billy Rose Theater Collection.

51. Swartz, *Oz before the Rainbow*, 65.

52. Robert Young and Cast, "Stars from the Wizard of Oz," *Good News of 1939*, Los Angeles, CA, KFI, June 29, 1939.

53. Tom Shales, "New Turn for Bolger," *Victoria Advocate*, March 7, 1976, p. 3.

2 "THE ROAD TO OZ"

FROM BOOK TO MOVIE MUSICAL

Benjamin Sears

When MGM undertook in 1939 to make a film version of L. Frank Baum's *The Wonderful Wizard of Oz*,[1] the studio was faced with the inevitable dilemmas that need to be addressed when adapting a novel for the screen. Such a transition, by the nature of the two media, is always one of compromise. A novelist has the option of revealing information at the pace and to the extent that she or he feels best suits the narrative; by contrast, a play or film has a limited time frame, usually ninety minutes to two hours, in which to tell the story. A novel may require a paragraph or more to portray a setting; in a play, it can be ascertained quickly by viewers; however, even with this visual information there is often much that can be learned only through dialogue. To prevent the dialogue from being overly time-consuming, an adapter needs to determine what and how much of the story to take to the new medium, and how best to use it. Perhaps most problematic is the visual expectations readers bring to a play or film; readers will have their own images of settings and characters that may not correspond to those of a playwright or filmmaker (the least solvable problem of all), particularly an illustrated book and one as vividly illustrated, by W.W. Denslow, as *The Wonderful Wizard of Oz*.[2] Metro-Goldwyn-Mayer faced these challenges in adapting L. Frank Baum's novel, solving them by trimming the book and making changes in focus.

Once the decision to film was made, *The Wizard of Oz* had a revolving door of writers with varying lengths of tenure and size of contribution. Yet, for all that has been written about this film, the various contributors have left behind very little commentary on the choices they made, and their reasons, in adapting the story from book to film.[3]

In most cases one writer did not see what others had done, yet most tended to take a similar approach as to how the book could become a film. In 1939, Florence Ryerson and Edgar Allen Woolf (who ultimately shared writing credits with Noel Langley) summed up some of the problems of adaptation. They give themselves a bit more credit than they deserve along with downplaying the changes made. This likely was part of the film's publicity, which explains the ingenuousness of some of their comments:

> No screen writer faces a more difficult task than the translation of a classic from the printed word into celluloid, and when the classic is for children, the difficulty is increased because many generations have read and loved that book.
>
> Of all children's books, *The Wizard of Oz* [*sic*] is most widely read, most dearly beloved. Hence, we daily received letters from fans warning us to follow the book and leave out no characters.
>
> Necessarily, a few things had to be sacrificed by selecting the most important incidents and characters and telescoping or combining others. When we had finished, we were amazed to realize how little had been left out. Only a few grotesque things, which might be amusing to read about, but would not be well to look at, were eliminated.
>
> We included Dorothy, the Wizard, the Scarecrow, the Tin Woodman, the Cowardly Lion, the Wicked Witch, Glinda the Good, the Munchkins, the Winkies, the Winged Monkeys, the trees which could take hold of people and the inhabitants of the Emerald City.
>
> Changes in the story were really minor. For example, in the book when the characters are overcome by poison in the poppy field, the field-mouse queen and all her mice rescue the characters. That, of course, couldn't be done on the screen. Instead, we have Glinda the Good send a snow storm to revive them. We also eliminated the wishing cap and have the characters merely seek the Witch's broomstick.
>
> We changed the scenes in the Witch's castle slightly, making them a little more dramatic. But all the episodes are there including the melting of the Witch and the final scenes where the Wizard proves a humbug and, then being on the spot, is forced to show the characters they really have the qualities they've been wanting. He is still a balloonist and flies away without Dorothy, and she clicks her heels and goes home.
>
> The only change in the ending is pointing up Baum's philosophy and having Dorothy repeat the words, "There's no place like home."[4] We also stress the Kansas farm sequences more than in the book, but do so to build character only.

We scenarists did have problems. But they were those that involved satisfying Oz readers. We left in the most memorable incidents, never altered the characters; and we inserted most of the magic. After that, it was the problem of those technical geniuses to figure out how to do those strange things. And they did.[5]

A brief history of *The Wonderful Wizard of Oz* on stage, outlined by Jonas Westover in Chapter 1 of this book, helps put the 1939 film, and Ryerson and Woolf's comments, into context. Mark Evan Swartz, in *Oz before the Rainbow*, posits that "the various pre-1939 dramatizations . . . left their stamp on [the 1939 film]. . . . They were the source of inspiration for, among other things, using the musical-comedy format to present Dorothy's journey, for adding the Kansas farm hands to the story, for having a snowstorm sent by Glinda to save Dorothy and her companions from the deadly scent of the poppies, and for turning Dorothy's adventures into a dream."[6] It is difficult, however, to determine exactly how influential these earlier versions, in fact, were.

Early Screen Adaptations

Baum himself was responsible for the earliest film versions, made during the silent era. The first, in 1908, was a multimedia stage presentation called *Fairylogue and Radio-Plays*, created for Baum to promote his Oz books.[7] Swartz reveals that "Baum functioned as the onstage narrator, presenting a travelogue of some of the fairy lands—hence the term *fairylogue*—that he had created in his books."[8] A combination of short films, drawn from the first three Oz books, and slides illustrated his talk.

A fifteen-minute short feature, based on the stage musical, was released in 1910 as *The Wonderful Wizard of Oz* with future film star Bebe Daniels as Dorothy. Then in 1914 Baum created his own production business, the Oz Film Manufacturing Company, which produced three films that year, all about Oz, but not direct adaptations of the original book: *The Patchwork Girl of Oz*; *His Majesty, the Scarecrow of Oz*; and *The Magic Cloak of Oz*. In 1921, after Baum's death, another film was contemplated, to be called *The Wizard of Oz*, but it never went beyond contemplation. In 1925, Baum's son, Frank Joslyn Baum, was involved in producing another film, also called *The Wizard of Oz*. It was written and directed by comedian Larry Semon, who was also featured in the cast as the Scarecrow, along with the young Oliver Hardy (pre–Stan Laurel, billed as Oliver N. Hardy) as the Woodman. The plot is far removed from the original book but does feature three farmhands who are blown to Oz by a tornado, where they adopt disguises as the Scarecrow, Tin Woodman, and Cowardly Lion. Significant to the 1939 film, this one introduced the idea that Dorothy's trip to Oz was a dream. (Baum always insisted that Oz was a real place, not a dream or a figment of Dorothy's, or anyone else's, imagination, even though few others than Dorothy ever go there.) It also is "the first to set much of the story in Kansas and to give the farmhands a role in the story."[9] In the 1920s and 1930s, other versions, not connected to Baum himself, were created. They included stage plays, a marionette show, radio broadcasts, and a Canadian film that was not released due to copyright issues. This brief history of early film adaptations shows that the 1939 MGM film did share earlier ideas for dramatizing Baum's book, both in adapting the story to a new medium and, drawing from the stage versions, bringing music into the story though, as previously noted, it is unclear how much was owed directly to these earlier works.

MGM's interest in filming the book dates from 1924 when the studio was still Metro-Goldwyn. The rights were owned by Baum's son Frank, with whom the studio was unable to reach a deal. The reconstituted Metro-Goldwyn-Mayer studio tried again with the younger Baum in 1933, this time with the intention of creating an animated film series based on the Oz books, again, with no result. In 1934, Samuel Goldwyn, having left his previous company before it was incorporated into MGM and now an independent producer, purchased the film rights to *The Wonderful Wizard of Oz* for $40,000.[10] This would prove to be a good investment. Three years later, director Mervyn LeRoy and up-and-coming producer Arthur Freed both expressed an interest in the book to MGM head Louis B. Mayer. According to Swartz, LeRoy had seen and enjoyed the 1902 musical; if so, it likely had some influence on his thinking regarding a film version of the book.[11] That same year, Walt Disney scored a success with the first full-length animated feature film, *Snow White and the Seven Dwarfs*. LeRoy and Freed's interest in *The Wonderful Wizard of Oz*, coupled with the need felt by MGM to produce a fantasy film of their own, led to serious consideration about filming the book. This is where Goldwyn's gamble was rewarded as MGM paid him $75,000 to secure the film rights.[12] Whether drawing on LeRoy's memories of the 1902 stage musical or in imitation of Disney's use of song in *Snow White*, the decision was made for the film to be a musical, and in 1939 the parade of writers began.

First Efforts to Create the Screenplay

Before any writers were on the scene, LeRoy "turned the book over to his assistant, William Cannon, in early January, to get his thoughts on how best to dramatize the story."[13] Cannon felt strongly that the use of magic in film should be kept to a minimum. He also thought the Scarecrow and Tin Man should be real humans in disguise; whether intentional or not, this reflects the 1925 film.

After this, Irving Brecher led off the parade of screenwriters but was done almost before he started as he was shifted to another film, *At the Circus*.[14] Next came Herman Mankiewicz, whose lasting fame would come with *Citizen Kane* in 1940. His initial work, between February 28 and March 3, 1939, was mainly on what came to be known as "the Kansas sequence."[15] All the various writers wanted a contrast between the drab world Dorothy lived in and the fantastic world of Oz,[16] with the result that this sequence and the concept behind it would remain consistent through to the shooting script—underscoring and expanding on that contrast. In his initial treatment Mankiewicz perceived Kansas as having "the grey nature of the landscape and Dorothy's daily life,"[17] expanding on the few pages Baum devotes to Kansas and his description of "the great grey prairie on every side."[18] Baum devotes only a few pages to Dorothy in Kansas, giving us almost no background on Dorothy's life there; nor does he philosophize on how the landscape affects its residents. Dorothy's only companions are Uncle Henry and Aunt Em, and her dog, Toto (even Toto, a black dog, lacks color). We learn nothing about neighbors, if any, nor are there any farmhands to assist Henry and Em, which no doubt contributes to their difficult existence. Baum's Dorothy apparently is no trouble for Henry and Em; he tells us little of their relationship. In book and film Dorothy apparently has no function on the farm.[19] Credit for Oz being in color was claimed by Mervyn LeRoy;[20] regardless of who should receive that credit, the expanded Kansas introduction and Oz in color were in the earliest concepts of the film and would be vital in the final production.

As Mankiewicz went on to write his first draft script (delivered, incomplete, on March 7), he started another process that would run through the gestation of the film: creating characters who do not appear in *The Wonderful Wizard of Oz*. Baum himself initiated this concept in his 1902 play and it is employed, in varying permutations, in the subsequent early film versions. Again, whether Mankiewicz's decision was based on knowledge of the 1902 play and subsequent films is not known.

In this treatment Mankiewicz contributed "a lost limousine containing a chauffeur, an obnoxious rich woman, her more obnoxious daughter, and the little girl's Pekingese."[21] In subsequent treatments the obnoxious rich woman becomes Miss Gulch and the obnoxious daughter also is subject to variations before disappearing from the scripts completely.

Mankiewicz, and several writers who followed him, also had to deal with Arthur Freed's desire to use MGM contract players, in particular Judy Garland, with whom he had worked on two previous films. In addition to Garland, he wanted to utilize two other young performers, Betty Jaynes and Kenny Baker. Garland's Dorothy would be " 'an orphan from Kansas who sings jazz,' and Jaynes would be Princess Betty of Oz, 'who sings opera'[22] and is in love with Grand

Duke Alan, to be portrayed by Baker. Now Dorothy was off to see the Wizard not only to return home but also to rescue this royal Munchkin couple imprisoned by the Wicked Witch of the West."[23] This first treatment did feature elements that ultimately would be in the film—not only the Kansas sequence but additionally midgets as Munchkins and the Wicked Witch of the West as Dorothy's adversary upon her arrival in Oz. Mankiewicz also gave indications for how and where music could be used in the story.[24]

Unbeknownst to Mankiewicz, on March 7, when he delivered his first efforts, Ogden Nash was hired to write a script; then on March 11, Noel Langley was brought to the project. Using multiple writers was not unusual as it provided producers with a variety of scripts from which to choose. Ultimately, Nash, after about five weeks of work, contributed nothing.[25] Langley had an initial treatment ready by March 22, which would be the basis, albeit with further development, of the final film. The obnoxious woman now is Miss Gulch in Kansas, later in Oz the Wicked Witch of the West; and newly introduced are two farmhands who will become the Scarecrow and the Tin Woodman. Echoing Cannon, Langley justified this use of the Kansas characters in Oz by telling the producers "you cannot put fantastic people in strange places in front of an audience unless they have seen them as human beings first."[26] This helps justify Dorothy's adventure in Oz being a dream. Michael Patrick Hearn calls this "Langley's most alarming violation of Baum's text,"[27] yet it had an antecedent in the 1925 film, which "was framed as a largely inappropriate bedtime story for a little girl."[28] Langley's knowledge of that film is questionable.

To further strengthen the connection between the real and fantasy characters, the farmhand who will become the Tin Man is stiff jointed[29] and called heartless by a new extraneous character, soda fountain girl Lizzie Smithers. Now Lizzie has to be given a place in Oz. Mankiewicz's obnoxious daughter in the limousine is removed from the script; her replacement, as such, is the son of the Wicked Witch of the West, who is the fantasy version of Uncle Henry from the Kansas sequence. Romance also has blossomed. Dorothy is in love with a farmhand, Hickory, later to be the Scarecrow. Hunk, who will become the Tin Man, is in love with Lizzie.[30] Freed would come to realize that any sort of romance adversely affected the story.[31]

The Witch's son will appear in subsequent treatments and scripts before being eliminated. Along the way he will cause the creation of more new characters, thus complicating matters further. In the March 22 Langley version, the Witch has a son, Bulbo. She wants him to marry a beautiful girl named Sylvia who is the Witch's prisoner. To force her hand, the Witch has turned Sylvia's real love, Florizel, into a lion with the intention that he will terrorize Sylvia into marrying Bulbo. She also wants to conquer the Emerald City. One can only imagine how long the film would be in order for this to play out.[32]

In this version Dorothy travels to the Witch's castle not with the Scarecrow and Tin Man, as might be expected, but rather with Lizzie Smithers and the Wizard himself. Dorothy has already found the Wizard to be a humbug, which apparently makes it acceptable for him to join this journey. He also becomes a comic character, which may have influenced the consideration, for the second time, of W. C. Fields for the role.[33] At the Witch's castle, Florizel returns to human form and it is he who kills the Witch. Ultimately, in this version, love, not home, is the denouement:

> Florizel [now returned to his proper shape] has Sylvia in his arms and we blend to the strain of their love song; Lizzie Smithers and the Tin Man have their arms around each other; and then, as Dorothy watches, the whole thing begins to go out of focus and start swirling and swaying and eddying. She tries to cry out to Toto, and then we dissolve right out and through to her lying on the ground calling, "Toto! Toto!" with Aunt Em bending over her weeping, and Hunk, Hickory, and Uncle Henry watching.[34]

In this Kansas sequence Aunt Em is more of a Miss Gulch type, stern and un-yielding toward Dorothy. In fact, it is she who wants to take Toto away from Dorothy after being informed, by Miss Gulch (now a schoolteacher), that Toto bit a pupil. It is little wonder that Langley, in this script, has Dorothy say that Em never wanted her and considers her ungrateful. Apparently, Dorothy has been adopted from an asylum and is not at all sure that life is better now.[35]

These early treatments and scripts move well away from Baum. As shown earlier, this has a basis in Baum himself who reworked his own stories when adapting them for the stage. As there is so little firsthand commentary, any at-tempt to unravel the thinking behind these sometimes drastic changes is purely speculative. Hollywood scripts more often than not stray from their literary source, so it is hardly unusual that doing so was contemplated for this film.[36] Also, Hollywood favored including some sort of love story, no matter how extraneous to the plot it might be. As shown, early treatments of The Wizard of Oz added a romantic element, presumably because it was thought that audiences expected it.

The reasoning behind the variety of extraneous characters is also left to specu-lation. From a simply practical production standpoint, replicating Baum's fantas-tical creatures, such as Kalidahs, Hammer-Heads, and people made of China, was impractical. These various humans fill Langley's goal of presenting characters that audiences accept because they are human, but the larger number of characters would be unwieldy and shift the focus away from Dorothy. Further work on the script trimmed away many of them.

Continuing Evolution of the Screenplay

The day after the March 22 treatment was completed, Mankiewicz was removed from the project. Langley continued on, turning his treatment into a script, finished on April 5 with further changes.[37] Florizel is now Kenelm the Lionhearted who inevitably becomes the Cowardly Lion. Langley returns to Baum's narrative and again has Dorothy kill the witch, but the Lion needs to prove his mettle by battling someone or something, so a dragon now joins the cast of characters. Harmetz points out that Langley consistently has the Lion proving himself by killing some sort of beast.[38] She rightly mentions the contrast of this with the harmless Lion of Bert Lahr, but in fact, Langley here does follow Baum. In the book the travelers meet with a variety of creatures who bar their way or even threaten to kill them; one of Dorothy's companions always finds a route out of their peril. The lion uses force when necessary and even kills; in the final film it is only the two witches who are killed.

Other characters get shuffled around, too, particularly in Kansas. Sylvia is the niece of the schoolteacher who is a now-married Mrs. Gulch, whose son, Walter, is particularly unpleasant. Fortunately, he will disappear from the ongoing development of the story as quickly as he appeared. By this time Langley had blended Baum's two Good Witches (North and South) into Glinda. Baum's Glinda (the Witch of the South) knows the power of the shoes, but Dorothy must seek her out. In the film she becomes, from her first appearance onward, a deus ex machina (or, perhaps, deus ex ebullio),[39] though if she does know the shoes' power, she does not reveal it in Munchkinland.

Langley, in various versions of his scripts, did make efforts to retain as much of Baum's story as was feasible.[40] One risk, of course, is that holding too closely to the book would result in a lengthy film. The solution was the change from a series of perils to a sole foe. Thus, Langley eliminated the many perils Baum has Dorothy face in Oz both before *and* after the Witch of the West is killed, changing Dorothy's adventures from perils to facing an implacable foe who is out to kill her and who must be vanquished. Some attempt was made to include some of the quartet's adventures; Baum's deadly poppy field remained, though with changes, as noted by Ryerson and Woolf.[41] Again this altered version has its roots as far back as the 1902 play in which Glinda intercedes to save the travelers by calling on the King of the Frost to bring the snow; Langley calls him the more colloquial Jack Frost. The book's fighting trees are also retained, appearing in later scripts.

In the midst of this, on April 16 Ogden Nash left the project, apparently, as noted, having written little or nothing in the five weeks he was involved. Three days later Herbert Fields was on the job for all of four days. He, too, contributed nothing.[42] In the meantime, Langley continued his work with a second script completed on May 4. Between then and May 14 he completed the third and fourth versions, submitting the fourth as ready for production.[43]

In a significant variation from the book, until the May 14 script the silver slippers have not been the means of returning Dorothy home. Here, the slippers, changed to the now-familiar ruby, return to the purpose Baum originally gave them. Why their function was removed in earlier versions is not clear, but by following the history of the script's development it certainly can be seen that excluding them was yet another change from Baum that was a misstep.[44]

As might be expected, the May 14 script proved not to be the final version, despite its "do not make changes"[45] status. Over the next few weeks, until June 4, there was constant tinkering with the script, now involving producer Arthur Freed, director Mervyn LeRoy, and lyricist E. Y. ("Yip") Harburg, the latter coming to play a significant role in the film's creation. The result was another final version which also was not final, though much of this script was used when the film did go into production.[46] This script would include the only time the witch explains why the ruby slippers are so important to her: "With those shoes I can destroy the Wizard of Oz with three clicks of my heels—as easy as that!—three clicks of my heels!"[47]

From the evidence at hand it seems that in the initial stages the various writers used the barest outline of the book's plot and left the rest to their imaginations. When the extraneous characters are trimmed, based on Langley's desire to return to Baum, it is almost as if a decision was made to reread the book. However it may have been decided, streamlining the story rather than keeping the various expansions was the right decision.

Yet Further Revisions

Now more writers were shuffled in and out. Samuel Hoffenstein spent four days producing a slightly altered storyline for the Kansas Sequence which, apparently, was never given serious consideration.[48] Next came the addition of Edgar Allen Woolf and Florence Ryerson. MGM writers for some time, their films prior to *The Wizard of Oz* have proven to be unmemorable, though Woolf had contributed to *Grand Hotel* without credit. Together they had previously written for the Judy Garland film *Everybody Sing* (1938). These two were brought in on June 3, and a week later Langley was removed. Ryerson and Woolf identified problems that would be resolved as development continued. They were the ones who gave the script its focus on what would be the two central aspects of the plot: Dorothy's wish to go home and the Witch's pursuit of the ruby slippers. In particular, they felt that Dorothy's "desperate desire to get home should be dramatized more fully."[49] "There's no place like home" was viewed by Freed as vital: "We must remember at all times that Dorothy is only motivated by one object in Oz; that is, how to get back home to her Aunt Em, and every situation should be related to this main drive."[50] It is, quite simply, homesickness, love for home itself, which motivates her. Film and theater historian Ethan Mordden takes a more cynical view: "Because MGM was the conservative studio, the home of 'family values' long before the term became a bigot's euphemism, *The Wizard* purports to teach a disaffected and slightly mutinous girl how to fit in at home, in her community—in the System. Dorothy's journey over the rainbow is meant to teach her that there's no place like home, that she must abandon the mutiny and take her place among the righteous."[51]

Though not addressed directly as a solution, sharpening this focus did ultimately resolve a problem in the earlier scripts, that being the loss of Dorothy's centrality to the story because of the addition of so many extraneous characters. By emphasizing Dorothy's need to go home, the story is hers. Ryerson and Woolf also felt that the Wicked Witch of the West should be better utilized in the story; it was their initial thinking that led to the Witch's appearances during the journey to, and then at, the Emerald City. Theirs was also the idea to have the Wizard appear "as a quaint old medicine man"[52] who would become Professor Marvel in the Kansas sequence, and also take on different guises in the Emerald City, giving the popular Frank Morgan more screen time.[53] One idea that did not take hold was for the audience to know "that the water will melt her [the Wicked Witch of the West] beforehand, and be hoping that Dorothy will find out."[54] This would have added another element of suspense in addition to the problem of whether Dorothy really could get home, but it would have eliminated the more effective element of surprise when Dorothy does douse the Witch with water.

Ryerson and Woolf quickly produced two scripts, the first on June 13, the second on July 5. The first continued the use of extraneous characters, now including a caged lion and a dwarf with Professor Marvel; the Wicked Witch has not only her son Bulbo, but a lion of her own in addition to a gorilla and a human Captain. Clearly, they were able to see the new complications they caused, and with the July 5 script extraneous characters disappeared from the story, which was all for the better.[55]

Ryerson and Woolf left the project on July 27, apparently having added little or nothing to their July 5 script. Langley immediately returned and replaced as much as he could of the Ryerson-Woolf dialogue with his own. He seems to have been able to do this overnight, as July 28 is the date of what was now the Ryerson-Woolf-Langley script, although he was not officially back on the job until July 30. The script now was close to what would be the shooting version, but changes were still to be made.[56]

FIGURE 2.1. E. Y. (Yip) Harburg and Harold Arlen. Credit: Photofest.

Enter E. Y. Harburg, Unsung Script Doctor

At this point the participation and influence of lyricist E. Y. Harburg solidified. An established songwriter by 1939, Harburg had worked successfully both on Broadway and in Hollywood. Previously he had been show doctor on two Broadway productions for which he initially provided only lyrics, *The Show Is On* and *Hooray for What?*[57] Furthermore, Freed trusted Harburg's instincts and judgment, which helped give the lyricist room to develop his ideas. Langley later said "I had no fears" with Harburg and composer Harold Arlen providing the songs,[58] so he was more likely to be receptive to Harburg's influence (see Figure 2.1). To Langley's benefit, Harburg preferred Langley's script,[59] so he was well positioned to keep both Langley and Freed happy. It was Harburg's work that made the final blend of Ryerson-Woolf and Langley possible, with additions of his own.

Harburg received no writing credit other than lyricist. Harburg's son Ernie, explained those contributions in an interview:

> Yip also wrote . . . dialogue in that time and the setup to the songs and he also wrote the part where they give out the heart, the brains and the nerve, because he was the final script editor. And he . . . pulled the whole thing

together, wrote his own lines and gave the thing a coherence and unity which made it a work of art. But he doesn't get credit for that. He gets lyrics by E. Y. Harburg, you see. But nevertheless, he put his influence on the thing.[60]

It is the sequence in Munchkinland and the introduction to the Emerald City that best show Harburg's influence on telling the story. The Munchkinland scene, in particular, is a mini opera, telling the story in song and rhyme to establish, in a way that dialogue could not, Oz-as-fantasy upon Dorothy's arrival. Similarly, by having the residents of Emerald City introduce themselves in song, the image of the City as a carefree place is much stronger than it could be through any spoken introduction. This use of song to delineate Oz gives the film a feeling of the fantastical quality of Baum's story that the early scripts were losing.

To make the songs work to his satisfaction, Harburg reversed what may seem the logical sequence of making the songs fit the script and adjusted the script to fit the songs as he, and Arlen, conceived them. This created an integrated musical in which lyrics, music, and dance all contributed to further the plot or, at the very least, not slow it down. Even the one star turn, for Bert Lahr, fills time as the travelers await the Wizard's answer, and it also gives insight into the Lion's character. Freed was in agreement with this approach, saying "Music can be a big help properly used as an adjunct and accent to the emotional side of the story, because the masses can feel it."[61]

Along with his contribution of song, as noted, Harburg did provide some dialogue, in particular the scene in which the Wizard confers the brains, heart, and courage on Dorothy's companions.[62] Baum has the Wizard give the Scarecrow a bag of pins and needles, the Tin Man a red silk heart, and the Lion a potion that instills courage. It is not clear if these items are, in fact, magical, or simply placebos that allow the recipients to realize their dreams. Harburg uses unambiguously symbolic gifts, an idea he called "satiric and cynical."[63] Satiric, yes, but sincere rather than cynical. Harburg makes the Wizard, who was fearsome in his first meeting with the travelers, into a lovable counterpart to the Wicked Witch of the West. The scene reaches its climax with the Wizard's moment of wisdom in saying "a heart is not judged by how much you love, but by how much you are loved by others."[64] While this is addressed to the Tin Man, it is true for Dorothy, the Scarecrow, the Lion, and even the Wizard himself. It resurfaces in the final scene in Kansas where Dorothy learns how greatly she is loved by others.

Harburg is also responsible for another significant change to the story: the rainbow, which he often pointed out receives no mention in the original book. Rainbows were a lifelong fascination for Harburg. He used the word—and concept—in one Broadway show title, six song titles, and the lyrics of another twenty-two songs. Rainbows represented joy and wonder for Harburg, signifying for him, and in turn Dorothy, the "dreams that you dare to dream."[65] With the song "Over the Rainbow," Dorothy indicates a desire for something beyond life on the farm. As Harburg explained, "This little girl thinks: *My life is messed up. Where do I run?* The song has to be full of childish pleasures. Of lemon drops. The book had said Kansas was an arid place where not even flowers grew. The only colorful thing Dorothy saw, occasionally, would be the rainbow. I thought that the rainbow could be a bridge from one place to another. A rainbow gave us a visual reason for going to a new land and a reason for changing to color."[66]

Harburg's blending of the Ryerson-Woolf and Langley scripts did not, however, end the parade of writers. Gag writer Jack Mintz worked for a month starting August 3, writing jokes for the Scarecrow, Tin Man, and Lion. Sid Silvers, a writer of light comedy films, came in for six days on October 17, assisting then-director Richard Thorpe by providing script changes as needed. Thorpe was fired and Silvers left also. When Victor Fleming came on as director he was assisted by John Lee Mahin, who also was uncredited for his work. Mahin made minor adjustments to the script as shooting went on, but his major contribution was the final version of the opening Kansas sequence. It was Mahin who conceived the scene of Dorothy running back to the farm after her altercation with Miss Gulch. Mahin also added Zeke, the farmhand who becomes the Cowardly Lion.[67]

Page and Screen: Baum's Oz and MGM's Oz

This history of the transitions from novel to screen has shown that from the first adaptation liberties were taken with the story, even by Baum himself. Ryerson and Woolf, as quoted earlier, claim that "changes in the story were really minor," a statement to which "yes" and "no" both apply. The trajectory of the film's story is in keeping with that of Baum's book. Dorothy, in her house, is blown by a tornado to Munchkinland in Oz. The house lands on the Wicked Witch of the East, killing her. Dorothy meets a good witch who advises her to go to the Emerald City by following the Yellow Brick Road and to ask the Wizard to return her to Kansas. Dorothy wears a pair of magic shoes which she learns are coveted by the Wicked Witch of the West. On the way to the Emerald City, Dorothy meets three fantastic characters: an animate scarecrow (who wants a brain), a man made of tin (who lacks and desires a heart), and a talking lion (not the mighty King of the Jungle, as he believes he has no courage). The four arrive at the Emerald City and meet the Wizard, who promises to give them brains, a heart, and courage, and to return Dorothy to Kansas. First, they must eliminate the Wicked Witch of the West, which is successfully done. The Wizard proves to be a humbug, but he does give Dorothy's three companions what they desire. The Wizard promises to take Dorothy home in a lighter-than-air balloon that departs before she can get into the basket. A good witch reveals that the shoes have the power to take her home, which they do.

As Swartz observes, "Never before had so many of the key elements of Baum's tale appeared in a single dramatic adaptation."[68] Yet, the variations from Baum are significant. In the book there are two Good Witches. The first (and nameless) Witch of the North does not know the power of the book's silver shoes, saying "The Witch of the East was proud of those shoes and there is some charm connected with them; but what it is we never knew."[69] She and Dorothy, nonetheless, are rather casual in their approach to the shoes. The Witch hands them to Dorothy, rather than magically transferring them to her feet. Dorothy, in turn, puts them aside, only later to step into them herself. Glinda, the Witch of the South, knows the shoes' power and is able to tell Dorothy how to use them to return to Kansas, but Dorothy must travel to her; she does not come to Dorothy. The film combines the Witches of the North and South into one, calling her Glinda, the Witch of the North. At the end of the film she reveals the shoes' power with the implication that she knew all along but that Dorothy "had to learn it for herself," a view the book's Glinda does not share.[70]

The book's Witch of the North does not come and go in a bubble, nor does she interrogate Dorothy. Her knowledge, in general, seems somewhat limited as she has to consult her magic slate for the advice to send Dorothy to the Emerald City. In both book and film this Witch does give Dorothy a magic kiss that will provide protection against evil magic.[71] Dorothy, in the book, accepts the magic of Oz quite readily and shows no surprise when the Witch of the North simply vanishes.[72] She also has no enemies specifically seeking to harm her because of who she is or because she possesses the shoes.

The Munchkins in the film are initially shy, eventually emerging in large numbers to salute Dorothy. Baum's Munchkins also show initial nervousness, but later they are quite hospitable to Dorothy, giving her room and board while she is in Munchkinland rather than immediately sending her on her way. Nor does she receive fanfare or a gala send-off from the locals.[73] Dorothy does encounter many perils, which range from a lack of food after she meets the lion, a ditch and a river that both seem impassable, to wolves, crows, bees,[74] fighting trees,[75] and fantastical creatures such as the Kalidahs and the Hammer-Heads, the latter using their heads as hammers to repel intruders, as well as the aforementioned deadly poppies.[76] In more than one instance, fantastic creatures not only block her way but attempt to kill her and her companions. Dorothy's progress is impeded fourteen times (not counting her stay with the Wicked Witch of the West), and in each case it is one of her comrades, not Dorothy, who saves the group, in some instances resorting to violence and killing. These violent episodes are eliminated in the film, with only the two wicked witches being killed, both inadvertently by Dorothy (as in the book). In the film, Glinda and the Witch of the West repeatedly insert themselves into Dorothy's progress; in the book they do not, and it is only the Wizard whom Dorothy meets on a second occasion.[77]

The film, on Dorothy's arrival in Oz, quickly presents the Witch of the West as her enemy. This Witch is the sister of the deceased Witch of the East and she seeks both to avenge her sister's death and to gain the powerful ruby slippers, goals satisfied only by Dorothy's death; she threatens Dorothy on more than one occasion. This is in contrast to the novel, in which the Witch of the West, not introduced until Chapter 12, views all four of the travelers as intruders into her country who, for that reason only, need to be destroyed.[78] When she meets Dorothy she also knows well (but Dorothy does not) that the mark of the kiss left by the Witch of the North on Dorothy's forehead prevents her from harming Dorothy.[79]

After the death of the Witch of the West, both book and film have the Wizard give Dorothy's companions the brains, heart, and courage they desire. He then offers to take Dorothy back to Kansas in a balloon (built from scratch in the book, apparently brought out of mothballs in the film), with disastrous results for Dorothy, as the balloon leaves without her. The film moves quickly to its end with yet another appearance of Glinda. Baum sends Dorothy, in her quest to find a way home, to one of the most powerful people in Oz, Glinda, the Good Witch of the South. Again, Dorothy faces many perils on the road and is aided by her companions in overcoming them. In both book and film, Glinda is the one who knows the shoes have the power to take Dorothy home. Having learned of the shoes' power, Dorothy uses them to return to Kansas. Baum relates her return across two chapters, comprising a total of only one page of text concluding with "And oh, Aunt Em! I'm so glad to be at home again!"[80] Hearn suggests that some commentators think the book is slowed down by Dorothy's encounters after she kills the witch.[81] However, arguably, killing the witch is a high point, but not the culmination of Dorothy's adventures. In the film it can be the culmination, as the witch has been her enemy from her initial arrival in Oz and her death effectively ends the adventure.

Baum, in fact, carefully structured the book so that no one adventure is a culmination. Michael Patrick Hearn points out that "dichotomy is important. . . . The exact center of the book is the discovery of Oz, the Terrible. He disappoints Dorothy twice: first, after she has killed the Wicked Witch of the East and he appears to her as the great head; second, after she destroys the Wicked Witch of the West and he escapes in his balloon. Far from being prosaically anticlimactic, the second half of the book reflects the first. Intelligence, kindness, and bravery, which are discovered within themselves on the journey to the Emerald City, must be tested on the trip south, once they have been given the outer symbols of brains, heart, and courage."[82]

The Wizard also changes from book to film. The reader learns that the Wizard "can take on any form he wishes. So that some say he looks like a bird; and some say he looks like an elephant; and some say he looks like a cat. To others he appears as a beautiful fairy, or a brownie, or in any other form that pleases him. But who the real Oz is, when he is in his own form, no living person can tell."[83] The Wizard grants individual audiences to the travelers, one each day, appearing in a different guise to each. MGM, no doubt to save narrative time, has the four meet the Wizard as a group. His appearance is also disguised in the film; drawing on the giant head Dorothy encounters in the book, MGM has him appear to the group as a large head amidst a swirl of smoke and flame.

In both book and film Dorothy wants to go home, though each present different views on her *need* to go home. Baum has her avow that need very simply, "I am anxious to get back to my Aunt and Uncle, for I am sure they will worry about me."[84] Her concern is a fairly practical one—her family will fret about her, even though she apparently feels reasonably safe in Oz, despite the adversities. In the film Dorothy is very aware of being uprooted and desires to return to the familiar.

Other changes, of a lesser nature, include Dorothy in the film meeting the Scarecrow specifically at a crossroad, not simply beside the road. The book's Scarecrow does not speak initially, but winks at Dorothy; the film's version allows for some comic relief. Often mentioned in discussions of the film is the fact that the Golden Cap which controls the Flying Monkeys is never explained; it does play a significant role in the book. As noted earlier, the two Emerald City Guardians of the Gates and the cabby were developed in the film to play to the strengths of Frank Morgan. In the book, everyone wears green glasses in the Emerald City; in the film the travelers are surrounded by green Art Deco splendor. Baum's Emerald City also has the Wizard living in a palace peopled by courtiers, making the Wizard a kingly, if unseen, figure. As well as can be determined, in the film he has only the Doorkeeper in his palace.

The film does not give any indication as to how long Dorothy is in Oz. Baum is not specific either, though clearly it is many days and more likely a number of months, which begs the question as to why Aunt Em, while emotional at Dorothy's return, appears nonetheless not to have been frantic during Dorothy's absence. Baum does let us know that the cyclone itself takes hours, but he is less clear on other passages of time. As the film is a dream, the passage of time is not an issue, thus allowing the film a vague timeline, though it is more than a single day. In the book Dorothy is shown hospitality during her travels and given places to sleep, and she either is given food or finds it for herself; in the film we never learn where she eats and sleeps.

The Two Views of Dorothy

Between them, Baum and MGM fill the tale with memorable characters, fantastic monsters, and colorful settings in Oz. For all of this, the story is about Dorothy. The film Dorothy reflects MGM's changes to the story, the casting of Judy Garland as preferred by Arthur Freed, and choices about her character made by the screenwriters. Changes in Dorothy were seen in the earliest treatments starting with Mankiewicz's envisioning her as an "orphan from Kansas who sings jazz."[85]

Baum is vague in his depiction of Dorothy; the reader can discern as much from Denslow's drawings as from Baum's writing. He never reveals her age, though he tells us that she is "a well-grown child for her age."[86] Denslow's drawings suggest a child much like Shirley Temple, at one time considered for the film role, rather than the more mature Judy Garland.

This Dorothy likely is seven or eight. She is merry, playful,[87] and well mannered. Whatever the grayness of her existence, she has not lost her laughter and "merry voice"[88] which provide the only contrast to the drab life she shares with the unsmiling Aunt Em and Uncle Henry. Indeed, Dorothy's laughter startles Aunt Em so much that she screams in reaction.[89] Dorothy shows anger only when she feels she has been treated unfairly by the Wizard and the Witch of the West, the latter instance causing the Witch's demise. Fear appears not to be part of her personality; she is undaunted by the many perils she faces on the road, maintaining her spirit throughout, and she does not hesitate to speak up to the authority figures of the Wizard and the Witch of the West.

MGM's Dorothy is more sentimental, though she shares her book counterpart's willingness to speak up when she feels wronged. Again, we never learn her age. This Dorothy does not have as playful a spirit, taking life much more seriously. Baum's Dorothy, for instance, would never consider running away from home, no matter how gray it is; however, that Dorothy also does not face Miss Gulch and the loss of Toto.

In both book and film Dorothy does not physically rescue herself and her companions, but she is able to face her adversaries. Like her anger, these moments of gumption occur when her sense of justice has been offended. She treats the lion like a bad pet by slapping him and exclaiming "you ought to be ashamed of yourself"[90] in the book and simply "shame on you" in the film.[91] In their first meeting with the Wizard in the film, she responds with "you ought to be ashamed of yourself"[92] to him when he turns down their requests. In the book, each of the four meets the Wizard separately, so Dorothy does not know that he has disappointed her companions. Later, in both, she does not hesitate to express herself to him: "you must keep your promises to us!"[93] in the book and "if you were really great and powerful, you'd keep your promise"[94] in the film. For all of this, though, it is only when she reacts to the burning of the Scarecrow that she acts in a way that results in saving herself and her three companions, and this in the film only.

Casting Judy Garland made Dorothy older, which helped render more believable her ability to imagine a world beyond Kansas, and Garland's trademark vulnerability elicited the audience's sympathy. This Dorothy does fall prey to fear. In the Witch's castle she calls out repeatedly to Auntie Em's image in the crystal ball, "I'm frightened!"[95] reflecting a sense of abandonment that Baum's Dorothy apparently never feels. Even when life threatening, the obstacles Baum's Dorothy faces are problems to be solved rather than cause for fear.

No matter how different they are, these two versions of Dorothy have the same goal: for Dorothy to return home. Ethan Mordden points out that "the film is built around her quest, and the ease with which she befriends the good, unmasks the phony, and defeats the vicious."[96] This is no less true of Baum's Dorothy, giving them another important commonality. Baum insisted that Oz was a real place, thus it is physically possible for Dorothy to return home. She only needs to find the means. MGM's Dorothy can return home because she never left it; her visit to Oz was a Technicolor dream. Whether Dorothy is practical (Baum) or sentimental (MGM), she wants to return home. In the end she does return home, glad to be there.

Conclusion

As shown in the history of MGM's adaptation of Baum's novel, Hearn's words were apt when he observed that "most of the troubles with the script were easily resolved by simply going back to what L. Frank Baum had done in *The Wonderful Wizard of Oz*."[97] Yet, also as shown, changes were necessary because of the shift in medium and the reinterpretations of the original by writers, directors, and producer. Ultimately, *The Wizard of Oz* is a new interpretation. Drawn heavily from Baum's novel, nonetheless it makes concessions to, and adaptations for, the screen. The tale is no longer a real-life adventure but the dream of a girl who yearns for color in her drab life. In that dream she reimagines the friends and foes of her daily life as friends and foes in a magical land over the rainbow. Being a "realistic" medium, film as a genre often has difficulty dealing with elements that may be perceived as not realistic. Because Dorothy's adventure is turned into a dream, there is no need to question the reality of what happens to her in Oz.

For all of this, however, the film retains the sense of a magical world and magical adventure that made Baum's *The Wonderful Wizard of Oz*, and the series of Oz books, so popular. Readers and viewers will continue to fall under the spell of that magic; a magic that ensures that neither book nor film are likely to fade from popular culture.

Notes

1. For clarity, I refer to the book as *The Wonderful Wizard of Oz* (its original title) and the film as *The Wizard of Oz*.
2. The "Wardrobe Department ... chose to follow as closely as possible the illustrations drawn by W. W. Denslow for Baum's book. . . . In several cases where Denslow's drawings were not explicit, costume designer Adrian followed Baum's text" (Aljean Harmetz, *The Making of The Wizard of Oz* [New York: Alfred A. Knopf, 1977; New York: Dell 1989], 209). However, changes in the look are inevitable.
3. Much has been written since 1939 about the creation of the MGM film. Even so, the creators of the film consistently prove frustrating in not divulging why they made the changes they did or in revealing their aims in rewriting Baum's story. Aljean Harmetz in her book on the creation of film was able to interview some of the writers and production staff, giving us a few glimpses into the creative process. Hers is the most thorough writing on the film, but other sources add to the story and were used in writing this chapter.
4. It is arguable how much of this is Baum's philosophy or, rather, the home-and-hearth–oriented philosophy of MGM, as argued by writers such as Ethan Mordden. Ethan Mordden, "I Got a Song," *New Yorker*, October 22, 1990, 125.
5. Quoted in Doug McClelland, *Down the Yellow Brick Road: The Making of The Wizard of Oz* (New York: Bonanza Books, 1976, 1989), 87, 90.
6. Mark Evan Swartz, *Oz before the Rainbow: L. Frank Baum's The Wonderful Wizard of Oz on Stage and Screen to 1939* (Baltimore: Johns Hopkins University Press, 2000), 3. "Many aspects of its preliminary treatments and scripts harkened back not only to the 1902 stage musical but to the various earlier film adaptations as well" (242). Of the deadly poppy scene, Swartz says, "They decided to copy the play's solution and have the Good Witch bring about the snowfall to freeze the flowers" (245). "Finally, the very fact that the 1939 film was conceived from the outset as a musical probably can be attributed to the success of the 1902 stage adaptation" (245).
7. There is speculation on why these were "Radio-Plays." Patrick Michael Hearn says it is a reference to "Michel Radio, the inventor of the early color film process, and not to wireless transmission" (Patrick Michael Hearn, Introduction to *The Wizard of Oz: The Screenplay* [henceforth "Intro"] [New York: Delta, 1989], 2). Fraser A. Sherman in *The Wizard of Oz Catalogue* concurs, though he also suggests

that "he [Baum] may have been joking" (Fraser A. Sherman, *The Wizard of Oz Catalogue* [Jefferson, NC: McFarland, 2005], 69). Swartz, however, speculates that this "is likely just another example of Baum's whimsy—using the word *radio*, which connotes something transmitted by radiant energy, to refer to his fairy films so as to make them seem exotic and technologically modern" (162; see also 162, fn2).

8. Swartz, *Oz before the Rainbow*, 161–162.

9. Sherman, *The Wizard of Oz Catalogue*, 146. The film is also an early example of blending animation into a live-action picture.

10. According to Swartz, his plan was "a Technicolor musical comedy starring Eddie Cantor as the Scarecrow, W. C. Fields as the Wizard, and either Helen Hayes or Mary Pickford as Dorothy." The mind boggles. Swartz says that the project did not proceed because Cantor was no longer the draw he had been in earlier years (Swartz, *Oz before the Rainbow*, 239).

11. "With the industry convinced that 'Snow White' will be a box-office success, there is a wild search by producers for comparable fantasies. Within the last ten days Samuel Goldwyn has received five offers for L. Frank Baum's 'Wizard of Oz,' the highest being $75,000" (*New York Times*, February 19, 1938, quoted in Harmetz, *The Making of The Wizard of Oz*, 3).

12. LeRoy said the deal "must go down alongside the Louisiana Purchase as one of the biggest bargains of all times" (Hearn, "Intro," 5).

13. Hearn, "Intro," 6.

14. Hearn says that Brecher was "consulted," which suggests his role was only to provide expertise in the early stages of script development ("Intro," 7).

15. Harmetz, *The Making of The Wizard of Oz*, 26. Hearn says that this early script goes "not far past the introduction of the Cowardly Lion, here on all fours" ("Intro," 7).

16. Harmetz, *The Making of The Wizard of Oz*, 26.

17. Quoted in Harmetz, *The Making of The Wizard of Oz*, 26. "The most important section of Mankiewicz's script to remain in the movie was the transition from Kansas to fairyland by contrasting the grayness of the farm with the colorful atmosphere of Oz" (Hearn, "Intro," 9).

18. Baum, L. Frank, *The Wonderful Wizard of Oz* (Chicago: George M. Hill, 1900), 3. Herman Mankiewicz drew on this in his original treatment: ". . . every effort should be made through tinting, to emphasize the grey nature of the landscape and Dorothy's daily life." Mankiewicz, quoted in Harmetz, *The Making of The Wizard of Oz*, 27.

19. She really has no chores? One would assume that on a small farm all the able-bodied would be put to work. This is an inconsistency of both the book and film.

20. Harmetz, *The Making of The Wizard of Oz*, 27.

21. Harmetz, *The Making of The Wizard of Oz*, 27.

22. MGM had previously done this with Garland in the short film *Every Sunday* in which she squared off with Deanna Durbin in a contest between jazz and opera.

There is no apparent winner. In *Babes in Arms* Garland engaged in another such contest with Jaynes herself, this time between opera and swing. Given the antics by Mickey Rooney with a cello, one has to give the nod to swing this time.

Jaynes was of the Durbin mold, having made her opera debut at the age of fifteen with the Chicago City Opera Company. Baker's greatest claim to fame was introducing the George and Ira Gershwin standard "Love Walked In" in *The Goldwyn Follies* (1938).

23. Hearn, "Intro," 8. Freed eventually would agree that Jaynes and Baker were not needed and that the extra characters cluttered up the story.

24. Hearn, "Intro," 9.

25. McClelland credits Nash with "a four-page précis that proved non-filmic" (*Down the Yellow Brick Road*, 86). Harmetz says "he turned in no written material" (*The Making of The Wizard of Oz*, 32).

26. Quoted in Harmetz, *The Making of The Wizard of Oz*, 34. "This angle in MGM's film marks a departure from the approach in Baum's book where the companions of Dorothy were fantastic, almost indestructible, figures" (Francis MacDonnell, "'The Emerald City was the New Deal': E. Y. Harburg and *The Wonderful Wizard of Oz*," *Journal of American Culture* 13, no. 4 [1990]: 73).

27. Hearn, "Intro," 10.

28. Hearn, "Intro," 3.

29. The stiff joints are not in the film, but all three farmhands show characteristics of who they will become in Dorothy's dream.

30. Ray Bolger was originally to be the Tin Man and Buddy Ebsen the Scarecrow. They switched roles and the character names switched with them.

31. This is in accord with Baum's original intention: "Baum firmly believed that romance didn't interest children and didn't belong in their stories" (Sherman, *The Wizard of Oz Catalogue*, 4). However, it was Baum who introduced romance in his 1902 play *The Wizard of Oz*: "Dorothy was now a young woman falling in and out of love and accompanied on her travels through Oz by her pet cow, Imogene" (Hearn, "Intro," 1). See also Sherman, *The Wizard of Oz Catalogue*, 64. Dorothy's farewell to the Scarecrow, "I think I'll miss you most of all," may well be a remnant of the discarded romantic additions.

Swartz points out that in the years between 1900 and 1939, Dorothy undergoes a variety of changes: "Dorothy . . . who in Baum's book is an innocent little girl, becomes first a young maid courted by a Poet, then again a child, then a flirtatious flapper who marries a prince and is crowned queen of Oz, and finally, in the MGM musical, a twelve-year-old girl just coming of age. And the Emerald City, which appears in Baum's book as a Victorian Orientalist fantasy and several times reappears in that guise in the adaptations, suddenly becomes a Middle European kingdom before emerging as an art deco world of splendor in the 1939 film" (Swartz, *Oz before the Rainbow*, 3).

32. Harmetz, *The Making of The Wizard of Oz*, 35.
33. The first time was in 1934 when Samuel Goldwyn acquired the rights (Swartz, *Oz before the Rainbow*, 239). Apparently Fields had a quality that producers deemed fitting to the Wizard. "To Freed and [lyricist E. Y.] Harburg, [the perfect choice] was W. C. Fields" (Harmetz, *The Making of The Wizard of Oz*, 119). "Harburg had written the Wizard's main speech to fit Fields' massive cynicism as he handed out the diploma in place of brains, a plaque in place of a heart, and a medal in place of courage" (120). This helps explain Harburg's view of the scene as "satiric and cynical" (58).
34. Langley script, quoted in Harmetz, *The Making of The Wizard of Oz*, 37.
35. Other than saying that she was an orphan, Baum gives no background on Dorothy's parents or why she lives with her aunt and uncle (or even which of them is her blood relative). The 1939 film also does not.
36. A few such films from just the 1930s include *The Gay Divorcee* (1934), *Anything Goes, Rose Marie, Show Boat* (1936), *Maytime, A Damsel in Distress*, and *Rosalie* (1937), among musicals. Nonmusical examples include *Frankenstein, Dracula* (1931), and *The Thin Man* (1934).
37. Harmetz, *The Making of The Wizard of Oz*, 37.
38. Harmetz, *The Making of The Wizard of Oz*, 38.
39. Langley came up with the idea of Glinda traveling in a bubble, a concept that went back to a 1918 film, *Queen of the Sea*.
40. "In the end most of the troubles with the script were easily resolved by simply going back to what L. Frank Baum had done in *The Wonderful Wizard of Oz*" (Hearn, "Intro," 24–25). Again, not entirely true, but valid as regards all the extraneous characters.
41. Harmetz, *The Making of The Wizard of Oz*, 51–52.
42. Harmetz, *The Making of The Wizard of Oz*, 23, 45; Hearn, "Intro," 10.
43. Harmetz, *The Making of The Wizard of Oz*, 37; Hearn, "Intro," 14.
44. Harmetz, *The Making of The Wizard of Oz*, 40–41.
45. Harmetz, *The Making of The Wizard of Oz*, 43.
46. Harmetz, *The Making of The Wizard of Oz*, 57.
47. Quoted in Hearn, "Intro," 14.
48. Harmetz speculates that, given Hoffenstein's status as a writer of light verse, he might be viewed as suitable for a fantasy tale (*The Making of The Wizard of Oz*, 45). His film credits, however, were for films of a serious nature including *Dr. Jekyll and Mr. Hyde* (1931), *Phantom of the Opera* (1943), and *Laura* (1944); he also was a writer of *Gay Divorce*, Fred Astaire's last stage show, and contributed to the groundbreaking Rodgers and Hart film *Love Me Tonight* (1932).
49. Quoted in Harmetz, *The Making of The Wizard of Oz*, 47.
50. Quoted in Hearn, "Intro," 12. "Freed was a sentimental man and demanded that Dorothy have a deep-rooted psychological need back home that would justify her

actions in Oz." This is at odds with Baum who gives precedence to her adventures, even though she does express a desire to go home.

In the book Dorothy does use the phrase when she says to the Scarecrow, "No matter how dreary and gray our homes are, we people of flesh and blood would rather live there than in any other country, be it ever so beautiful. There is no place like home" (Baum, *The Wonderful Wizard of Oz*, 44–45). Note how Baum alludes to the song "Home, Sweet Home" in this passage. Later, when she comes to use the shoes in order to go home she says "take me home to Aunt Em" (258) rather than "there's no place like home." MGM, however, transforms it to become the moral theme of the film.

51. Mordden, "I Got a Song," 125.

52. Harmetz, *The Making of The Wizard of Oz*, 47.

53. It seems plausible to me that all of these Emerald City characters are, in fact, the Wizard, using these disguises to keep tabs on the doings of his domain. Sherman is the only source I have found which posits this theory: "Woolf . . . and Ryerson . . . had the Wizard appear in multiple roles" (*The Wizard of Oz Catalogue*, 150). Baum's Wizard behaves in quite the opposite way, saying, in two different instances, "usually I will not see even my subjects . . ." (*The Wonderful Wizard of Oz*, 185), and later ". . . ever since this palace was built I have shut myself up . . . " (188). If these film characters are all the Wizard in disguise it may not be in keeping with Baum's Wizard, but works well for the film's Wizard.

54. Harmetz, *The Making of The Wizard of Oz*, 48–49. In both book and film Dorothy's killing of the witch is inadvertent. In the film it is to save the Scarecrow; in the book "Dorothy [was] so very angry that she picked up the bucket of water that stood near and dashed it over the Witch, wetting her from head to toe" (Baum, *The Wonderful Wizard of Oz*, 154).

55. Harmetz, *The Making of The Wizard of Oz*, 49, 50.

56. Harmetz, *The Making of The Wizard of Oz*, 57; Hearn, "Intro," 22.

57. Harold Meyerson and Ernie Harburg, *Who Put the Rainbow in "The Wizard of Oz"? Yip Harburg, Lyricist* (Ann Arbor: University of Michigan Press, 1993), 124. Harburg and Arlen also were familiar with Bert Lahr, having tailored two songs in Broadway shows for him, "The Song of the Woodman" and "Things."

58. Quoted in Meyerson and Harburg, *Who Put the Rainbow in "The Wizard of Oz"?*, 119.

59. Harmetz, *The Making of The Wizard of Oz*, 54.

60. "A Tribute to Blacklisted Lyricist Yip Harburg: The Man Who Put the Rainbow in The Wizard of Oz," *democracynow.org*, November 25, 2016.

61. Hearn, "Intro," 16.

62. He does draw on a passage in the book: "Oh, no, my dear; I'm really a very good man; but I'm a very bad Wizard, I must admit" (Baum, *The Wonderful Wizard of Oz*, 189).

63. Meyerson and Harburg, *Who Put the Rainbow in "The Wizard of Oz"?*, 153. See fn32.

64. Noel Langley, et al., *The Wizard of Oz* (New York: Smithmark, 1990, script copyright 1939 by Loewe's Incorporated, renewed 1966 MGM), 150.

65. It has always fascinated me that Dorothy heard of the land "over the rainbow" only one time ("once in a lullaby"). Was this simply because Harburg needed an extra syllable to fit the music or is it yet another reflection on life in Kansas being so difficult that even lullabies are a luxury?

66. Quoted in Harmetz, *The Making of The Wizard of Oz*, 80–81.

67. Harmetz, *The Making of The Wizard of Oz*, 58; Hearn, "Intro," 24.

68. Swartz, *Oz before the Rainbow*, 243.

69. Baum, *The Wonderful Wizard of Oz*, 25. Other than their ability to take Dorothy home, we never learn what their power is in either book or film.

70. "There is one miscalculation in the final moments in Oz, however, when Glinda reveals that Dorothy always had the power to return home, by knocking the magical ruby slippers together. Well, why didn't Glinda say so in the first place? Because then there would have been no movie" (Mordden, "I Got a Song," 125).

71. Baum, *The Wonderful Wizard of Oz*, 28.

72. Baum, *The Wonderful Wizard of Oz*, 28.

73. Baum, *The Wonderful Wizard of Oz*, 24, 34–35.

74. Baum, *The Wonderful Wizard of Oz*, 75–76, 77, 79, 87–92, 141–142, 143.

75. Baum, *The Wonderful Wizard of Oz*, 222–223. In the earlier quote, Ryerson and Woolf take credit for this, but it was Langley who had the initial idea of the trees fighting Dorothy and the Scarecrow (Harmetz, *The Making of The Wizard of Oz*, 43). Ryerson and Woolf utilized this change to provide comic relief. The trees also serve a practical function in that Dorothy's search for an apple brings her to the Tin Woodman. In the novel the trees are violent, rather than comic. Overall, the film trims away the book's violence.

76. Baum, *The Wonderful Wizard of Oz*, 80–81, 93–105, 246–248.

77. First in Chapter 11, second in Chapter 15.

78. ". . . the Wicked Witch was angry to find them in her country . . . " (Baum, *The Wonderful Wizard of Oz*, 141). She incites her various minions to tear the intruders to pieces.

79. Baum, *The Wonderful Wizard of Oz*, 149–150.

80. Baum, *The Wonderful Wizard of Oz*, 261.

81. Hearn, *The Annotated Wizard of Oz*, 306, fn1. However, he cites only Salman Rushdie and Russian translator Alexander Volkov. The latter went so far as to remove chapters he deemed unnecessary, though he did also add two of his own.

82. Hearn, *The Annotated Wizard of Oz*, page xcix. This is not quite accurate. There are twenty-four chapters in the book, with the Witch appearing in only Chapter 12; the Wizard is unveiled in Chapter 15, thus we move toward the Witch in the center

of the story and then away from her. Dorothy twice has to face adventures after being involved in the death of a Wicked Witch, thus the Witch's proper place is in the middle of the book.

83. Baum, *The Wonderful Wizard of Oz*, 113.
84. Baum, *The Wonderful Wizard of Oz*, 25. One can wonder why, in both book and film, Dorothy desires so strongly to return home to a drab existence and, in the film, also still facing the danger of Miss Gulch who, we must assume, is soon to arrive with the Sheriff, warrant in hand. Perhaps vanquishing the Wicked Witch has given Dorothy the courage to face this adversary. We will never know.
85. Hearn, "Intro," 8.
86. Baum, *The Wonderful Wizard of Oz*, 20.
87. "Toto played all day long, and Dorothy played with him." Baum, *The Wonderful Wizard of Oz*, 13.
88. Baum, *The Wonderful Wizard of Oz*, 13.
89. "Aunt Em had been so startled by the child's laughter that she would scream and press her hand upon her heart . . ." (Baum, *The Wonderful Wizard of Oz*, 12–13).
90. Baum, *The Wonderful Wizard of Oz*, 67.
91. Langley, *Wizard of Oz,* 83.
92. Langley, *Wizard of Oz,* 119.
93. Baum, *The Wonderful Wizard of Oz*, 183.
94. Langley, *Wizard of Oz,* 144.
95. Langley, *Wizard of Oz,* 129.
96. Mordden, "I Got a Song," 125.
97. Hearn, "Intro," 24–25.

3

"ARLEN AND HARBURG AND MORE, OH MY!"

THE CUMULATIVE CREATION OF THE *OZ* SONGS

Laura Lynn Broadhurst

Anybody who approaches the creative process on an assembly line basis
must have some glandular, nervous structure for turning a thing out that is
an assembly line product. . . . That's why [these people in Hollywood are] able
to do so many pictures a year, songs a year, whatever it is. They turn them out
like gloves or fur coats.[1]

—E. Y. "YIP" HARBURG, *lyricist, February 1959*

Even in those days [in Hollywood], when we made a lot of money, we still had
no prestige. We were considered just song writers. George Gershwin, too. . . .
You would write as well as you could. Hand it in. Walk away. They would do
anything they pleased with your song. They would change the tempo or throw
it out if they felt like it. Anyhow, once a song leaves you it thumbs its nose at
you and develops a life of its own.[2]

—HAROLD ARLEN, *composer, August 1961*

In early May 1938, when Harold Arlen and Yip Harburg began their
fourteen-week assignment to write the songs for MGM's *The Wizard
of Oz*, they were, by all accounts, thrilled to have landed the job.
Crisscrossing the country during the previous few years, the songwriting team had enjoyed successes on Broadway and were gaining a
foothold in Hollywood.[3] *Oz* would be their best job yet on the West
Coast—their first chance to work on a big-budget project for the era's
largest and most extravagant studio. "We were very excited about the
film, we loved it," Harburg recalled. "For the first time we'd gotten
something that we both felt had the feeling of being fun."[4] Among
their elite set of songwriting colleagues, *Oz* was a coveted opportunity: MGM lavished nearly $2.8 million and eighteen months on
the picture (an enormous budget and time frame for the period),
conceived from the outset as their live-action, Technicolor rival to
Disney's 1937 animated triumph, *Snow White and the Seven Dwarfs*.
Apparently not expecting to turn a profit, studio executives hoped at

least to break even by making a "prestige" film that would show up well at the Academy Awards.[5] *Oz* would be an *original* movie musical of L. Frank Baum's popular novel—not a transfer of a preexisting stage show—and would serve as the first major vehicle for MGM's ascending prodigy, sixteen-year-old Judy Garland.[6] Arlen and Harburg knew they would be working primarily for Arthur Freed—*Oz*'s fledgling, uncredited associate producer and a lyricist himself—who (atypically for Hollywood) would nurture their talents. In fact, Freed gave them more creative freedom than was customary, even allowing Harburg the unusual opportunity to influence the screenplay.[7] Moreover, the partners realized that several big-name contenders had been considered for *Oz*, including their friend Jerome Kern, who evidently had turned MGM down.[8] As Arlen recollected, "There were plenty of other major songwriters who were damned unhappy and shocked when they heard that we'd gotten [*Oz*], because they'd all been sitting around, waiting for that job."[9]

Completing their assignment by mid-August 1938, the duo moved on to new opportunities, while production on *Oz* continued for another year until its August 1939 premiere. In retrospect, Arlen and Harburg's achievement for *Oz* evinces a brilliant musico-dramatic trajectory—a strong narrative structure in which songs deftly delineate character and arise effortlessly from the exigencies of plot. Appreciated by both adults and children, theirs are storytelling songs of the highest caliber: Dorothy's bittersweet ballad ("Over the Rainbow"), the vaudevillian soft shoe for the Scarecrow, Tin Man, and Lion ("If I Only Had a Brain"/"a Heart"/"the Nerve"), the joyous traveling theme ("We're Off to See the Wizard"), etc. Throughout the remainder of their careers, the partners looked back upon these songs with pride, always grateful for their fortuitous hiring and the profound legacy of the film.

An explanation is necessary, then, for the team's negative comments about the motion-picture industry cited at the opening of this chapter. Like most studio-age songwriters, it seems, the duo had a love-hate relationship with Hollywood. Granted, motion-picture money was plentiful, especially compared with the squeezed, Depression-era Broadway market. But luxury amid California sunshine came with a price: the loss of creative control. In contrast to the customary practice on Broadway, even veteran Hollywood songwriters were generally powerless over the fate of their songs. Once submitted, songs could be significantly altered or dropped at any stage, depending on the powers-that-be. According to one of today's foremost theatrical orchestrators, Larry Blank—an expert in studio-era production practices—such a modus operandi was reluctantly accepted by Broadway tunesmiths bound for the West Coast: "Although songwriters probably didn't like giving up artistic control, it was part of the deal. . . . Going to Hollywood meant 'selling our souls' (for a very large amount of money). The obscene fees offered by the studios made it easy to turn a blind eye to the *de rigueur* of 'Hollyweird.'"[10]

One could find the occasional exception, of course.[11] Nevertheless, *Oz* provides a compelling case study of the typical songwriting scene in mid-twentieth-century Hollywood: after Arlen and Harburg turned their songs in to MGM, they essentially lost artistic control. Primary materials suggest they had little (if any) input on the arrangements and orchestrations of their songs, which were completed subsequently by several different studio personnel. And although most of their numbers were retained in the completed film, a substantial percentage of their work was unceremoniously deleted during *Oz*'s preview period, two months before the picture's release. It was actually during the preview stage that Garland's now-iconic performance of "Over the Rainbow" almost ended up on the cutting room floor. The song's early quest for survival has become the stuff of legend: Hollywood lore suggests some MGM executives believed it undignified for their new star to sing in a barnyard, while others felt the number slowed down the prologue's narrative. The ballad was dropped and reinserted at least once, with most versions of the story granting Freed the greatest credit for demanding its permanent restoration. So distraught over the song's near-extraction, Arlen would never again attend a preview for a picture on which he had worked.

Woven around Arlen and Harburg's songs is *Oz*'s orchestral underscoring, much of which is thematically based on the duo's material, although a good deal of original music and quotations from familiar pieces are also incorporated. Therefore, in its entirety, the score for MGM's *The Wizard of Oz* is a single, fully orchestrated entity, comprising two, interdependent components: the songs (by Arlen and Harburg) and the underscoring (by MGM music director Herbert Stothart and a staff under his supervision). These two elements—songs and underscoring (sometimes termed "song score" and "background music")—constitute the scores for most Hollywood and Broadway musicals of this time. Thus, with respect to their constituent parts, at least, studio-era screen musical scores are somewhat similar to their stage musical counterparts. But first and foremost, movie musicals are obviously *films*, and are therefore distinguished from stage musicals by the nature of their medium. And filmmaking during the heyday of Hollywood's studio system—for movie musicals or straight dramatic films—consisted of numerous, fairly well-defined stages contained within three principal production phases, much like an assembly line:

- Pre-production: casting, screenplay development, set design, and other activities;
- Production: the actual filming;
- Post-production: special effects, editing, and so forth.

The construction of original film musical scores typically conformed to these established phases, resulting in a unique process of score production—one also consisting of many quasi-assembly line stages. These sequential stages are illuminated by tracing the assemblage of movie musical *songs*, as one component of the score overall. An outline of the *Oz* songs' creation illustrates this process:

- Pre-production: genesis of the songs (by Arlen and Harburg); arrangement (by MGM staff); orchestration (by yet different personnel); prerecording (with orchestra);
- Production: shoot-to-playback (songs filmed);
- Post-production: underscoring (by Stothart and staff—a stage essential to an accurate understanding of the songs' formation); continued development of the songs (by Stothart and staff); previews (including musical editing); final cut released.

Barring a few anomalies, the majority of the film's songs traversed this path. But does the piecemeal assembly of the songs have an effect on their status as individual "works," and (perhaps even more intriguingly) on their authorship? And what types of primary sources have survived over the decades that afford us insight into the creative process? In the following section, we briefly address these issues; the conclusions drawn from this short discussion significantly impact the remaining body of this chapter, which is devoted to an in-depth exploration of the songs' creation.

Sources, Work, and Authorship

Regrettably, for one undertaking the first source study of the *Oz* songs, a considerable amount of archival material no longer exists.[12] In 1969, MGM sent the songs' original orchestrations and separate instrumental parts to a landfill, along with hundreds of other manuscripts from classic MGM films. Some *Oz*-related artifacts have fortunately survived: numerous studio piano-vocal manuscripts, a few piano-conductor parts, Harburg's draft lyrics, a handful of Arlen holographs, draft screenplays, production records, *Oz*'s original music tracks, correspondence, contemporaneous journal articles, and other materials. These items are presently scattered in numerous archives, including the Cinematic Arts Library (University of Southern California), the Irving S. Gilmore Music Library (Yale), the Warner Brothers Corporate Archive (San Fernando Valley/undisclosed location), the Lilly Library (Indiana University), the Margaret Herrick Library/ Academy of Motion Picture Arts and Sciences (Beverly Hills), and the Library of Congress (Washington, DC).

As a source study, this project has led naturally to the oft-debated question of what constitutes a "work," famously tackled (among others) by literary theorist Roland Barthes and (in a well-known exchange) between musicologist Richard Taruskin and philosopher Lydia Goehr. From this large body of discourse, the present study borrows Barthes's theoretical concept of a "work" as a "closed" entity—a phenomenon comprised of individual instances or snapshots of a continuously unfurling, unlimited "Text" that remains "open" to interpretation.[13] Such a notion offers an especially useful model for an archival examination of the *Oz* songs: indeed, since *Oz* is obviously a film, each song eventually came to a fixed form—the result or "product" of the assembly line–like process by which it was created. The subject of authorship, also much discussed, has been at the center of recent archival scholarship on the Broadway musical. In a valuable 2015 article, Dominic McHugh documents the various collaborative procedures of several mid-twentieth-century Broadway songwriters and their largely uncredited associates (arrangers, orchestrators, etc.). Thereby McHugh convincingly concludes, "We might decide to refer no longer to Broadway 'composers' but rather to 'composer-collaborators.'"[14]

Similarly, many hands were involved in creating most studio-age film musical songs. Yet while "collaborative" is an accurate assessment of the Broadway songwriting environment of this era, the term is not wholly applicable to contemporaneous Hollywood. Collaboration implies that songwriters worked together with other members of a team—that is, somewhat simultaneously. But from the perspective of most songwriters, Hollywood musicals were generally *not* a collaborative endeavor. Arlen himself, recalling the near-deletion of "Over the Rainbow," alluded to the lack of teamwork in Hollywood vis-à-vis Broadway:

> I realized [then and there] the fundamental difference between pictures and shows. When you're doing a show, everybody's in there pitching. It's your show and everyone else's. But it's never your picture. You're just getting paid.[15]

Naturally, while under contract for *Oz*, Arlen and Harburg occasionally collaborated with other personnel, especially since Harburg contributed to the screenplay. Still, sources suggest such interaction was relatively infrequent (far less than for Broadway shows) and did not always constitute direct, genuine collaboration. Furthermore, once their fourteen-week contracts expired, they had little else to do with *Oz*, save for a few exceptions.

Certainly, the *Oz* songs stem primarily from the combined creative gifts of Arlen and Harburg. But determining the authorship of these songs—whether within the context of the movie or as individual entities apart from that setting—is no easy task. This challenge is further complicated if one considers the songs' *legal* authorship: soon after Arlen and Harburg submitted each song to MGM, its legal authorship was firmly attributed to them by copyright law. Their names are clearly listed as the songs' sole legal authors at the Library of Congress's Copyright Office (where piano-vocal copies were deposited during *Oz*'s production) and on the film's all-important "cue sheet" (the studio's detailed log of every musical cue in the movie, which determined who received royalties). Interestingly, though, the songs' copyrights were actually held by MGM's parent company, Loew's Incorporated. In essence, Loew's "owned" the songs, not Arlen and Harburg. (For all practical purposes, the songwriters—by the terms of their 14-week, "work-for-hire" contracts—relinquished control of their intellectual property to MGM/Loew's.) Additionally, Loew's owned MGM's publishing company, Leo Feist, which (even before *Oz* was released) published six of the *Oz* songs, with Arlen and Harburg's names prominently indicated as sole authors. Larry Blank offers additional details about this admittedly complex business arrangement: "When the studios hired or bought songs from songwriters, they were by contract the songs' publishers. Therefore they owned the publishing rights and ASCAP/BMI publishing royalties from the songs. This was *significant* income for the studios and the primary reason they made musicals in the first place."[16]

But if we put aside all such legal and financial matters, and instead consider the songs only as they exist within the confines of the completed picture, Arlen and Harburg—while unequivocally principal authors—are *not* sole authors. Primary sources show that after the partners submitted their songs, several fairly independent and mostly uncredited staff developed and modified their original materials throughout the ensuing months—without the duo's direct involvement—resulting in the songs as we know them in the finished movie. Thus, the *actual* authorship of each song—within the context of the picture—is best described as "cumulative"—a term that conveys additive authorship, acquired over a period of time by a chain of separate contributors.[17]

The following argument draws together the above threads regarding work and authorship: each *Oz* song within the completed film—as an individual, fixed "work"—was created via cumulative authorship along a figurative assembly line. Through many discrete developmental stages, every work changed significantly over time, in part because the music was adapted to suit the film's needs, but also due to the different talents of multiple creators. (A note of clarification: each song as an entity *outside* the film's parameters—for example, in a cover version—is arguably a different work, with its own authorial configuration, from the work as it exists within the finished movie.)

Based on the study of surviving materials, our discussion now turns to a detailed account of the songs' cumulative creation. We will follow the outline given earlier in this chapter of the numerous assembly line stages within *Oz*'s three production phases.

PRE-PRODUCTION (c. January—mid-October, 1938)

Genesis of the Songs

Although Arlen and Harburg's *Oz* contracts are dated June 17, 1938, they indicate that their fourteen-week term was "deemed to have commenced on May 9, 1938."[18] This May date was probably their first day at MGM, although they might already have been in preliminary meetings, perhaps with *Oz*'s associate producer, Arthur Freed. Whether on or before May 9, the songwriters walked into an evolving situation. By this point, the screenplay had gone through innumerable drafts under various hands; it would be revised (often daily) over succeeding months by at least fourteen writers, including Harburg.

Upon arrival, the team was given a copy of the screenplay—certainly a draft dated May 14, 1938 (to which Harburg referred later that summer), if not also earlier versions.[19] The May 14 draft was one of several substantial scripts submitted by Noel Langley, who received screen credit for adapting Baum's novel, and who (with Florence Ryerson and Edgar Allan Woolf) contributed more significantly to the finished screenplay than *Oz*'s many other writers. Langley's May 14 script already included numerous song spots—suggested slots where musical numbers could later be added. Without doubt, Langley received continual guidance from Freed regarding song placement. In all likelihood, a second figure assisted Langley: the multitalented (yet uncredited) Roger Edens—an accompanist and arranger who had previously worked with Freed and Garland at MGM. Early on during pre-production, Freed had assigned Edens as *Oz*'s "musical supervisor"—a job Edens later recalled included determining how to insert songs into a picture, from the inception of its script.[20]

From all available evidence, Freed and Edens (long before Arlen and Harburg came on the scene) pushed for a song score with a strong narrative quality—one in which musical numbers would support the overall drama. Songs would therefore grow naturally from the narrative's demands and develop characters, rather than interrupt the storyline. (This dramatic concept is commonly referred to as "integrated"—a term that has rightly been problematized by recent musical-theater scholarship.)[21] By early spring 1938, Edens himself had attempted two such narrative songs for *Oz*, perhaps with the hope of landing at least part of the film's songwriting assignment: (1) the lyrics for an opening number for Dorothy entitled "Home Sweet Home in Kansas" (each refrain, beginning "Mid pleasures and palaces," would possibly be set to the familiar music of "Home, Sweet Home"); and (2) the lyrics and music for an extended Munchkin routine welcoming Dorothy to Oz.[22]

Arlen and Harburg surely reviewed Edens's *Oz* numbers and the script's tentative song placement. Hence, they were influenced by the desire to adopt a narrative approach. But the surviving sources provide no evidence that the duo genuinely *collaborated* with Freed and Edens on the songs' genesis. When it came to writing the movie's songs, they were basically left alone. As Harburg recalled, they typically worked away from their MGM bungalow:

> [Harold and I] didn't have to go to the studio. Mostly we worked at home. . . . We worked a good deal at night. . . . [It was] better for creation.[23] [*Oz*] was a chance to express ourselves in terms we'd never been offered before. I loved the idea of having the freedom to do lyrics that were not just songs, but *scenes*.[24]

In the earliest stages of a song's genesis, Arlen and Harburg certainly discussed the number's potential musical style, dramatic purpose, and so on. But one wonders what happened next. Eventually, the inevitable question arises: which came first—music or lyrics? For some of the *Oz* songs, Arlen seems to have composed the music first. This was certainly the case for "Brain"/"Heart"/"Nerve," which (under the title "I'm Hanging On to You") was an unused trunk song written for *Hooray for What!*, their 1937 Broadway show; for *Oz* the following year, Harburg created new lyrics for Arlen's preexisting music. Harburg's discarded ideas for this number are especially delightful.[25] His draft lyrics for the Scarecrow, for example, include such charming couplets as:

> And to you my darlin' Dorothy—
> I'd be Bergen—not McCarthy—
> If I only had a brain.

Or the following:

> I would be no small potatoe—
> I would think out things like Plato—
> [etc.]

Yet while music clearly came first in this instance, no uniform pattern of creation can be definitively determined for the seasoned *Oz* duo. Instead, their artistic interactions likely ran the gamut of collaborative possibilities. As Harburg told Walter Cronkite about working specifically with Arlen:

I don't think the creative process has any formulas or any recipes. . . . You could start a song with a word. You could start it with a title. You could start it with just a four-bar line of music. You can start it by a man giving you the whole chorus, and saying, "Here it is." Or you can start it by my having four lines of lyric, and giving it to him. Everything is fair. . . . Anything that sets off the spark for a song is right.[26]

In a later interview, Harburg confirmed that his collaborative method with Arlen encompassed a great deal of back-and-forth: "We'd instinctively give each other clues about what we were thinking. I'd incorporate his ideas into my lyrics. He'd incorporate my ideas into his music."[27] And as it happens, a few of Harburg's draft lyrics for *Oz* suggest that at least in some cases, textual ideas might have preceded music. In fact, his *Oz* sketches reveal that he frequently brainstormed several ideas in the early stages of his work—quickly jotting down his first thoughts for a given number before setting them aside in an incomplete state, perhaps to share later with Arlen. For instance, Harburg's initial jottings for "If I Were King of the Forest" include such unmetered (and eventually discarded) phrases as "Call me Rex" and "I wanna Be King," as well as single words and phrases that ultimately made it into the finished number (e.g., "Rhinoceros," "Impposerous," and "Monarch of all I survey"). For the duo's Munchkin routine, Harburg's early drafts range from short phrases like "Ding Dong—Ding" and "Sing Ho—The Merry Oh" (both of which, in slight variation, found their way into the completed number), to strictly metered couplets that went unused (e.g., "Eenie Meenie Minny Moe"/"Catch a Witch by her Toe"). Such examples reveal that Harburg may occasionally have offered Arlen a word, phrase—or even a fairly complete line—in order to get a song started. And once a number was on its way, the partners (by their own accounts) appear to have worked both independently and in direct collaboration until a song was completed.

At this point, a third party entered the picture—one whose role is revealed first with this study. Virtually all the extant MGM piano-vocal manuscripts for the *Oz* songs include the phrase "Transcribed by Sam Messenheimer" beneath Arlen's name. However, the remaining sources offer no additional information concerning a figure named Messenheimer, who (by his ASCAP entry) was apparently a composer, saxophonist, and pianist who had also arranged

songs for numerous MGM musicals.[28] Fortunately, Messenheimer's surviving
stepson—K. Cochran, who was remarkably an eyewitness to the last stages of
the songs' genesis—kindly agreed to several interviews during which he vividly
recalled details of his stepfather's contributions. A college student in the late
1930s, Cochran remembered "tagging along with my stepfather" to numerous
late-night sessions in the small music den of Arlen's home in Laurel Canyon,
where he observed his stepfather working with the duo near the piano. From
Cochran's recollections, it appears that Messenheimer served as an amanuensis
to Arlen and Harburg, taking down the contents of each song by listening repeatedly to Arlen's playing. Arlen—a top-notch singer as well as pianist—may
very well have sung the lyrics to Messenheimer many times, probably with
Harburg singing along. According to Cochran, Messenheimer often sat beside
Arlen on the piano bench, making sure music and lyrics were notated precisely
as the songwriters wished. Messenheimer surely worked very quickly; therefore,
his original "take downs" were probably rather messy. Presumably, then, nearly
all the surviving studio piano-vocal manuscripts are Messenheimer's fair copies
of his original drafts. In turn, Arlen and Harburg likely proofed these fair copies
before submitting them.

Arlen's use of a transcriber for *Oz* is apparently representative of his typical working method: two documents at the Library of Congress confirm that
throughout his career, he regularly worked with a musical secretary.[29] Arlen was
not unique in this respect. Many songwriters of the era (e.g., Kern, Porter, Berlin)
routinely employed the services of such assistants, although the degree of input
from these amanuenses varied considerably, depending (among other factors) on
the level of musical training and/or the preferences of the individual composer. In
Arlen's case, he definitely possessed the expertise to notate his own compositions,
but likely found the task tedious and time-consuming. Having songs transcribed
as quickly as possible clearly proved far more expeditious, and in the case of film
musicals, swiftly moved the numbers to their next developmental stages at the
studio. Moreover, Arlen had come to stage and screen musicals from many years
in the jazz world, both as a young artist and during his early songwriting days for
Harlem's famed *Cotton Club*. He was at heart an improvisatory musician. A secretary nearby (or the knowledge that one would be provided) probably freed him
up at the keyboard.

Even with such information at hand, the *exact* extent of Messenheimer's
contributions remains unknown. He appears to have transcribed what was
effectively finished; therefore he should not be considered a collaborator.
Furthermore, given Arlen's musical proficiency and superb keyboard skills, the
composer was in all likelihood very specific about how his ideas were notated.
Thus, Messenheimer probably strove for accuracy above all else. That said, we

must allow the possibility that Messenheimer suggested ideas such as voice leading or practical harmonic voicings for the accompaniments (e.g., keeping left-hand stretches within an octave for the average pianist), especially since some of the MGM piano-vocal manuscripts were marked specifically for publication. In fact, some rather persuasive evidence supports this possible scenario: the few available Arlen holographs with harmonic indications (for *Oz* and other productions) suggest that the composer seldom notated accompaniments in full, preferring instead to sketch a minimum number of vertical sonorities by means of chord symbols and/or single-stemmed harmonies in closed position. For *Oz*, then, we should strongly consider the possibility that Messenheimer provided at least some degree of authorial input within the cumulative process, since he may have made accessible piano arrangements for the numbers, and in so doing, might have slightly modified the partners' essentially completed (yet not fully notated) ideas. But even if cumulative authorship is too generous a designation, Messenheimer still served as a crucial conduit—a means of transmitting the duo's songs to the studio and publisher in written form.[30]

Over the course of the duo's assignment, Harburg occasionally stepped away from the songs to collaborate with some of *Oz*'s screenwriters. In a unique role for a studio-era lyricist, Harburg wrote the lead-in dialogue for the songs (smoothly inserting them into the narrative), helped edit the script, and even rewrote one of Langley's slated song slots as a comedic dialogue scene: the lightly satirical section in which the Wizard, although revealed to be a humbug, still grants the wishes of Dorothy's comrades in a mock "awards ceremony."[31] But even in these periodic collaborations, Harburg seems to have worked somewhat independently. In addition to the "awards ceremony," many screenplay drafts include individual song scenes submitted separately by Harburg.

Perhaps most significantly, Harburg is primarily responsible for successfully adapting *Oz*'s evolving screenplay to suit the film's songs, thereby achieving the strong narrative structure desired by Freed and Edens. As Harburg explained:

> I knew how to change plot around to make the plot fit the songs. . . . Not until the songs came in did you know how to eliminate. . . . And lots of things not in the script have to be invented to make the songs work. All the songs in Wizard were plot.[32]

The different types of authorship discussed thus far (cumulative versus collaborative, in various degrees and contexts) should be distinguished from the closely related concept of influence—a topic frequently deliberated within scholarly discourse concerning the intertextuality among musical compositions. (Indeed, one often wonders where influence ends and authorship begins.) As briefly mentioned, various MGM personnel provided an immediate influence on Arlen and Harburg. More specifically, the extended format of Edens's Munchkin welcome (a multipart, operetta-like song-and-patter routine, completely in rhyme) impacted the design of the duo's own "Munchkin Musical Sequence": a multisection song-and-patter routine, entirely in rhyme, in which numerous episodes ("The Lullaby League," "The Lollipop Guild," etc.) are contained within a roughly six-minute frame, centered around "Ding-Dong! The Witch Is Dead." Certainly, the extent of Edens's influence is such that he deserves some credit as a contributing author of this sequence.

Perhaps more intriguing are the myriad *external* influences that kindled the partners' creativity, especially those stemming from their individual backgrounds. Their *Oz* song score owes much to the spirit of vaudeville, particularly their treatment of Dorothy's three companions. Vaudeville echoes are hardly surprising: Ray Bolger, Jack Haley, and Bert Lahr (as well as Garland and Frank Morgan, for that matter) were ex-vaudevillians, and the songwriters had previously worked with Bolger and Lahr in New York. Markedly, the repetitions of "Brain"/"Heart"/"Nerve" give each performer a vaudevillian "turn" at the soft-shoe number. Many other songs reflect the distinctive imprint of Gilbert and Sullivan: for their Munchkin routine, the partners brought Edens's operetta-inspired structure to an entirely new level of musical/textual sophistication, now adding (among countless elements) a whimsical wordplay and gentle parody fundamentally indebted to Harburg's lifetime passion for the British pair. Furthermore, while the Lion's "If I Were King of the Forest" is clearly vaudevillian at its best, the first section of this "mock aria" also seems an affectionate send-up of "Tit-Willow" from *The Mikado*—an influence noted as early as 1939 by the musicologist and film critic Bruno David Ussher.[33] Arlen's jazz background is sprinkled throughout the film in subtle tinges, felt in the understated blue note of "Ding-Dong! The Witch Is Dead" (the flat 7 on the central word "witch," in m.6 of the chorus), and in the swinging rhythmic motive that opens "Brain"/"Heart"/"Nerve"—which in turn is directly (and likely intentionally) related to the analogous motive in "We're Off to See the Wizard" (which was written subsequently).

And what should we say about the influences manifested in "Over the Rainbow"? Might the ideas of a past author linger within the duo's most famous composition? Curiously, the ballad's overall musical character seems far more indebted to late Romantic opera than to Arlen's typical manner, even given the great stylistic diversity of his oeuvre. Interestingly enough, an investigation has yielded a possible operatic inspiration for this Arlen anomaly: the chorus's familiar 8-bar [A] section bears a striking resemblance to the refrain of the "Song to the Moon," from Dvořák's opera *Rusalka* (1901). Aside from the obvious parallels in textual imagery, these eight-bar strains share an analogous melodic contour (an octave leap followed by a gradual scale-wise descent back to the tonic), a similar harmonic progression (which is essentially identical in mm.1–3: from I-iii-IV), and the same formal structure (two symmetrical four-bar phrases: [2+2] + [2+2]).[34] The possibility of Dvořák as a "before-the-fact author" grows more intriguing when one considers dramatic context: in each case, a young female protagonist—near the beginning of a musical-theatrical fairytale—directs her song of yearning toward a celestial object. This theory of influence is substantiated (if inconclusively) by several *Oz* screenplays from early June 1938, which strongly suggest the duo originally wished to emulate the dramatic/textual content of "The Land Where the Good Songs Go" (1917)—a Kern/Wodehouse wanderlust ballad whose often-included verse begins with a prominent lunar reference: "On the other side of the moon." These screenplays also indicate that the partners initially considered adopting the "wishing on a star" trope, drawn from "beyond the last little star," also within the Kern/Wodehouse verse.[35] By mid-June, however, the term "rainbow" first appears among the extant *Oz* screenplays—not during the barnyard scene, but within the screenwriters' descriptions of Munchkinland—an idea Harburg seems quickly to have borrowed in lieu of the "star" device.[36] Meanwhile, Arlen was evidently struggling to find a broad, long line for Dorothy's number. All such cosmic ideas might very well have reminded him (consciously or subconsciously) of Dvořák's aria—a piece he surely knew. (Among possible channels of familiarity: the influential African American musician Will Marion Cook, one of Arlen's mentors in New York, had studied with Dvořák.) Such a suggestion does not ipso facto discredit Arlen's story about the opening ideas for "Over the Rainbow" occurring to him outside Schwab's Pharmacy, the legendary soda fountain where (according to Hollywood mythmakers) numerous stars were discovered—no more than inspiration outside Schwab's would discredit the idea that the musical source was Dvořák.[37]

By the second week of August 1938, Arlen and Harburg had turned in all their numbers except one (discussed below). Accordingly, the date of the last screenplay bearing substantial evidence of their continuous involvement with *Oz*—August 8–12, 1938—corresponds with the conclusion of their fourteen-week contractual period, which had begun on May 9.[38] This August 8–12 script discloses the duo's original musico-dramatic conception for the film—a seamless narrative structure. Throughout the first two-thirds of this draft screenplay (and discounting a few minor deviations), Arlen and Harburg's song placement unfolds in much the same manner as in the finished movie:

- "Over the Rainbow": defines complexity of adolescent protagonist; provides dramaturgical set up for Oz sequence

- "Munchkin Musical Sequence": action continuously carried forward by many song-and-patter episodes within extended frame
- "You're Off to See the Wizard": first statement of film's traveling song achieves transition between scenes as Dorothy leaves Munchkinland and sets out for Emerald City
- "If I Only Had a Brain"/"a Heart"/"the Nerve": along the Yellow Brick Road, repetitions distinguish identities of Dorothy's companions: all sing virtually same chorus, but with individualized lyrics; repetitions function as ongoing reprise, linking three scenes
- "We're Off to See the Wizard": tune now becomes unifying theme: reprised after Dorothy acquires each friend, pushing travelers onward
- "Choral Sequence to 'Gates of Emerald City'": off-screen heavenly choir ushers comrades into Emerald City, beginning with well-known line, "You're out of the woods"
- "The Merry Old Land of Oz": citizens explain city's carefree attitude; companions spruced up for visit to Wizard
- "If I Were King of the Forest": faux coronation aria further delineates Lion's character

In the completed film, the Lion's "aria" marks the conclusion of Arlen and Harburg's song score. However, the screenplay of August 8–12, 1938, indicates that the songwriters created a significant amount of material to follow the Lion's showcase: a major ensemble to prepare the narrative's climax, followed by several vocal reprises during the final third of the movie to complement the story's falling action and dénouement. In fact, if we consider what they submitted by mid-August 1938, their song score would have continued along as follows:

- "The Jitterbug": as travelers enter Haunted Forest, this song-and-dance routine—an up-tempo swing tune conceived as the only substantial ensemble exclusively for the four singing principals—occurs just before the plot's climactic events of Dorothy's capture and the Witch's subsequent melting

"The Jitterbug," in turn, is balanced by three reprises:

- "Over the Rainbow": while captive in Witch's castle, Dorothy sings partial reprise
- "Ding-Dong! The Witch Is Dead": after Witch's melting, Dorothy's return to Emerald City marked by choral reprise (followed a few scenes later by Harburg's awards ceremony)[39]

- "The Merry Old Land of Oz": before Dorothy clicks heels together, crowd begins soft reprise; never recorded or shot; likely intended as choral finale, bringing closure to duo's projected cyclical structure and setting up smooth transition to Kansas epilogue

With the above concept in mind, Arlen and Harburg completed their *Oz* contracts, entrusting their efforts to the hands of many talented others down the line. Evidently, they were briefly called back to the *Oz* set (perhaps on a few separate occasions) from late November through December 1938. During this period they would accomplish the following: recording rehearsal demos for "Munchkin Musical Sequence" and "Choral Sequence to 'Gates of Emerald City'" (both of which correspond quite faithfully to the songs' respective piano-vocal manuscripts but *not* to the completed film—further evidence they were uninvolved with arrangement and orchestration); and writing "Follow the Yellow Brick Road"—their only substantial addition to the song score after mid-August 1938.[40]

Arrangement

During the arrangement stage, the significance of Roger Edens's authorial input emerges again. Edens—an extraordinary pianist who had been Garland's coach and accompanist for years—later recalled that he had done a great deal of "arranging" for *Oz*, without specifying precisely what he meant by this often-ambiguous term.[41] While surviving records provide no further clarification, by "arranging," Edens presumably meant "routining" (described momentarily)—a duty for which he is well remembered.[42] Indeed, Edens performed this task on numerous MGM musicals, both before and especially after *Oz* as part of what would soon become MGM's celebrated "Freed Unit." In this capacity, he seems to have served as an intermediary figure who took the reins from Arlen and Harburg and—likely in consultation with MGM's music director Herbert Stothart—developed the duo's songs before they were orchestrated and prerecorded.

For film musicals, the first steps of routining usually involved coaching and rehearsing: determining appropriate keys and tempi, working on interpretation, and so on. Given his wide-ranging skills, Edens was an ideal candidate for such work. As Larry Blank explains:

Edens was a major accompanist and "arranger" with singers and artists before going to the Hollywood studios. Pianists for singers were automatically arrangers in that they would adjust keys and accompaniments for vocalists.[43]

While coaching Garland for *Oz*, then, Edens was the individual most likely to have suggested she sing "Over the Rainbow" in A-flat major for the movie—an exceptionally warm key that sits so beautifully in her voice. (Messenheimer had taken down the ballad in E-flat major, its published key.) But routining entailed additional duties: laying out the overall format of numbers with choreographers and/or directors, possibly inserting modulations, timing the songs (adding necessary extensions to accommodate staging or choreographic demands), and other required details to prepare the songs for orchestration.

The film's solo songs and small vocal ensembles seem to have been routined during September—after Arlen and Harburg completed their contracts.[44] Other numbers (mostly the larger ensembles) were surely routined later—during *Oz*'s production—even further from the duo's departure. Considering such information, chances are slim that the partners collaborated with Edens on the songs' routining.

Orchestration

Progressing along the assembly line, the vague term "arranging" requires further clarification: within the context of commercial music, "arranging" is sometimes used interchangeably and/or conflated with "orchestration." In reality, though, these duties are distinct. Arranging for film musical scores involves creating "settings" or "backgrounds" for songs: planning the overall format of numbers (sometimes overlapping with routining, as described above), possibly modifying harmonic content and/or adding original material (thereby blurring the lines between arranging and composing), perhaps even borrowing from earlier works. Orchestration (if strictly defined) is more specific, and refers to assigning instruments within a composition. For movie musicals, arranging and orchestration are generally carried out by the same person—an "arranger/orchestrator." Again, Larry Blank provides further insight:

The orchestrators [of the *Oz* songs] . . . were naturally arrangers as well as orchestrators. None of them simply assigned notes to the instruments. They all created backgrounds for the singers and countermelodies. It was part of the job. . . . Arranger/orchestrators could include anything that came to their imagination or fingers, using quotes from existing material, classical or popular, other works from the same composers and anything that they [themselves] might have created.[45]

The French émigré Murray Cutter (credited on screen) arranged and orchestrated all of Arlen and Harburg's songs in the completed movie except "Munchkin Musical Sequence," which was arranged and orchestrated by another French transplant, Leo Arnaud (uncredited). Almost certainly, the songs' orchestrations were completed after Arlen and Harburg left *Oz*: as we shall discover, some songs were prerecorded with orchestra in late September/early October; the orchestrations for these numbers were likely created shortly beforehand. The songs' remaining orchestrations were clearly written months later, during post-production. As with Edens during the arrangement stage, Cutter and Arnaud therefore surface as contributing authors, even if the duo (especially Arlen) was informed of their work or knew them professionally.

Prerecording

According to studio documentation, *Oz*'s vocal leads—Garland, Bolger, Lahr, and Buddy Ebsen, who was later replaced by Jack Haley—spent several days between September 30 and October 11, 1938, in prerecording sessions with the MGM studio orchestra. During this initial round of sessions they recorded their solo numbers ("Over the Rainbow," "Brain"/"Heart"/"Nerve," etc.) and small vocal ensembles (e.g., "We're Off to See the Wizard").

Some of the more complicated numbers were prerecorded during *Oz*'s subsequent production phase—with piano accompaniment alone, and with piano and vocals on separate tracks (e.g., "The Merry Old Land of Oz"). The tracks were eventually combined, forming "piano/vocal tracks." After these more intricate numbers had been shot to playback—using the combined piano/vocal tracks—the separate piano tracks were discarded, and replaced during post-production with recently written orchestrations on new tracks that had been recorded independently. Also during post-production, some numbers involving a choral component were post-dubbed in orchestral sessions with choir (e.g., "Choral Sequence to 'Gates of Emerald City,'" which by that time had acquired a separate title, "Optimistic Voices").[46]

By one account, Edens supervised the numerous prerecording sessions, during which many "takes" of individual numbers were recorded.[47] Clearly, whoever decided which takes would be used for the film (likely Edens and/or Freed, possibly among others) may be considered contributing authors of the songs, since their judgment helped determine what we hear in the completed movie.

PRODUCTION (c.mid-October, 1938—mid-March, 1939)

Shoot-to-Playback

Throughout *Oz*'s production phase, the various prerecordings (made with orchestral or piano accompaniment) were played back through loudspeakers on the set, as vocalists lip-synched to the music. *Oz*'s sole credited director—Victor Fleming—shot all of Arlen and Harburg's numbers in the finished movie except "Over the Rainbow," which was filmed near the end of production by King Vidor, the picture's fifth director.

A consideration of this developmental stage must account for the contributions of *Oz*'s performers, especially Garland, Bolger, Haley, and Lahr. To a great extent, the *Oz* songs are inextricably connected to these gifted artists. Etched indelibly in our collective memory is Garland's inimitable performance of "Over the Rainbow"—a cinematic moment so powerful that vestiges of that performance remain in virtually every subsequent rendition of the ballad by other artists, and even by Garland herself. The same can be said to a lesser degree of Bolger's "Brain" and Haley's "Heart." Although Nathan Lane and others have successfully delivered the Lion's "Nerve" and mock aria, Lahr's masterful portrayal of the character's pseudo prowess is permanently attached to this material. For each song in the completed film, the combined visual and prerecorded audio components arguably create yet another layer (perhaps even a new "text") of the "work." Consequently, the film's vocalists (particularly the four singing principals)—along with directors Fleming and Vidor—must be added to the ever-increasing chain of authors.

In fact, we owe a debt of gratitude to Fleming for "Follow the Yellow Brick Road." While shooting "Munchkinland" in December 1938, he apparently requested additional music and lyrics to help set up "You're Off to See the Wizard"—the Munchkins' send off to Dorothy.[48] Accordingly, Arlen and Harburg returned to the film to write the now-familiar introduction. Fleming clearly seems to have acted as a collaborator during this number's genesis, although once submitted, the music was subject to the cumulative input of future arrangers, orchestrators, and others.

POST-PRODUCTION (c.mid-March—mid-August 1939)

Underscoring

Shortly after production wrapped, the footage taken during that five-month period was assembled into a two-hour "rough cut" (the first print of a movie after preliminary editing). *Oz* would require even further editing to bring its timing down to the desired range. Yet it was this lengthy rough cut that MGM music director Herbert Stothart received and for which he and his staff created the movie's underscoring. A good percentage of *Oz*'s background music is based on material already provided by Arlen and Harburg's songs. As might be expected with a narrative film, most of their songs are employed leitmotivically. The frequent leitmotivic fragments are integral to the delineation of *Oz*'s characters or representation of ideas, often accumulating or changing in significance as they recur in new contexts. *Oz*'s underscore also includes numerous quotations of well-known repertoire (from Schumann and Mussorgsky to popular songs like "Home, Sweet Home"), and a considerable amount of original writing. (For a detailed discussion of *Oz*'s underscore, see Chapter 4 of this volume by Nathan Platte.)

FIGURE 3.1. Shown in the studio: composer-conductor Herbert Stothart. Credit: MGM/ Photofest.

Continued Development of the Songs

During this time, Stothart and his staff contributed directly to the ongoing evolution of the film's songs. For example, they created orchestrations for those numbers that had been shot only to prerecorded piano/vocal tracks, such as "The Merry Old Land of Oz": by post-production, the piano track of this prerecording was pulled and replaced with a track of Murray Cutter's colorful orchestration, recorded May 8, 1939. The post-production musical team provided other details as well: as necessary, introductions or tags were added to the partners' numbers. Perhaps the most significant of such background music is Stothart's "Introduction to 'The Rainbow'" (composed by early April 1939, then orchestrated by Cutter and recorded April 13, 1939), which accompanies Dorothy's dialogue immediately preceding "Over the Rainbow."[49] Stothart's underscoring begins in the middle of Aunt Em's reprimanding exit line (" . . . and find yourself a place where you won't get into any trouble!"), and eventually encompasses Harburg's wistful lines that lead into the song (beginning, "It's not a place you can get to by a boat or a train . . ."). Providing fluid continuity with the duo's ensuing chorus, Stothart's introduction thus comprises an integral element of the ballad in the completed movie.

Several post-production modifications were far more substantial, as illustrated by "If I Were King of the Forest": in August 1938, Arlen and Harburg submitted a lengthy, multipart aria for the Lion, including his "soliloquy" on courage that remains in the finished film as the number's last segment. For this spoken recitative portion, Arlen had written a decidedly abstract accompaniment: a series of ambiguous tone clusters that grow more and more unstable, providing a custom-tailored backdrop for the Lion's increasingly bizarre rhetorical questions (building to such absurdities as "What puts the 'ape' in apricot?"). But apparently, someone along the assembly line deemed Arlen's abstruse music unsuitable for the Lion's recitative.[50] By post-production, Stothart and his associates replaced Arlen's enigmatic setting with underscoring that eventually introduces an Elgarian march (beginning, "What makes a king out of a slave?"—a march actually constituting an arrangement of Arlen's material from the aria's second section).[51] Throughout *Oz*'s various production stages, numerous other alterations were made to the duo's initial conception for this number, confirming the piecemeal assemblage of the finished work.

Previews

The weeks during and after *Oz*'s preview phase (c. mid-June—mid-August 1939) saw the elimination of several key portions of Arlen and Harburg's song score (including the aforementioned *near*-deletion of "Over the Rainbow"). From the duo's perspective, the most drastic permanent cut came early on: "The Jitterbug" was deleted after *Oz*'s first preview, even though the elaborate number had taken five weeks and roughly $80,000 to shoot. At some point after *Oz*'s third preview, two of the three reprises originally planned by the partners were extracted as well: Dorothy's partial recap of "Over the Rainbow" in the Witch's castle and the choral return of "Ding-Dong! The Witch Is Dead," which escorted Dorothy and company back to Emerald City after the Witch's melting. (By now this reprise had been entitled "Ding-Dong! Emerald City," and had been fashioned by Stothart and staff into a medley incorporating three of the duo's songs.)[52]

Final Cut Released

By *Oz*'s premiere in mid-August 1939, approximately twenty minutes had been deleted from the rough cut, bringing the finished picture down to 101 minutes. Still, the excisions of "The Jitterbug" and the two reprises had abruptly truncated Arlen and Harburg's original dramatic arc, leaving the last third of the film dependent upon underscoring to achieve a sense of musical closure. Not surprisingly, Harburg was quite upset about the overall dramatic integrity of the completed movie: "I am always disappointed when I see [*Oz*], because they deleted several songs at the end of the picture and they made it a chase and I feel the loss of music there."[53] On another occasion he was more emphatic: "[Because 'The Jitterbug' was cut,] the movie suffers musically in the final third of the story.... When will they ever learn?"[54]

Harburg's feelings are understandable, especially since so many decisions were made after his contract expired in mid-August 1938. Nevertheless, Stothart's scoring mitigates these cuts to some extent: due to the songs' frequent leitmotivic presentation throughout the film's concluding half-hour, bits and pieces of the partners' numbers are heard within the underscore until the very end of the movie. Moreover, sometimes these leitmotivic fragments are substantial enough to function as underscored reprises, thereby replacing the vocal reprises that might be expected during the last third of *Oz*. Partial orchestral reprises of "Over the Rainbow" are heard, for instance, when the comrades are temporarily denied entry to the Wizard's Palace, and when Dorothy is trapped in the Witch's castle.

The cumulative creation of the *Oz* songs—from their genesis by Arlen and Harburg through the numerous assembly line stages beyond the duo's artistic control—did in fact stop with the completion of *Oz*'s final cut. Each finished "work," as a fixed entity, is encapsulated within this singular, edited version of the film. Yet while every work is certainly completed, the chain of authorship endures ad infinitum. Indeed, these songs were forever released into the future when *Oz* debuted, and have since unfolded continuously toward receptive audiences— past, present, and future. In turn, each audience member now becomes a contributing author, bringing, as musical-theater scholar Jim Lovensheimer observes, "his or her own social and historical identity to the experience."[55] In this way, attentive audiences share an ongoing dialogue with the many talented individuals who originally created the songs, spawning a potentially infinite number of interpretations. And surely, for the vast majority of audiences, these miniature masterpieces represent not only cherished memories from childhood, but priceless treasures for a lifetime.

Notes

I am grateful to the following individuals who read this chapter and made many helpful suggestions: Dominic McHugh, Danielle Birkett, Carol Oja, Mark Eden Horowitz, Larry Blank, and especially Rufus Hallmark.

Abbreviations

IU   Indiana University—Lilly Library—Wizard of Oz mss., 1938–1939
USC   University of Southern California—Cinematic Arts Library
WBCA   Warner Brothers Corporate Archive—Oz materials

1. Harburg, "Reminiscences of E. Y. 'Yip' Harburg" (February 1959), Popular Arts Project, Columbia Center for Oral History, Columbia University, 24–25.
2. Arlen, to Murray Schumach, "Composer Tells of Movie Abuses," *New York Times*, August 10, 1961.
3. Prior to *Oz*, Arlen and Harburg had each worked with other songwriting partners. As a team, however, their pre-*Oz* collaborations include (among other endeavors) the hit song "It's Only a Paper Moon" (pub. 1933, with Billy Rose credited as co-lyricist), two Broadway shows (*Life Begins at 8:40*, 1934; *Hooray for What!*, 1937), and three "B" movies for Warner Brothers, all released in 1936 (*The Singing Kid*, *Stage Struck*, and *Gold Diggers of 1937*). Additionally, in 1935, Harburg created lyrics for a song Arlen had previously composed on his own— what would ultimately be published under the title "Last Night When We Were Young."
4. Harburg, to Max Wilk, *They're Playing Our Song* (1973: Westport, CT: Easton Studio Press, 2008), 296.
5. Aljean Harmetz, *The Making of The Wizard of Oz* (1977: Chicago: Chicago Review Press, 2013), 19.
6. Garland turned seventeen during *Oz*'s production.

7. Several reliable sources confirm that Arlen and Harburg knew Freed would serve as *Oz*'s associate producer, and they provide details verifying that Freed himself hired the duo. See, for example, Harmetz, *The Making of The Wizard of Oz*, 71–74; and Edward Jablonski, *Harold Arlen: Rhythm, Rainbow, and Blues* (Boston: Northeastern University Press, 1996), 121–124.

8. Stephen Banfield, *Jerome Kern* (New Haven, CT: Yale University Press, 2006), 63.

9. Arlen, to Max Wilk, *They're Playing Our Song* (1973: Westport, CT: Easton Studio Press, 2008), 169.

10. Author's correspondence with Larry Blank, October 2016.

11. One figure who seems to have escaped the studio moguls' typically dismissive attitude toward songwriters was Irving Berlin, who, as musical-theater scholar Jeffrey Magee explains, "was unusual [among Hollywood songwriters] in insisting on creative control in an industry where songwriters (as in early Broadway) were seen as makers of raw material that producers and directors could use as they saw fit." See Jeffrey Magee, *Irving Berlin's American Musical Theater* (New York: Oxford University Press, 2012), 194. Another exception to the usual loss of creative control among Hollywood songwriters is illustrated by Rodgers and Hammerstein's *State Fair* (released August 1945), the team's only musical written expressly for the screen. Interestingly enough, although *State Fair* was filmed in California, Rodgers and Hammerstein wrote its songs on the East Coast. By this point in their partnership, they had clearly established themselves as a team on Broadway with the debuts of *Oklahoma!* (in spring 1943) and *Carousel* (spring 1945). Moreover, they had already formed the Rodgers and Hammerstein copyright and organization. Thus, when their "product" arrived in Hollywood with *State Fair*, they were extremely wealthy and had acquired a great deal of power and artistic control over their work.

12. Laura Lynn Broadhurst, "Wizards of Song: Arlen, Harburg, and the Cumulative Creation of the Songs for *The Wizard of Oz* (1939)," PhD diss. in progress, Rutgers University.

13. Roland Barthes, "From Work to Text," in *Image-Music-Text*, edited and translated by Stephen Heath (New York: Hill and Wang, 1977), 155–164. For a succinct definition of Barthes's concept of the "work," see Matthew Creasy, "Manuscripts and Misquotations: Ulysses and Genetic Criticism," *Joyce Studies Annual* (2007): 48.

14. Dominic McHugh, "'I'll Never Know Exactly Who Did What': Broadway Composers as Musical Collaborators," *Journal of the American Musicological Society* 68, no. 3 (2015): 648.

15. Arlen, to Lewis Funke, "Arlen the Tunesmith," *New York Times*, July 4, 1943, X4.

16. Larry Blank correspondence with author.

17. "Cumulative" is adopted from literary scholarship, where the term has been applied (by Theresa Tinkle and others) to the authorship of folk tales and Chaucer's *Canterbury Tales*.

18. The duo's *Oz* contracts, MGM Music Dept. Collection, *USC*, PR/1A, 1B.

19. May 14, 1938, screenplay, *WBCA*; mentioned by Harburg in two documents (July 30, 1938; August 1, 1938), *IU*, 3/7, 3/8.

20. Albert Johnson, "Conversation with Roger Edens," *Sight and Sound* 27, no. 4 (Spring 1958): 179.

21. For example, see Tim Carter, *Oklahoma! The Making of an American Musical* (New Haven, CT: Yale University Press, 2007), esp 173–174, 185–186, 206–211. Carter demonstrates here how Rodgers and Hammerstein promoted the idea that their musicals were "integrated" for commercial reasons rather than actually buying into the concept.

22. Edens's materials are in the Roger Edens Collection, *USC*, Box 12A.

23. Harburg, to Harmetz, unpublished notes for *The Making of The Wizard of Oz*, Yip Harburg Foundation, New York.

24. Harburg, to Wilk, *They're Playing Our Song*, 296.

25. Harburg's draft *Oz* lyrics are in the E.Y. Harburg Collection (mss. 83), Irving S. Gilmore Music Library, Yale University, I. Writings 1929–1968, 2/14.

26. Harburg, to Walter Cronkite; February 9, 1964, episode, *The Twentieth Century* (CBS-TV).

27. Harmetz, *The Making of The Wizard of Oz*, 80.

28. "Messenheimer, Sam," in the *ASCAP Biographical Dictionary*, 4th ed. (New York: R.R. Bowker, 1980), 343–344.

29. See Edward Jablonski, "Harold Arlen: Rainbow's End," Library of Congress, Edward Jablonski Papers, 11/2; and Letter of July 23, 2004, Lawrence Stewart to Gary Carver, Library of Congress, George and Ira Gershwin Collection, 135/7.

30. My thanks to William Rosar for his kind assistance in the search for Messenheimer's stepson and for his feedback concerning Arlen's use of an amanuensis.

31. Typescript drafts, Harburg's awards ceremony (July 30, 1938; August 1, 1938), *IU*, 3/7, 3/8.

32. Harburg, to Harmetz, *The Making of the Wizard of Oz*, 87, and within Harmetz's unpublished notes provided by the Harburg Foundation, New York.

33. Bruno David Ussher, "Music in the Films," *Los Angeles Daily News*, August 11, 1939.

34. A comparison of these details is facilitated by music theorist Allen Forte's close analysis of "Over the Rainbow," which reveals the [A] section's fundamental melodic contour and underlying harmonic rhythm, both of which strongly resemble Dvořák's refrain, particularly in mm.1–3. See Allen Forte, *The American Popular Ballad of the Golden Era, 1924–1950* (Princeton, NJ: Princeton University Press, 1995), 232–233.

35. Script portions of June 9 and 10, 1938, *IU*, 1/8, 1/9.

36. Script portions of June 16 and 18, 1938, *IU*, 1/8.

37. For an example of Arlen's account, see Edward Jablonski, *Harold Arlen: Rhythm, Rainbows, and Blues*, 131. The possible Dvořák-Arlen connection in "Over the Rainbow" is fully explored within my dissertation in progress, where the discussion

includes further archival documentation to support the claim, as well as a consideration of various counterarguments.

38. August 8–12, 1938 screenplay, MGM/Turner Script Collection, Margaret Herrick Library, Beverly Hills and *WBCA*.

39. In August 8–12, 1938 screenplay, reprise entitled, "The Wicked Old Witch Is Dead."

40. The recording dates for these two demos are not available among the extant sources. However, both demos are commercially available on the following CD set: *The Wizard of Oz (1939): Original Motion Picture Soundtrack*, Rhino R2 71964/Turner Entertainment Co., 1995. According to the track information included with this set, the demo of "Munchkin Musical Sequence" was recorded on November 22, 1938; the demo for "Choral Sequence to 'Gates of Emerald City'" (incorrectly listed as "Optimistic Voices" on the Turner/Rhino track listing) was recorded on December 13, 1938.

41. Johnson, "Conversation with Roger Edens," 180.

42. A scholarly definition of "routining" appears not to have been published. For further discussion of the topic, see Stephen Banfield, *Sondheim's Broadway Musicals* (Ann Arbor: University of Michigan Press, 1993), 86, 359–364; and Todd Decker, *Music Makes Me: Fred Astaire and Jazz* (Berkeley: University of California Press, 2011), 16, 69–95, 238–239.

43. Larry Blank correspondence with author.

44. A rehearsal/recording schedule (September 22, 1938) supports asserted time frame, Arthur Freed Collection/Wizard of Oz, *USC*, 56/1.

45. Larry Blank correspondence with author.

46. Conrad Salinger arranged and orchestrated the deleted "Jitterbug" number. Information regarding the songs' orchestrations and prerecordings gleaned from a comparative study of numerous sources, including the film's Pre-Recordings log, Daily Music Reports, and original music tracks—all held at *WBCA*; additional copies of *Oz*'s Pre-Recordings log and Daily Music Reports at MGM Music Dept. Collection, *USC*.

47. Hugh Fordin, *The World of Entertainment! Hollywood's Greatest Musicals, The Freed Unit at MGM* (Garden City, NY: Doubleday, 1975), 20.

48. Fleming's principal role, confirmed by inter-office memo (December 21, 1938), Freed Collection/Wizard of Oz, *USC*, 25/1.

49. Piano-conductor part, "Introduction to 'The Rainbow'" (April 11, 1939), *WBCA*.

50. A piano-vocal manuscript (August 2, 1938) at *WBCA* indicates Arlen's accompaniment was deleted.

51. A piano-conductor part (April 24, 1939) at *WBCA* shows the underscoring for the number's concluding recitative.

52. Information regarding deleted scenes, previews, and release: Harmetz, *The Making of the Wizard of Oz*, 85, 282–288; and John Fricke, Jay Scarfone, and William Stillman, *The Wizard of Oz: The Official 50th Anniversary Pictorial History*

(New York: Warner Books, 1989), 115–122. Bolger's dance routine following "Brain" was also deleted.

53. Harburg, to Paul Lazarus, WBAI, March 2, 1980; cited by Harold Meyerson and Ernie Harburg, *Who Put the Rainbow in The Wizard of Oz?: Yip Harburg, Lyricist* (Ann Arbor: University of Michigan Press, 1993), 152.

54. Harburg, holograph annotation, piano-vocal manuscript, "The Jitterbug," Yale Harburg Collection, I, 2/14.

55. Jim Lovensheimer, "Texts and Authors," in *The Oxford Handbook of the American Musical*, edited by Raymond Knapp, Mitchell Morris, and Stacy Wolf (New York: Oxford University Press, 2011), 27.

4 "SOUNDS MUST STIR THE FANTASY"

UNDERSCORE AS SPECIAL EFFECT IN *THE WIZARD OF OZ* (1939)

Nathan Platte

When Dorothy opens the door of a farmhouse to find Oz beyond its threshold, Technicolor sweeps away sepia tone, and an uneasy hush gives way to a delicate bloom of violins, woodwinds, horn, and harp. In the conductor's part, MGM composer Herbert Stothart writes "Exquisite lento. . . . She opens the door, the scene is enchanting."[1] The poignance of this transition hinges on the conjunction of a narrative event with a shift in cinematic technology. It is not only Dorothy and Toto who gaze from one world into another. It is also the spectators, similarly situated in one realm while observing a second, who see and hear their film changing around them. The illusion suggests that Oz is so sensationally immersive—so great and powerful—that it can reconfigure the cinematic apparatus itself.

When critics first reacted to MGM's film, many dwelt on its use of special effects to render the fantastic world of Oz through the inherently fantastic medium of cinema. After attending multiple previews, Nelson B. Bell of the *Washington Post* promised readers that "the mechanical trickery in *The Wizard of Oz* is almost unbelievable" and that "the extraordinary effects they achieve onscreen must have presented the most acute technical and mechanical problems with which the motion picture industry ever has been confronted."[2] Writing for the *New York Times*, Frank Nugent noted the conflation of cinematic and Oz-specific fantasies: "By courtesy of the wizards of Hollywood, *The Wizard of Oz* reached the Capitol's screen yesterday as a delightful piece of wonderworking which had the youngsters' eyes shining and brought a quietly amused gleam to the wise ones of the oldsters."[3] Nugent wanted his readers to know that, as a member of the latter, he did not wholly abandon his critical faculties: "Even such great wizards as those who lurk in the concrete caverns of California are often tripped in their flights of fancy by trailing vines of piano wire and outcroppings of putty noses."[4] Even so, Nugent averred that "it is clear enough that Mr. Dawn, the make-up wizard, Victor Fleming, the director-wizard, Arnold Gillespie, the special effects wizard, and Mervyn LeRoy, the producing wizard, were pleased as Punches with the tricks they played. They have every reason to be."[5] As Hollywood's largest and richest studio, MGM had leveraged nearly every special effect at its disposal to make *The Wizard of Oz* a prestige picture.[6] Among the visual effects, there were miniatures, mechanically manipulated props, on-set projection tricks, and multiple color schemes, among others.[7]

Special effects were a means of flaunting studio power, and in a prestige film devoted to fantasy, their presence was expected. But effects were not limited to the visuals. Publicity notices also explained that extraordinary time and expense were devoted to rendering the film's complicated orchestral accompaniment, which fitted among the film's songs. Herbert Stothart, who headed a team of composers and arrangers for the film,[8] explained that "music and sound [for this film] must be highly imaginative, unreal while super-realistic. Here sounds must stir the fantasy."[9] In another interview, Stothart argued that color cinematography required a different approach from black-and-white films: "a too-somber note, or too-heavy quality seems incongruous with the life and light of color photography."[10] For a photo caption of a recording session, a staff publicist emphasized both special musical sounds and the technical difficulties of integrating them: "There are musical effects to go in behind the dialogue and the thousands of sound effects for *The Wizard of Oz*. Herbert Stothart is conducting a symphony orchestra playing over four channels, each with a microphone which a sound mixer juggles to bring up some instruments, diminish the others, and blend the whole."[11] If close attention to extramusical effects helped guide the music team, they are still of use today. Music's multivalent relationship with visual and sonic effects in *Oz* remains an important yet unexplored factor.[12] As Kevin J. Donnelly has noted, "While film music traditionally has been conceived as part of narration, working for film narrative, in some ways it would be better to see it as part of the film's repository of special effects."[13] To be sure, these issues are confronted when considering either numbers from film musicals or the slippage between music and sound effect in science fiction and horror genres.[14] Given that the MGM film is a fantasy musical spiced with dashes of horror, it is not surprising that music and special effects enjoy a cozy relationship. But as the film blends qualities from multiple genres and seeks to reach multiple audiences—namely, the youngsters and oldsters identified in Nugent's review—its shifting modes of address make it especially interesting. Music and special effects not only stir the fantasy, but they also manage and control it—revealing the limits of seemingly unlimited power: a message that applies to both the narrative and the experience of cinema itself. This paradox nestles comfortably among the film's other contradictions in character, tone, and genre. The relationships brokered between music and effects in *Oz* encourage revelry in these ruptures rather than resolution. This chapter contextualizes such idiosyncratic impulses by looking first to Oz's creator, L. Frank Baum, whose interest in visual and sonic attractions persisted throughout his career, shaping his source novel and effects-laden films. Next, several case studies from the MGM film show how Stothart, his assistants, and studio sound engineers crafted a soundscape that upheld and extended Baum's aesthetic, with new effects stirring and soothing the film's most fantastic elements.

Special Effects, Attractions, and Oz

Scott Bukatman's *Matters of Gravity: Special Effects and Supermen in the 20th Century* traces cinematic special effects to the origins of the medium: "Cinema is, of course, a special effect, and that is how it was regarded by its initial audiences."[15] Bukatman argues that the continued reliance on special effects reflect the resilience of a "cinema of attractions," a term adopted by Tom Gunning to complement (and correct) scholarly discourses that treated film primarily as a vessel for narrative.[16] Gunning stressed that cinema's initial, pre-1906 appeal lay in "its ability to *show* something," whether that might be a distant locale, an unfamiliar individual, or a film-enabled magic trick.[17] As narrative became a more common preoccupation among audiences and filmmakers, the "cinema of attractions" did not disappear but shifted. Gunning points to techniques of avant-garde cinema and the visual spectacle of select genres—like the musical—as proof of its abiding presence.[18] Subsequently, scholars of visual effects like Bukatman and Julie A. Turnock have invoked the "cinema of attractions" to understand the pleasure and meaning that effects bring to film beyond their service to narrative.[19]

L. Frank Baum, who wrote his novel *The Wonderful Wizard of Oz* (1900) during the cinema of attractions' heyday, was uniquely suited to comprehend and contribute to its proliferation. By the late 1890s, the forty-something Baum had already pursued an astonishingly variegated career in theater, retail, and writing. In 1897, he began to publish *The Show Window*, a monthly magazine devoted to transforming storefront window displays into sites of attractions. Among his many words of advice to storeowners, Baum enthusiastically recommended the creative application of special effects.[20] In *The Art of Decorating Dry Goods Windows and Interiors*, a book published the same year as *The Wonderful Wizard of Oz*, Baum noted that "people will always step out to examine anything that moves . . . and will enjoy studying out the mechanics or wondering how the effect has been obtained."[21] Baum continued to think about window displays as he labored on *The Wonderful Wizard of Oz*—and it is easy to register in both the story and its presentation in book form an "attractions" sensibility. Chapters announce either eye-catching tableaux—"The Cyclone," "The Rescue of the Tin Woodman," "The Deadly Poppy Field"—or curiosity-quenching explanations as to how effects were obtained—"How Dorothy Saved the Scarecrow," "The Magic Art of the Great Humbug," "How the Balloon was Launched." The initial edition of the book was also a handheld attraction. Baum biographer Rebecca Loncraine notes that Baum's text and W. W. Denslow's illustrations were set "in an unusual way, with color images blended into the text. The walls of Dorothy's wooden house, for instance, merge into the text that describes it. Words reach up into the blue sky of Munchkinland . . . and run along the yellow brick road up to the gates of the Emerald City."[22] In *Land of Desire: Merchants, Power, and the Rise of a New American Culture*, Michael Leech notes that Denslow's "colored plate inserts, which grew ever richer as the story unfolded," culminate in Emerald City, "where the pages seem to drip and glisten with tiny emeralds."[23] It was, Leach notes, "the most 'colorful' children's book published to this time."[24]

With the novel's success, Baum was quick to extend Oz's effects to other entertainments. In addition to his production of the wildly successful 1902 Oz "musical extravaganza" (see Chapter 1), Baum also realized Oz as a mixed media spectacle in 1908. Whimsically titled *Fairylogue and Radio-Plays*, the entertainment starred Baum, "attired in a white Prince Albert suit," and blended narration, pantomime, hand-colored slides, and twenty-three short films.[25] As with the source novel, which had used color coding to distinguish Kansas (gray) from the various regions of Oz (yellow, red, brown, blue, and green), Baum's films featured hand-colored footage. "The entertainment starts by a youngster stepping out of a picture book containing fairy stories," wrote a *Variety* journalist. "The series of pictures ultimately comes to life. The entire performance is garbed in illusions."[26] Indeed, the short films featured a variety of magical effects, an approach that aligned the production with the fairy tales and magic-trick films released by French filmmaker and magician Georges Méliès.[27] In an interview for the *New York Herald*, Baum carefully described the tricks behind various effects—such as how the storybook characters came "alive." His enthusiasm revealed both familiarity with the special effects themselves and an abiding desire to share such attractions with audiences.[28] In the mid-1910s, Baum also ran the Hollywood-based Oz Film Company. From their first film, *The Patchwork Girl of Oz* (1914), the company placed emphasis on using cinema's trick effects. An early scene of *The Patchwork Girl* features a pile of rags that magically coalesces in the form of a girl.

Baum's desire to produce cutting-edge Ozian attractions extended to orchestral music as well: a consequence, perhaps, of his own work as an actor, playwright, and occasional composer. (While in his twenties, he had written the songs for his melodrama *The Maid of Arran* [1883]—he also directed and starred in the play.[29] For his Oz-based stage musicals, Baum frequently provided lyrics.) For the *Fairylogue*, Baum took what was then an uncommon step of commissioning an original orchestral accompaniment. Nathaniel D. Mann, one of the composers with whom Baum had collaborated on his 1902 musical, wrote the score.[30] The *Chicago Tribune* acknowledged the musicians' presence as an attraction by clarifying that "a fairylogue is a travelogue that takes you to Oz instead of China. A radio-play is a fairylogue with an orchestra at the left-hand corner of the stage."[31] For *The Patchwork Girl of Oz*, Baum hired another composer from his stage musicals—Louis Gottschalk—to provide "specially written" orchestral scores for the films, which still remained exceptional in 1914.[32] Gottschalk's music was featured in multiple advertisements for the film (see Figure 4.1). Of course, not all of Baum's ideas about Oz and its relationship to visual and musical effects pertain to the MGM filmmakers' decisions regarding music and effects in their adaptation. Nonetheless, Baum's devotion to attractions clearly informed his novel, its physical presentation, and the subsequent adaptations of it through musicals and films. In selecting Baum's novel for adaptation, MGM's production teams took on not only a particular narrative but also an attractions-based aesthetic that Baum had cultivated across his Oz oeuvre.

In his consideration of cinema *as* special effect, Scott Bukatman argues that special effects reinforce cinema's reflexivity. In science fiction films, Bakutman explains, special effects represent a "technology of technology, a cinema of cinema."[33] Furthermore, Bukatman shows that effects-enabled vistas from films like *2001: A Space Odyssey* and *Close Encounters of the Third Kind* provide an "immersive, overwhelming, and apparently immediate sensory experience" that simultaneously evokes the sublime while controlling it through narrative and the cinematic apparatus itself. Terror is contained because audiences know they are watching a movie. MGM's *Wizard of Oz*, in extending Baum's penchant for granting viewers access to an extraordinary realm through extraordinary means, does similar work, but with different expressive goals. In *Oz*, encounters with the sublime are hastily qualified, even overturned, allowing Bukatman's notion of reflexivity to bubble quickly to the surface.

When considering effects and music in *Oz*, several complementary case studies illustrate different roles music might play as it both engages special effects and serves as effects across these categories. For the film's most elaborate visual effects sequence—Dorothy's ride through the cyclone—the musical accompaniment

Ojo Discovers the Magic Brains

Scenes from the
Wonderful Feature Film
of L. FRANK BAUM'S
Whimsical Fairy Tale,

"THE PATCHWORK GIRL OF OZ"

Just completed. A marvelous filmization that will make the whole world wonder, laugh, and be happier and brighter through its influence. Complete musical score composed to fit every scene by Louis F. Gottschalk.

The Oz Film

STUDIO AND

Santa Monica Boulevard

LOS ANGELES,

The Crooked Magician Completes the Magic Powder of Life

FIGURE 4.1. An advertisement for Baum's film, *The Patchwork Girl of Oz*, emphasizes wonder and music. Printed in *Moving Picture World*, August 1, 1914, 648. Courtesy of lantern.mediahist.org.

emphasizes a tripartite structure through conspicuous stylistic shifts that alter music's relative placement within the soundtrack and relationship to onscreen events. The second case study treats music *as* effect by considering the manipulation of singing voices across the Oz soundscape. The final case study considers the ways in which music affiliated with magical characters is both signaled and contained through a savvy balancing among special effects, musical attributes, and narrative trajectory. In all three cases, musical effects depend on special recording technology and sound editing as well as compositional decisions for their impact. These music-and-effect encounters offer productive opportunities for exploring music's varied functions within the broader discourse of special effects and cinema.

Musical Cyclones

In Baum's source novel, the cyclone is set at the beginning of the story, and it greatly resembles Alice's tumble down the rabbit hole in Carroll's *Alice's Adventures in Wonderland*.[34] Surprise gives way to idle curiosity before boredom and sleep ensue. In Denslow's illustration for Baum's novel, Dorothy is shown sleeping on her bed as the house—tilted at an unusual angle— flies to regions unknown (see Figure 4.2). In the film, the cyclone follows a substantial prologue set

FIGURE 4.2. W. W. Denslow's illustration for Baum's *The Wonderful Wizard of Oz* (1900) shows Dorothy sleeping peacefully during the cyclone—a consequence of boredom.

in Kansas, and it is within the cyclone that Dorothy witnesses the metamorphosis of Miss Gulch into the Wicked Witch. Dorothy's journey in the film also begins with a violent blow to the head, rendering Dorothy unconscious—precisely the conditions the MGM special effects team required to wreak mischief of all kinds. In a sequence under two minutes in length, the studio drew upon miniature sets, an elaborate, mechanically operated tornado funnel, double-printing, and projection tricks.[35] Music—as arranged by George Bassmann and orchestrated by George Stoll—plays throughout.

The entrance of the cyclone music is synched to match the colliding of a window with Dorothy's head. The pain of impact is passed experientially to the audience through music: an accented, bitonal smash that reels into disorienting runs and sustained trills as Dorothy falls to the bed. A series of disjointed textures in a Stravinskian mold follow. Rapid meter changes and destabilizing brass exclamations challenge metric structure. A glistening alto flute solo plays against symphonic wind effects of tremolo and whirling ostinati in strings and winds. (For this portion of the sequence, almost all of the "wind" on the soundtrack is provided by orchestra.) This layering of asynchronous instrumental textures aligns with the superimposition of unanchored images: multiple close-ups of Dorothy's profile, the whirling smear of the cyclone, and a farmhouse that flies upward as garish trombone glissandi plunge downward.

When Dorothy awakes and takes notice of the goings on beyond her window, the orchestral accompaniment relaxes into a much simpler style. Wind effects—previously suggested through laborious and repetitive gestures in the orchestra—are handed to the sound department. With simulated wind effects higher in the mix, music no longer monopolizes the soundtrack. In his essay on the film, Salman Rushdie notes that Dorothy occupies at this moment the position of a spectator at a film (see Figure 4.3). The music provides clues as to what kind of film she may be watching.[36] As people whiz by her window with nary a word, each animal is announced with the correct livestock sound effect. The absence of human speech and the curious presence of isolated sounds recalls the silent cinema, in which onscreen actors are mute, but animals could be voiced through sound effects furnished by live musicians.[37] To fit this conceit, the musical accompaniment here mimics compiled scores from the silent era: the children's song "Reuben, Reuben" (William Gooch and Harry Birch, 1871), is playfully passed between solo trumpet and clarinet over plunking accompaniment before trombones interject with a selection heard previously in the Kansas scenes: Robert Schumann's "The Happy Farmer" from his *Album for the Young*, Op. 68 (1848). Thus, music has shifted from accompanying Dorothy's dream state and images of the hurtling house to accompanying the film within the film, where it cedes its domination of the soundtrack to ambient noise. This shift not only showcases the film's

FIGURE 4.3. During the cyclone sequence in MGM's film, Dorothy is situated as a spectator at the cinema.

trick-printing techniques with double-printed images and rear projection: it also signals a change in cinematic address that juxtaposes startling, spectacular visuals with the more whimsical characters that populate Dorothy's window. There is a productive irony here, in that this sequence, enabled by considerable technological finesse and effort, serves a backward-looking gesture. The pairing of quaint musical accompaniment and rocking-chair grannies suggests that this technological tornado has given Dorothy and the audience a rare encounter with an endearing, nonthreatening past.

The appearance of Mrs. Gulch ruptures the paradigm. Her taunting theme accumulates menace through repetition, instrumental doubling, and flutter tongue trumpet snarls. Like the other characters, she is initially mute. When another visual effect turns her from bicyclist to broom rider, a triumphant cackle shatters the vocal barrier and triggers a series of destabilizing sonic and visual events. Screams from Dorothy, shots of a tumbling farmhouse, and frantically rising fanfares from the brass section—indebted to Paul Dukas's apt *Sorcerer's Apprentice* (1897)—culminate in an anticlimactic exclamation as the house hits ground, the wild ride suddenly over.

Music and effects work in tandem across this scene both to unsettle and assuage spectators. As the scene progresses from depicting an unconscious

Dorothy in the cyclone, to Dorothy as window spectator, to Dorothy in waking nightmare, shifts in musical style, in timbre, and music's position in the sound-track underline different visual effects. Not surprisingly, this virtuosic musical passage received special attention at all levels of realization. The copyist of the conductor's part penciled tendrils of wind turbulence on the word "Cyclone," printed at the top of the page.[38] A larger orchestra of ninety musicians was called to record the piece.[39] After it was recorded, some sections were removed and repositioned during dubbing, further heightening the sense of disparate musical juxtapositions. But the scene and its music offer much more than just a flourish of MGM's production talent. As a visual-musical event, the cyclone sequence aptly illustrates Bakutman's ideal of "combined sensations of aston-ishment, terror, and awe that occur through the revelation of a power greater, by far, than the human."[40] Cinematic effects, however, did not embody the sub-lime so much as gesture toward it. Bukatman notes that cinematic effects "are designed to inspire awe, but always within a reassuring sense of play. Rapture replaces terror."[41] In the case of MGM's film, rapture is accompanied by self-reflexive cinematic play.

Hearing Voices

If the cyclone sequence shows the multilayered integration of music into a clearly defined set piece of sonic and visual spectacle, the manipulation of singing voices serves a broader and more diffuse special-effect function. Its function resembles that of a background matte painting, which characterizes visual space without necessarily dominating the visual frame. These are not instances when central characters break into song but rather the recurring entrance of myste-rious voices—mostly female, and frequently wordless—that waft through the Oz soundscape. Much like the aggressive color scheme, their recurring role as additions to and disruptions within the film's orchestral accompaniment do double duty: they reinforce Oz's otherworldly aura, but they also chip away at the well-worn conventions of musical accompaniment in film. In this way, they link the surprise of characters within the story with the wonder of spectators enthralled by a film that refuses to behave as others do.

The idea of using voices as a "special effect" within an otherwise instrumental score is not unique to Oz or even film music. MGM's music department had incorporated wordless choruses into background scores for other large-budget productions, including *Night Flight* (1933) and *Anna Karenina* (1935). In addi-tion, MGM staff drew from a robust tradition of symphonic works that incor-porate textless choral parts to suggest the magical, the dream-like, the visually expansive, and the sublime. Examples include Tchaikovsky's *Nutcracker* ballet (another story of a girl's magical journey to an exotic fantasy world, 1893), Debussy's "Sirènes" from *Three Nocturnes* (1899), Scriabin's *Prometheus: Poem of Fire* (1910), Delius's *Song of the High Hills* (1911), Ravel's *Daphnis et Chloé* (1912), Holst's "Neptune" from *The Planets* (1916), and Vaughan Williams's *A Pastoral Symphony* (Symphony No. 3, 1922), among others. In the film, a female word-less chorus is first heard during the main title sequence, singing the melody—but not the words—to "Come out, come out," Glinda's song to the Munchkins. The women's chorus is not heard again until Dorothy herself has entered the colorful world of Oz. In the conductor's part, the interspersed choral parts for this scene are alternately marked as "heavenly" and "eerie," grounding the choir's function in evoking that which is not of this world—or at least not the world of Kansas. As Dorothy moves about Munchkinland, solo and choral textures arranged by Ken Darby slip in and out of the orchestral accompaniment. Some of the vocal lines were further processed through an echo chamber, giving them an acoustically distinct spatial quality that contrasts with the rest of the score.[42] The presence of voices in the background orchestral score marks both excess—voices are not part of standard orchestral scores—and absence. Why do we hear voices in a village that appears deserted?

But this sequence is only the first of many in which voices—disembodied and otherwise—are set as special effect. There are the Munchkins themselves, whom Dorothy hears before seeing. "What was that?" she asks Glinda, unable to identify their offscreen laugh as sounds belonging to a "who," not "what." In this way, the Munchkins' vocal peculiarity anticipates and then intensifies their physical difference. Vocal director Ken Darby had the Munchkins' voices dubbed with manipulated recordings performed by others, rendering a twice-removed relationship between onscreen bodies and heard voices. Without the aid of magnetic tape let alone digital processing, this effect took considerable effort. Ken Darby explained:

> I worked it out mathematically, using a metronome. Then I went to the head of the sound department, Doug Shearer. I told him that if we could record at sixty feet per minute instead of the normal ninety feet per minute and if we sang at a slower pace in a different key, when we played it back at ninety it should sound right. He said there was no way to do that because we didn't have a variable-speed recorder. Then he said he would try to manufacture a new gear for the sound recording machine. And it worked.[43]

After Dorothy embarks on her Oz journey, voices continue to trail her. At times, the vocal enhancements mirror those of Dorothy's initial arrival in

Munchkinland. When Dorothy and her friends gaze on the Emerald City for the first time, wordless chorus and full orchestra help gild a matte painting of the city with evocations of the sublime. Although the musical affect achieved here is hardly original, capturing the performance of it strained the technological limits of sound recording, with orchestra and chorus overloading the microphones.[44]

Vocal effects also carry over to the film's songs, where both texted and untexted vocals provide unexpected comment. When the Tin Man imagines having a heart, he is surprised—but only momentarily—when a girl's voice interjects.

> TIN MAN: Picture me
>   A balcony
>   Above, a voice sings low . . .
> OFFSCREEN VOICE: Wherefore art thou, Romeo?
> TIN MAN: I hear a beat—
>   How sweet!

The voice is Adriana Caselotti's, better known as the voice of Disney's Snow White. Given that MGM's *Oz* would be frequently compared to *Snow White and the Seven Dwarfs* (1937), which had been released just two years earlier, it was a savvy and self-aware selection that fits *Oz*'s predominant timbre of youthful femininity. (Caselotti received $100 for her vocal cameo.)[45] Perhaps most memorable are the voices that buoy the travelers as they leave the poppy field to complete their journey to the Emerald City. Described in the conductor's part as both "optimistic" and "heavenly," the female trio's entrance on the soundtrack initially alarms the Scarecrow, who ducks reflexively and looks about for the source. But a few beats later the entire team is gamely bouncing in time to the lyrics: "You're out of the woods, you're out of the dark, you're out of the night . . ." In both cases, the onscreen characters' ready acceptance of offscreen voices is a cheerful affront to cinematic protocol. In musicals, onscreen characters may break into song. Acousmatic voices are not at liberty to join them. The fact that they do so here points not only to the oddness of Oz, but to MGM's film, which makes no attempt to justify the unprepared entrance of a popular women's trio—The Debutantes—in a field of poppies.[46] Under different circumstances, this effect might be more unsettling. Drawing on sound theorist Michel Chion, Stan Link argues that "the sound of the *acousmêtre* is the quintessence of horror: a power derived from disembodiment, invisibility, ambiguity, immateriality and authority."[47] In Oz, however, a self-reflexive musical effect both invokes and seemingly winks at this concept—illuminating a presumed rule about film music by playfully undermining it.

Music for Magic

The use of music to alternately enhance and tame cinematic representations of the fantastic is most vivid through the deployment of music and effects around the film's witches and wizards. As the earlier examples illustrate, MGM's film often provocatively conflates characters' onscreen encounters with the fantastic and audiences' relationship to the fantastic dimensions of cinema itself. This sense of elision between the story world and its cinematic rendering is palpable when considering the film's supernaturally endowed characters, who serve as extensions of the behind-the-camera "wizards" managing effects, cinematography, and sound. It is an elision that Baum or, rather, Baum-as-wizard modeled in his role as narrator for the *Fairylogue and Radio-Plays*.

As with other effects sequences in the film, music is not merely summoned to make magical individuals more incredible, fantastic, or spectacular. Humor and self-deprecating reflexivity also keep the scenes featuring these individuals safely grounded in familiar cinematic and pre-cinematic expressive registers. As a result, these sequences accommodate differing reactions. "Youngsters" may be enthralled, even frightened, by the sights and sounds of individuals possessing remarkable powers; "oldsters" may be more curious and bemused, wondering of the filmmakers, "how did they do that?" The music affiliated with each inhabits a variety of roles that are not limited to associative motives reflecting inherent, stable character qualities.[48] Instead, the music swirling about these characters alternately extends and moderates characters' cinematic presence as rendered through visual effects.

When it came to enshrouding characters with music, Stothart and his compositional team turned to Russian composers like Modest Mussorgsky, Nikolai Rimsky-Korsakov, and Igor Stravinsky. Their settings of fairy tales provided abundant examples of music signaling both the power and vulnerability of magically imbued characters. Glinda's six-note motive, placed prominently at the very beginning of the film's main titles, is a case in point. Set as a declarative fanfare figure in trumpets and violins, the last four notes outline two tritones (an interval with long-standing associations with the supernatural) and collectively comprise a fully diminished seventh chord. The straight eighth note rhythm, melodic contour, and harmonic content closely align with the end of a short, recurring motive in Stravinsky's "Infernal Dance of the King Kashchei" from *The Firebird* (1910) (see Examples 4.1 and 4.2). The passage in question involves competing magical characters: the evil sorcerer Kashchei is bewitched through an intercessory spell from the Firebird, a scenario that roughly corresponds to Glinda's role in *Oz*.

EXAMPLE 4.1. Glinda's six-note motive repeats, growing in volume as her bubble approaches Munchkinland.

EXAMPLE 4.2. A recurring motive from Stravinsky's "Infernal Dance" in *The Firebird* (mm. 17–18, Suite, 1919 version). The concluding pair of tritones exhibit the same contour as the tail end of Glinda's motive.

Stothart's admiration for Stravinsky's music is a matter of record. He had already drawn on *The Firebird* for his early score for *The End of St. Petersburg* (1928).[49] Stravinsky himself toured the MGM studio in 1935. During the visit, which has been carefully documented by William Rosar, Stothart honored the composer in a laudatory speech and received from Stravinsky a signed copy of the score to *Petrushka* (1911).[50] Shortly before working on *The Wizard of Oz*, Stothart argued that he and his colleagues "do not stress melodic themes as much as we seek musical effects that generate certain impressions. Stravinsky does it on the concert stage, and he has the ideal picture technique."[51] Indeed, sounds of Stravinsky resonate elsewhere in the score—Robert Stringer's music for the Poppy Field features a creative reworking of "The Shrove-Tide Fair" from *Petrushka* that incorporates snatches of "We're Off to See the Wizard." And when Dorothy clicks her heels and Glinda waves her wand, Stothart again draws on *The Firebird* by including a swerving trombone glissando—a conspicuous orchestral "effect" from "The Infernal Dance of King Kashchei."[52]

Glinda's music reveals other special characteristics. For one, her theme registers her supernatural aura, not her physical presence. In her first scene, set in Munchkinland, the six-note figure—now given a brilliantly hued setting in celesta and harp—repeats as a cycling ostinato while Dorothy watches Glinda's bubble approach. As the bubble grows larger, the orchestration transforms. A rustling shimmer behind the six-note motive grows louder as more instruments and a wordless chorus enter. Seconds before Glinda appears in human form, the accumulating sonic force dissipates. Rather than reflect Glinda's character, then, the motive underscores Glinda's means of travel and, by extension, the efforts of the special effects department: drastic changes in dynamics and texture grant a bobbing bubble a mysterious and commanding quality.[53] When Glinda returns to bubble form and floats away from Munchkinland, the textural effect is reversed. In these settings, the motive's delicate setting in harp and celesta (and occasionally doubled by solo woodwind instruments) recalls less Stravinsky's Kashchei and more Stravinsky's teacher, Rimsky-Korsakov. In the opera, *The Legend of the Invisible City of Kitezh and the Maiden Fevroniya* (1905), Rimsky-Korsakov also calls upon harps, celesta, and solo woodwind voices to perform a twinkling ostinato of falling fourths that play as the city magically disappears. They return later as the city becomes visible once again (see Example 4.3). In Oz, the motive is not limited to comings and goings—it also plays as Glinda sends life-saving snow to the poppy field and later helps Dorothy transmigrate from Oz back to Kansas. Its presence signals her extraordinary powers—wielded by a witch and rendered through MGM's effects.

In a land populated by exceptional individuals, Glinda stands out—she is the only major figure who lacks a Kansas counterpart and, unlike the Wicked Witch and the Wizard, her authority is never inadvertently overturned (although she is curiously selective about when to invoke her powers). Glinda appears—in classic deus ex machina form—only when moments of great uncertainty necessitate her presence. Her antithesis, the Wicked Witch of the West, is a persistently disruptive force with a penchant for halting choral numbers on their penultimate chord.

EXAMPLE 4.3. Rimsky-Korsakov's music for the disappearing and reappearing city of Kitezh may have served as a model for the shape and instrumentation of Glinda's motive. (*The Legend of the Invisible City of Kitezh and the Maiden Fevroniya*, Act IV, five measures after rehearsal number 316.)

"Just try and stay out of my way. Just try!" she cackles at Dorothy. This over-weening presence demanded different musical strategies to embody and frame her powers.

Although *The Wizard of Oz* is predominantly a fantasy musical, the Wicked Witch's presence invokes the horror genre. Her role upholds the narrative paradigm of horror, in which an abnormal individual (i.e., witch, monster) poses an existential threat to society and must be confronted to secure social stability and narrative resolution.[54] Timothy Scheuer notes that composers for horror films often deployed contrasting musical characteristics to reinforce oppositional binaries between normative and deviant characters. The theme for the Wicked Witch upholds this expectation and is introduced when Miss Gulch is shown riding her bicycle to the Gales' farm. Stothart's title for this particular music cue—"Miss Gulch, 'The Ultimate Witch'"—foreshadows the theme's role in Miss Gulch's cyclone transformation and its continued presence in Oz. As with Glinda's motive, the theme cycles repetitively—an apt accompaniment for bi-cycle riding—and its opening three phrases also emphasize the tritone interval. But in contrast to the graceful leaps built into Glinda's motive, the witch's theme scuttles in half-steps from note to note. Assistant composer Robert Stringer explained that the witch's theme was devised by inverting and distorting the opening motive for "We're Off to See the Wizard" to resemble a sneer.[55] In quite explicit terms then, the witch's music embodies disfigurement—an uneasy muta-tion from a more affirming musical sentiment.

If Glinda's motive served exclusively as the "sound" of extraordinary powers that are never challenged or qualified, the accompaniment for the wicked witch is more conventional—even clichéd. When she is onscreen or discussed by other characters, her theme plays in the underscore: a musical calling card that reinforces her one-dimensional role as disrupter to the journey. (An exception is when her theme plays as Dorothy sees the feet of the crushed Wicked Witch of the East. Here it misleadingly affirms Dorothy's erroneous impression that the house has finished off Miss Gulch's over-the-rainbow avatar.) The music for the witch's explosive entrance and exit from Munchkinland shows that even well-worn musical tropes can have complicated repercussions. When the witch emerges from the smoke, Stothart writes music that is marked "mysterioso-terrifying" in the conductor's part. There are string tremolos, grotesque wood-wind runs (marked "guttural snarl"), a "squealing" descending line in the violins, and muted brass who ironically intone "Ding-Dong! The Witch Is Dead." The orchestral calamity rapidly disperses, allowing a pizzicato setting of the witch's theme to be performed—per Stothart's instructions—"in marked time like old villain music." Although the cue title is "Threatening Witch," the music provides a strong caveat. She is threatening within the story world of Oz but her "old villain" accompaniment places her evil effects within quotation marks. For youngsters, she may continue to exert a fearful pressure on the narrative, but the knowing music conveys to older viewers a stagey humor redolent of theatrical melodrama.

This contrary impulse of symphonically enhancing the witch's powers one moment while qualifying them the next continues in the haunted forest and the Witch's castle. In the oppositional grammar of the horror genre, these sites affiliated with the Wicked Witch must contrast with the surrounding locale, offering a "secondary setting . . . where the evil flourishes."[56] Among the haunted forest's unusual events and effects, the accompanying music invokes both Hector Berlioz and cartoon specialist Carl Stalling—two composers who used special orchestral effects to connote the supernatural and the super silly. Sustained string tremolos, the eerie wail of a flexatone, a pizzicato setting of the Witch's theme, violin glissandi and harmonics, and muted brass chords create an atmosphere appropriate for a Witches' Sabbath. But abrupt shifts among musical textures, plunking iterations of "If I Only Had a Brain/a Heart/the Nerve," and the hammy staging gives the sequence a cartoonish veneer. Bemusement and fear do battle—even among the characters. When the Tin Man declares that spooks are "silly," he is whisked off the ground by a magical force and dropped in a clattering heap. Seconds later, an optical trick shot of the Wicked Witch studying the scene through her crystal ball reveals that she has been watching Dorothy's friends all along. Amid the various visual, musical, and sonic effects, it is her abiding presence—sitting, as it were, in the audience—that marks the scene's most unsettling revelation.

The castle itself presents an inversion in sound and visuals of Munchkinland. Instead of smaller individuals with artificially raised voices, the castle hosts Winkie guards: exceptionally tall individuals whose singing voices are artificially lowered by reversing the recording process that Ken Darby and Douglas Shearer had used for the Munchkins. In place of the expansive, kaleidoscopically colored Munchkinland set, the witch's castle depends on several dismally lit matte paintings and claustrophobic interior sets. Even the Winkies' stirring "Marzia grotesque" features a melody that distortedly resembles the "Tra-la-la-la-la" fragment from the conclusion of the Munchkins' chorus. Once again, however, music serves to diminish the threat of the Witch and her Winkies as much as enhance it. When Winkies sneak up behind the Lion, Tin Man, and Scarecrow, Stothart requests "Old-fashioned villain music" and pens a passage that is a clear allusion to J. Bodewalt Lampe's "Mysterioso Pizzicato," an onomatopoetic impression of tip-toeing that was published in the *Remik Folio of Moving Picture Music* (1914).[57] For Toto's escape from the castle, Stothart set Mendelssohn's "Scherzo" from *Three Fantasies*, Op. 16, No. 2. For the frantic liberation of Dorothy from the locked room, Roger Edens provided a reorchestrated version of Rimsky-Korsakov's arrangement of Mussorgsky's *Night on Bald Mountain* (1886). These selections do not serve as special effects or support specific special effects, but their aggregation in the Witch's castle contextualizes—and therefore delimits—the Witch's special powers. However genuinely evil or terrifying the Witch's effects-enabled powers might strike other characters or audiences, her music—and the music for her castle and guards—is firmly grounded in conventional modes of theatrical villainy. Much like the use of musical quotations in the cyclone sequence, the presence of these works harkens back to earlier practices of music directors working in theatrical melodrama and silent cinema.[58] This qualifying accompaniment may not register to all audience members, but it reflects a concerted effort on Stothart's part to grant the Witch a musical identity that was cogent, reassuringly familiar to some, and therefore readily contained.

If the Witch's powers are dampened through music—anticipating that final bucket of water—the Wizard's powers are purely illusive, even within the fiction of the film. For this ultimate special effects man, Stothart's music props up faked authority while slyly indicating its emptiness. The Wizard's theme is a reverent brass chorale that, like the Witch's theme, takes its inspiration from another song. In this case, it is the "Ha, ha, ha, ho, ho, ho" passage from "The Merry Old Land of Oz." Whereas the Witch's theme incorporates chromaticism and repetition to suggest a deviant corruption of "We're Off to See the Wizard," the Wizard's theme shrouds buffoonish laughter in Wagnerian majesty. The first iteration of the Wizard's theme—played when Glinda invokes his name in Munchkinland—prompts the Munchkins to bow in respect, but the melodic source already anticipates his incompetence. Another musical double entendre unfolds when Dorothy and her companions begin to process down the hallway to the Wizard's chamber. As with the Witch's castle, Mussorgsky serves as a model. Drawing on Mussorgsky's music for the coronation scene from the opera *Boris Godunov* (1869–1872), Stothart builds suspense by alternating between harmonically distant chords played by horns and trombones over a sustaining pedal. While the slowly chiming chords suggest the sonic weight of massive, tolling bells, their commanding endorsement is deliberately misplaced. Boris's ascent to power is problematic—as is the Wizard's.

The Wizard's introduction to the group and audience unfolds as a series of effects. As with the Munchkins and the various disembodied singing voices heard on the soundtrack, his booming voice issues from offscreen as he orders Dorothy's group to "come forward!" The room is illuminated with magical eruptions of fire. Above these, an image of a floating head emerges and begins to speak, confirming the previous voice as that of the Wizard's. "I am Oz, the Great and Powerful," the head avers. Instead of the Wizard's theme, however, the accompanying music serves the visual effects through a series of elaborate stinger chords. In a cue aptly titled "Magic Smoke Chords," the opening measures feature a series of pedal tones blasted by trombones, an orchestral imitation of the combustive huffs heard before each burst of onscreen fire. The initial articulation is followed by a spray of triadically arranged pitches, a musical emulation of the fiery blasts themselves. Each chord is different, as the highest note ascends sequentially, but all contain a devilish mix of tritones. The chords are strategically placed to sustain the Wizard's supernatural presence beyond the limits of the visual frame. As the scene is structurally organized, shots either show the flame-wreathed head or reverse shots of the visitors' terrified faces. Chords are timed always to enter when the camera focuses on the group. The thunderous, magically laced sounds offer an aural proxy for the thunderous, magical images that are temporarily not visible during the reverse shots. Only when the Wizard promises to grant their wishes does his beneficent brass chorale enter. With the chorale now heard after the performance of "Merry Old Land of Oz," its derivative and capricious character is more readily apparent.

There are other qualities in the scene's music that lightly mock the Wizard's special effects even as they extend them. There are, for instance, too many "magic smoke chords." Their repetition pulls the scene—along with the Wizard's penchant for alliteration—toward self-parody. Indeed, the number of chords heard in the film exceeds those indicated in the conductor's score. The score includes five, with the highest voice ascending a half-step with each chord. But in the film, six chords are heard. The second chord is played before *and* after the third chord, breaking the chromatic ascent and indicating a hastily applied solution that—whether inadvertent or not—is delectably appropriate for the Wizard's inflated performance, which begins to resemble the Lion's delusional grandeur ("If I Were King of the Forest"). When Dorothy and her friends return with the broomstick, Oz's power already appears diminished by the conspicuous absence of any empowering music. Not until the man behind the curtain is discovered does a rueful arrangement of "Merry Old Land of Oz"—and *not* the brass chorale version—begin accompanying the "very bad" Wizard's lines.

Conclusion

Across all three case studies, musical effects lend an empowering energy to the visual spectacle. Monumental sounds from orchestra and chorus affirm the grandeur or terror of the spectacular while drifting female voices infuse other scenes with a spirit of mystery. But if musical effects can energize the sensorial impact of visual effects, they can also divert it toward whimsical ends, in the case of the

FIGURE 4.4. The Wizard's power, it is revealed, flows from a microphone and a machine.

silent-film accompaniment heard during the cyclone, the "old villain music" accompanying the Wicked Witch, and the chipper "optimistic voices" from the poppy field. These instances point to a distinctive quality within the MGM film that connects with notions of power and authority as they are perceived, exerted, and ultimately overturned—both within the film, and *as* film. Nowhere is this more forcibly demonstrated than in the case of the Wizard, whose superpower depends on a poorly concealed vocal technology that—in contrast with the predominant vocality of Oz—brims with patriarchal bluster (see Figure 4.4). Unlike the other voices discussed in this chapter, the artifice of the Wizard's voice *is* revealed within the film,[59] throwing into question not only his power but the very point of Dorothy's odyssey and—by extension—audience investment in the film's narrative. "What's the point?" one might reasonably ask. For many, the film's deservedly famous songs and Judy Garland's performance of "Over the Rainbow" provide ample justification. But even the background score and the film's many visual effects provide much more than mere window dressing for a fantastical narrative. Instead, story, effects, and music engage in a much more intricate dance— a dance initiated by Baum that entreats old and young to revel in the illusory charms of film spectatorship itself. In Oz, musical effects stir more than fantasy; they echo back our abiding fantasy of film itself.

Notes

Earlier versions of this chapter were presented at the Spring 2017 American Musicological Society Midwest Chapter Meeting hosted at Drake University and the 2017 Music and the Moving Image Conference hosted at New York University. Special thanks go to film music historian William Rosar and archivist Edward Comstock (University of Southern California), who helped locate and share archival resources that were critical to this study.

1. Herbert Stothart, "Munchkinland, Prod: 'Wizard of Oz' No. 1060," conductor's part, April 10, 1939, 1. The conductor's parts for *The Wizard of Oz* are held in the archives of Turner Entertainment. Copies of the conductor's parts were kindly provided by William Rosar.
2. Nelson B. Bell, "Prelude to the Coming of a Rare Achievement in Cinematography," *Washington Post*, August 20, 1939, AM 3; Nelson B. Bell, "*Wizard of Oz* Takes Rank with *Snow White*," *Washington Post*, August 9, 1939, 6.
3. Frank S. Nugent, "The Screen in Review," *New York Times*, August 18, 1939, 16.
4. Nugent, "The Screen in Review," 16.
5. Nugent, "The Screen in Review," 16.
6. For more on MGM's relative standing among studios in the late 1930s, see Thomas Schatz, *The Genius of the System: Hollywood Filmmaking in the Studio Era* (New York: Henry Holt, 1989, 1996), 252–270.
7. Aljean Harmetz's *The Making of The Wizard of Oz: Movie Magic and Studio Power in the Prime of M-G-M—and the Miracle of Production #1060* (New York: Hyperion, 1977, 1998) remains the definitive account of the film's production. An entire chapter is devoted to the efforts of the special effects department, and other "effects"—such as music and Technicolor—are treated in individual chapters. See Chapter 3, "The Brain, the Heart, the Nerve, and the Music"; Chapter 8, "Below the Line"; and Chapter 9, "Special Effects."
8. In addition to songwriters Harold Arlen and E. Y. Harburg, a number of musicians contributed to Oz's music, including Leo Arnaud, George Bassman, Murray Cutter, Ken Darby, Paul Marquardt, George Stoll, Roger Edens, and Robert Stringer. See Harmetz, *The Making of the Wizard of Oz*, 92. See also Hugh Fordin, *M-G-M's Greatest Musicals: The Arthur Freed Unit* (New York: Da Capo Press, 1975, 1996), 551–552.
9. Bruno David Ussher, "Music," *Los Angeles Daily News*, May 3, 1939.
10. "Natural Color Brings Changes in Film Music," *Washington Post*, July 23, 1939, A3.
11. "After Cameras Cease Turning . . . at Metro-Goldwyn-Mayer on *The Wizard of Oz*," Metro-Goldwyn-Mayer Collection, Margaret Herrick Library. A copy of this photo caption was kindly provided by William Rosar.
12. Previous studies that examine the orchestral background score to *The Wizard of Oz* include Ronald Rodman, "'There's No Place Like Home': Tonal Closure and Design in The Wizard of Oz," *Indiana Theory Review* 19 (Spring/Fall 1998): 125–144; Fiona Ford, "Be It [N]ever so Humble? The Narrating Voice in the Underscore to The

Wizard of Oz (MGM, 1939)," in *Melodramatic Voices: Understanding Music Drama*, edited by Sarah Hibberd (Burlington, VT: Ashgate, 2011), 197–214; and Nathan Platte, "Nostalgia, the Silent Cinema, and the Art of Quotation in Herbert Stothart's Score for *The Wizard of Oz* (1939)," *Journal of Film Music* 4, no. 1 (2011): 45–64.

13. Kevin. J. Donnelly, *The Spectre of Sound: Music in Film and Television* (London: BFI, 2005), 2.

14. For one discussion of this phenomenon, see Stan Link, "Horror and Science Fiction," in *The Cambridge Companion to Film Music*, edited by Mervyn Cooke and Fiona Ford (Cambridge: Cambridge University Press, 2016), 200–215.

15. Scott Bukatman, *Matters of Gravity: Special Effects and Supermen in the 20th Century* (Durham, NC: Duke University Press, 2003), 90.

16. Gunning drew the concept of "attractions" from the writings of director Sergei Eisenstein. See Tom Gunning, "The Cinema of Attraction: Early Film, Its Spectator, and the Avant-Garde," first printed in *Wide Angle* 8, nos. 3–4 (1986): 63–70. Reprinted in *The Cinema of Attractions Reloaded*, edited by Wanda Strauven (Amsterdam: Amsterdam University Press, 2006), 381–388.

17. Gunning, "The Cinema of Attraction," 382.

18. Scott Paulin has also drawn on Gunning's "cinema of attractions" to consider concert music that has been described as "cinematic." With careful adjustments made to Gunning's theory, Paulin compellingly proposes a "music of attractions" that "would acknowledge music's attraction to spectacle while resisting the lure of narrative." See Paulin, " 'Cinematic' Music: Analogies, Fallacies, and the Case of Debussy," *Music and the Moving Image* 3, no. 1 (2010): 12.

19. Bukatman, *Matters of Gravity*; Julie A. Turnock, *Plastic Reality: Special Effects, Technology, and the Emergence of 1970s Blockbuster Aesthetics* (New York: Columbia University Press, 2015), 4–5.

20. William Leach, *Land of Desire: Merchants, Power, and the Rise of a New American Culture* (New York: Vintage Books, 1993), 60.

21. L. Frank Baum, *The Art of Decorating Dry Goods Windows and Interiors* (Chicago: Show Window Publishing, 1900), 7; quoted in Leach, *Land of Desire*, 60.

22. Rebecca Loncraine, *The Real Wizard of Oz: The Life and Times of L. Frank Baum* (New York: Gotham Books, 2009), 172.

23. Leach, *Land of Desire*, 252–253.

24. Leach, *Land of Desire*, 253.

25. "Living Pictured Fairy Tales," *Variety*, October 10, 1908, 11. Mark Evan Swartz provides an engrossing account of the event's details in *Oz before the Rainbow: L. Frank Baum's* The Wonderful Wizard of Oz *on Stage and Screen to 1939* (Baltimore: Johns Hopkins University Press, 2000), 161–172. Biographer Rebecca Loncraine disputes Baum's claim that "radio" referred to "Michel Radio," a French inventor who worked on coloring the film. According to Loncraine, there is no indication that anyone named Michel Radio worked on the film or, for that matter,

even existed. Loncraine argues instead that "radio" in 1908 was "vague and ambiguous ... [suggesting] radiant energy, an exotic higher plan on which stories as well as spirits were sloshing about" (Loncraine, *The Real Wizard of Oz*, 232).

26. "Living Pictured Fairy Tales," 11.

27. Baum's indebtedness to Méliès is noted by both Loncraine (*The Real Wizard of Oz,* 229–230) and Swartz (*Oz before the Rainbow*), who also registers the influence of American filmmaker Edwin S. Porter (161). In his essay on the *Fairylogue*, Artemis Willis also cites Porter and Méliès as models, noting that the illusion of bringing characters in a book to life had been achieved by Méliès in both *Le Livre Magique* (1900) and *Les Cartes Vivantes* (1905). See Willis, "'Marvelous and Fascinating': L. Frank Baum's *Fairylogue and Radio-Plays* (1908)," in *Performing New Media, 1890–1915*, edited by Kaveh Askari, Scott Curtis, Frank Gray, Louis Pelletier, Tami Williams, and Joshua Yumibe (New Barnet, UK: John Libbey, 2015), 147.

28. Loncraine, *The Real Wizard of Oz*, 233. Lengthy excerpts of the interview are reprinted in Michael Hearn, "Introduction to *The Annotated Wizard of Oz*," in *The Annotated Wizard of Oz* (New York: W. W. Norton, 1973, 2000), lxvii–lxx.

29. Katherine Rogers, *L. Frank Baum: Creator of Oz* (New York: St. Martin's Press, 2002), 9.

30. Swartz, *Oz before the Rainbow*, 37 and 162.

31. "L. Frank Baum in Fairylogue," *Chicago Daily Tribune*, October 3, 1908, p. 10.

32. J. C. Jessen, "Oz Company Finishes First Release," *Motion Picture New*, August 8, 1914, p. 40. For a detailed discussion of the surviving musical materials from *The Patchwork Girl of Oz*, see Eric Dienstfrey, "Synch Holes and Patchwork in Early Feature-Film Scores," *Music and the Moving Image* 7, no. 1 (2014): 40–53.

33. Bukatman, *Matters of Gravity*, 109.

34. Carroll died in 1898, shortly before Baum began work on his novel. Reviewers of Baum's work frequently compared his stories to Carroll's. See Loncraine, *The Real Wizard of Oz*, 161, 164, and Hearn, "Introduction," xliii.

35. These effects are explained in Harmetz, *The Making of The Wizard of Oz*, 246–250.

36. Salman Rushdie, *The Wizard of Oz* (London: BFI, 1992), 30.

37. See, for example, the reprinted description in *Silent Film Sound* of sound effects provided by a theater drummer for a single vaudeville program. For filmed "rural scenes," the drummer imitates three wild birds and three barnyard birds, each with its own whistle. Rick Altman, *Silent Film Sound* (New York: Columbia University Press, 2004), 104–105.

38. This page is reproduced in Harmetz, *The Making of The Wizard of Oz*, 96.

39. This estimate is based on George Bassman's recollection, as recounted in Harmetz, *The Making of The Wizard of Oz*, 94.

40. Bakutman, *Matters of Gravity*, 91.

41. Bakutman, *Matters of Gravity*, 109.

42. Herbert Stothart, "Munchkinland," conductor's part, mm. 22–23.

43. Harmetz, *The Making of The Wizard of Oz*, 97.

44. Robert Stringer, as interviewed by William Rosar, "My Years at M-G-M" (1983), unpublished, 22. William Rosar kindly provided a copy of the transcript.

45. Musicians' expenses, *The Wizard of Oz*, Prod. 1060, MGM Music Department Collection, Cinematic Arts Library, University of Southern California.

46. Musicians' expenses, *The Wizard of Oz*, Prod. 1060, MGM Music Department Collection.

47. Link, "Horror and Science Fiction," 214.

48. Justin London, "Leitmotifs and Musical Reference in the Classical Score," in *Music and Cinema*, edited by James Buhler, Caryl Flinn, and David Neumeyer (Hanover, NH: Wesleyan University Press, 2000), 90.

49. William Rosar, "Stravinsky and M-G-M," in *Film Music 1*, edited by Clifford McCarty (New York: Garland, 1989), 121.

50. Rosar, "Stravinsky and M-G-M," 116.

51. Herbert Stothart, "Film Music," in *Behind the Screen: How Films Are Made*, edited by Stephen Watts (London: Arthur Barker, 1938), 144.

52. Rosar, "Stravinsky and M-G-M," 121.

53. The optical effect used to create the Witch's bubble involved moving a camera closer to a stationary silver ball, then processing and imposing the footage over the Munchkinland shot. See Harmetz, *The Making of The Wizard of Oz*, 254–255.

54. Timothy E. Scheuer, drawing on the work of Stuart Kaminsky, summarizes these trends in *Music and Mythmaking in Film: Genre and the Role of the Composer* (Jefferson, NC: McFarland, 2005), 176–178.

55. Stringer and Rosar, "My Years at M-G-M," 6.

56. Scheurer, *Music and Mythmaking in Film*, 181.

57. This passage from the conductor's part is reproduced in Platte, "Herbert Stothart's Score for *The Wizard of Oz*," 50. The author thanks William Rosar for noting this connection.

58. Fiona Ford connects these practices to theatrical melodrama in "Be It [N]ever so Humble," 202–203; I also consider their relationship to silent cinema in "Herbert Stothart's Score for *The Wizard of Oz*."

59. This special moment has been singled out by others. John Belton notes that this sequence illustrates how "the identification of a voice with a body can be delayed," and "create suspense, both in the area of voice/dialogue and in that of sound effects, calling attention to sound *as a device* by playing with our perception of it" (Belton, "Technology and Aesthetics of Film Sound," in *Film Sound: Theory and Practice*, edited by Elisabeth Weis and John Belton [New York: Columbia University Press, 1985], 65). Kevin J. Donnelly posits that the "wizard . . . might serve as an apt metaphor for cinema. . . . He is large, loud, and impressive. She and her companions assume the unity of the booming voice and strange visuals as a 'real' and highly singular powerful being. This is all an illusion, achieved by a man with a machine" (Donnelly, *Occult Aesthetics: Synchronization in Sound Film* [New York: Oxford University Press, 2014], 7).

5 "DANCING THROUGH OZ"

CHOREOGRAPHIC CONTEXT IN *THE WIZARD OF OZ* (1939)

Claudia Funder

The Cultural Impact of *The Wizard of Oz*

The dance sequences in *The Wizard of Oz* are a wonderful feature of the film. They embellish the narrative and portray an emotional state, helping to define the characters, while also being entertaining. On closer examination, however, one realizes that there is very little dancing in the movie. There are brief choreographic sequences such as the recurring skipping down the Yellow Brick Road, and the dance tableaux presented by the Munchkins to Dorothy. The Munchkins and the people of Oz march and twirl in grand parading scenes with the full chorus. Although these scenes create tremendous spectacle and energy through color and movement, they are not really dancing, per se, and there are few dance solos or extended group work in the film as a whole. When dance sequences do appear, however, they bring a warm energy and their strength captivates the viewer.

This chapter explores the social and cultural significance of the choreographed numbers in *The Wizard of Oz*: how they contribute to the film and its immense popularity over the last seventy-five years. It argues that traditional and contemporary dance forms provide familiarity and cultural resonance for audiences and that the appeal of these elements, juxtaposed with an imaginative setting, contributes to the popularity of the film over time. Specifically, the jitterbug scene places an emerging, new social dance of the 1930s into the imaginary world of Oz. It becomes a direct link between the real and the imagined. This scene and other choreography are discussed, including the Yellow Brick Road recurring skipping motif and the Scarecrow's solo routine. The chapter also speculates on why neither the jitterbug sequence nor the Scarecrow's routine appeared in the commercial release of the film and argues that these exclusions resulted in a diminished and unclear role of dance in the film. There is little extant evidence regarding the planning or writing of the dance sequences, partly because filmed sequences simply did not survive and also due to the lack of a written documentation process for dance and the lack of specific, standardized nomenclature for dance work.

The Wizard of Oz has proven to be one of the most enduring, popular films of the twentieth century. It beautifully couples old world storytelling with new technology. It has the best elements of fairy tale along with the structure of a fable; the status quo is interrupted and an adventure to wondrously strange places with folkloric characters ensues in order to teach a lesson. The onset of Technicolor, used in the 1939 film, dazzled audiences by heightening familiar fairy-tale elements with color, setting, and pageantry. The highly colored painted set evokes pantomime or stage, placing the audience on familiar ground. Audiences understand the fairy-tale trope, but this time the color, the set, the costumes, the scale "on the big screen" confirmed and supplanted those in our imaginations. The effects of the twister uprooting the house, the Witch appearing and disappearing, the effects of flying monkeys, red smoke, the horse of changing colors, and the melting Wicked Witch of the West are etched into people's minds generation after generation. If the "wonder elements" are the technical achievements of color and effects, then, along with the familiar elements of fairy tale, the choreography also offers us a specific visual area where we are at home. None of the choreography is modern or groundbreaking but refers to the popular oeuvre of dance styles from vaudeville and social settings. In the context of the wondrous world of Oz, the familiar choreography immediately anchors the audience's personal experience and culture into that on the screen, giving a very entertaining frame of reference. The dance sequences demonstrate physically that their culture is our culture. We are delighted when we see familiar dance forms recontextualized in an imaginative setting, where the wonder of the new is balanced by the comfort of the familiar. The dancing in the *The Wizard of Oz* is a strong contributing factor to our connection to the film and its enduring popularity.

Dancing in the Film

The Wizard of Oz has no specifically credited "choreographer," and although very much a musical, it is not a "dance movie" as such. It was never intended to have numerous virtuosic dance numbers. In the original onscreen credits and on the Internet Movie Database (IMDb) we see "Musical Numbers staged by Bobby Connolly." Dona Massin and Arthur Abel (uncredited in the film) are each listed on IMDb as "Assistant to Mr. Connolly." In addition, Dona Massin is listed as an uncredited "Assistant Choreographer." As there is no actual choreographer, this is somewhat ambiguous. Who is she assisting? Or, given the title is uncredited, was it added in afterward to acknowledge a piece of work Massin was given? The distinction is important. The term "choreography" refers to the actual dance steps and the design of such steps and sequences of these that make up a dance routine, whereas "staging musical numbers" refers to the movement and flow of a whole dance scene but does not concern itself with an individual's footwork. Connolly was not credited as writing the routines because that was not his role. Although these titles come across as vague, the producers were in fact trying to be accurate. There is no general, overall choreographer credited to the film because there wasn't one. This becomes problematic in trying to understand the place that dance held in the film.

Bobby Connolly was known for designing musical numbers that had large choruses requiring systematic coordination as they created predesigned patterns for an impressive overall visual effect. Within this vision, the detailed footwork was always very generic. In all Connolly's film work he is never listed as a choreographer per se but is given credits such as "Dances," "Dance Director," "Musical Numbers Staged by," "Ensembles Directed by," or "Songs and Dances Directed by."[1] Unlike clear roles within a music department (words by, lyrics by, music arranged by, music composed by, etc.), there were no uniform terms for people working on dance numbers. We can see from the vague and differing descriptions that a formal nomenclature did not exist. While all music work is listed under a music department heading, people doing dance work are not collated into a group but appear uncredited, usually under the heading of "miscellaneous." The writing, arranging, and production of dance was little documented and not in any uniform manner. Despite the difficulty in titles, Connolly's jobs from film to film were consistent. Four years before working on *The Wizard of Oz*, Connolly designed numbers for "Lonely Feet" and "You Were the Girl from over the Way" for the film *Sweet Adeline* (1934). "Lonely Feet" sees two large staircases at the back of the stage on the left and right of a center fountain. The scene is romantic and elegant, set in a formal ballroom. The women's chorus enters from the back of the fountain, center back of the stage, and they spill around to the front and base of the staircases. They wear white floating ball gowns. The men's chorus enters descending the steps of both staircases. They are also formally dressed, in black buttoned tails, white ruffled shirts, and white military trousers (the film is set in the Spanish-American war). The gents descend the stairs to take their partners with military precision. The beautiful visual achievement is one of blocks of colors moving into a zigzag of black and white on the dance floor.[2]

Contrasting with this, the large chorus pieces in *The Wizard of Oz* are much more complex. In the scene where Glinda the Good Witch of the North calls the Munchkins out to meet Dorothy ("It Really was no Miracle"), the chorus of Munchkins similarly enter from the rear of the set. Distance and height here are created largely by the camera angles and the bigger set rather than the staircases of *Sweet Adeline*. There are little steps at various levels leading to the Munchkins' mushroom-like houses which have rooftops of varying heights. In this scene, the chorus filters in at doorways, from the back or side wings of the stage, and there are at least four different entrances onto the set. Costumes are colorful and mixed and there are no geometric patterns being formed. The task here is to create the busyness and hubbub of a village rather than the formal, measured proceedings of a ball. On close examination, the Munchkins' formations are dictated with military, timed precision as chorus members line up, cluster in small groups, or stand in doorways and on the little bridge in the background.[3] By the time the horse and carriage arrive with the soldier Munchkins marching behind, the stage is bursting with hundreds of people, animals, and moving props all requiring coordination. Despite great differences in filming techniques and logistical complexity for each of these films, Connolly's task is essentially the same. He designs and coordinates the comings and goings of the chorus and other moving parts, directing it to operate smoothly to achieve the desired visual and narrative effect. The actual footwork is very basic in both scenes because it needs to be. A do-si-do for the Munchkins of Oz, a simple waltz for the ballroom scene in "Lonely Feet." The design of both scenes is to look grand and impressive, to evoke atmosphere rather than highlight a dance number. Connolly's design of the flowing movement in the Munchkin scene, its vivid color, and joyous village atmosphere all combine to delight audiences and stimulate our imaginations as we are introduced to the Munchkins for the first time.

In *Broadway Melody of 1940*, Connolly is credited as miscellaneous crew: "Bobby Connolly: Dances."[4] The dance coordination for this film, made shortly after *The Wizard of Oz*, is more akin to what Connolly did for *Sweet Adeline*, but in a more contemporary, upmarket, swing music setting. In the number for "Begin the Beguine," the stage could be that of "Lonely Feet"; the staircases have been removed and a simple mirror backs the stage. The live band is behind the camera and reflected in the mirrors, while the camera at center focuses on the singers and then the dancers. As the quartet sings "Begin the Beguine," chorus girls are seated in a semi-circle at the back. The singers sway a little, executing a shift of weight, and walk forward as the chorus tap dances exiting stage left. The emphasis here is on the song, not the dance, which is saved for Fred Astaire and Eleanor Powell. In this context, it is highly likely that the soloist dancers in *The Wizard of Oz*, just like dancers in other movies, utilized their current repertoire, devising their sequences in liaison with the director. The creative choreographic detail was therefore the responsibility of the principal dancers rather than someone else. Just as in vaudeville or onstage, in the early movies, dancers were employed to bring their skills and repertoire, providing steps and routines fitted to the scene and character, which is why the film didn't need an overall choreographer.

There is little extant evidence for the choreographic process for *The Wizard of Oz*. Indeed, finding evidence for any dance process is inherently problematic. While music and scripting have long-established, internationally accepted, uniform and readable documentation systems (those of writing and Western music notation), nothing similar exists for writing a dance routine. Choreographers make notes and some have invented elaborate documentation systems, but none of these have endured such that they can be read and the dance re-created accurately by others. Most notes are simply used as an aide de memoir for the creator. While the subject of performance practice in music is an enormous movement of academic debate among musicologists, there is, of course, the written manuscript itself to refer to (and possibly drafts for that matter). If the interpretation of performance style is not written down, the notation is. Not so for the writing of dance. Perhaps this is why the accreditation nomenclature is so variable; documentation of music is well established but there is no set process for dance.

Despite a lack of written documentation, we are given an insight into Fred Astaire's personal approach to creating his choreography for film projects. While Astaire stands out as an absolutely extraordinary talent, he learned his trade in vaudeville like many dancers of his time. He is not an exception to the rule in terms of process; all vaudeville acts or performers such as Ray Bolger and Jack Haley (the Scarecrow and Tin Man, respectively) worked up their own material. Although we do not have documentation of the processes Bolger or Haley used, we do have insight into the way Astaire worked on choreography for film, described by pianist Hal Borne at the piano, in a reflection of the creative process for the film *Fancy Free*, released in 1935:

> Hermes' contribution was always great. . . . Sometimes they'd walk around in circles scratching their heads. No one would talk and I wouldn't play. I just let them figure out what they were trying to figure out. Fred would say, "Let's try this: You go over there and you'll be the Ginger part." And he would start. It was hard to figure out who contributed what to the choreography.[5]

Although "it was hard to figure out who contributed what," we can see there was no overall separate "choreographer" in the room or a director for that matter. The dancers wrote their own choreography and it was part of the role. Cyd Charisse compares Gene Kelly to Fred Astaire: "In my opinion, Kelly is the more inventive choreographer of the two. Astaire, with Hermes Pan's help, creates fabulous numbers—for himself and his partner. But Kelly can create an entire number for somebody else."[6] Here, again, we see quite clearly that performers choreographed routines for themselves and their partners. Astaire himself comments that he "had to do his own choreography . . . with help from various choreographers."[7] General dance directors or those who staged dance numbers like Bobby Connolly or the more famous Busby Berkeley were not concerned with the minutiae of dance routines. There is a strong argument that *The Wizard of Oz* was no exception in this regard. While Connolly was putting the large chorus scenes together, the solo dancers brought their current routines and repertoire, devising their own routines in liaison with the director. Expert dancers such as Bolger and Haley were expected to bring their skills and repertoire to a project, providing routines as befitted the scene and character. Although Busby Berkeley was contracted to *The Wizard of Oz* to work on a routine for the Scarecrow, it is feasible that Ray Bolger had a large degree of input to the number's footwork. No choreographer is listed at all in the IMDb entry for *The Wizard of Oz* among other accreditations, which are mostly very specific, and this lack supports the argument that no choreographer was employed to work on the dance detail across the whole film. This reflects the usual practice of the time—which was for artists to create their individual sequences. Ultimately, this means there was no central vision for the choreographic language of the film.

Skipping Down the Yellow Brick Road

The choreography for the Yellow Brick Road transitions Dorothy simply from walking around the Yellow Brick Road spiral to the commencement of her journey. As Dorothy is invited to "follow the Yellow Brick Road" to Oz, her initial uncertain steps evolve into an accelerated skipping motion. The movement establishes confidence and a change of pace, indicating acceptance and determination to go on a journey to find the Wizard. The bouncy confidence repeated within the skipping structure, a continuous loop, tells us that Dorothy has the courage to set off and keep going until she finds an answer. Culturally, the skip in the film is associated strongly and specifically with the character of Dorothy. The rising overhead camera shot of Dorothy skipping down the Yellow Brick Road with the Munchkins behind her is one of the everlasting images of the film (see Figure 5.1). Dorothy is at the front. She's setting out, following the road with optimism and quite literally a skip in her step. The Munchkins dance behind her. The use of skipping reflects Dorothy's youth and innocence. The step suits her. It is optimistic, bouncing, confident, and energetic, and so is she. The step itself is

FIGURE 5.1. Dorothy (Judy Garland) and Toto bid farewell to the Munchkins as they set off down the Yellow Brick Road.

not just a simple child's skip. Choreographically it is far more complex than that and quite constructed. The movement is launched from a placement of the foot behind, not in front. This is not easy by any means because to step behind every couple of steps is not a naturally forward moving device. Why not use a straight-forward plain forward cantering skip? Visually, the extra complexity in the foot-work boosts the energy and "bounce" effect. This is achieved by neat footwork and nimble, controlled weight placement. Dance director Connolly no doubt wanted a sequence that looked good. It needed to have energy and versatility so it could be used as a traveling figure as well as one that could be executed in place. He tasked Assistant Dona Massin to devise the step.[8] Although the reasons be-hind the step being used are practical, perhaps the inclusion of a backward foot placement reflects the difficulty that Dorothy is about to encounter. Although she is skipping forward, seemingly confident, the choreography seems to hint that her journey will take a step backward before she can go forward. Indeed, Dorothy is literally taking one step back for every two steps forward.

The other important function of the skipping sequence is as a device to unite key characters after they meet. It is danced four times in total, estab-lished as Dorothy's own motif and then reprised as the Scarecrow, Tin Man, and Cowardly Lion are introduced to the group. When each character decides to join the journey, the skip returns at the end of the scene as a choreographic coda, drawing the characters together. The skip only occurs when trust is established, appearing for this purpose repeatedly as the group grows. The skip thereby reinforces the theme of friendship over and over again. Emotionally, the skipping motif establishes optimism for each new character after he turns from personal despair to united hope when Dorothy assures him that the Wizard can fulfill his personal goals. As the entire group skips together, we know they're now a team. The skip is a visual device to demonstrate to the audience the galvanizing of new friendships, a uniform optimistic outlook, their shared agency, and the physicality of travel.

While the skip is a natural movement for Dorothy, it is not for the others. Had the Scarecrow, Tin Man, and Cowardly Lion not met Dorothy, one could not imagine those characters skipping. In doing so, they are adopting her attitude. The skip shows that the Tin Man has lost his stiffness, the Scarecrow has gained physical control over himself, and the Cowardly Lion has discarded his threatening bravado attitude. The audience sees that in joining in the skip, the others are acquiescing to Dorothy's ideas and leadership. Indeed, she is the character who establishes the step and she is the one who fully "owns" it. It is her attitude, leadership, and dance motif that drives the group forward. When other characters take on Dorothy's signature piece of choreography, the audience knows the group has bonded and they now have a unity of purpose, emotionally and physically, joining in her journey.

The Munchkins

The Munchkins participate in both large chorus work for grand effect and small ensemble dance pieces: the choreography here helps the viewer to understand the Munchkins' community. At the presentation in Munchkinland, Dorothy and her friends are treated to a balletic tableau from the Lullaby League and a cockney-style "Lambeth Walk" (a contemporary fad dance from the 1937 stage musical *Me and My Girl*) by the Lollipop Guild. These dances demonstrate the cultural mix of society in Munchkinland from perceived "lowbrow culture" with working-class men to "elite arts" shown by the trained ballerinas. They draw on our own culture, parodying class and gender types where women are extensively adorned and graceful in movement while the men wear their regular clothing, are rather awkward, and find dance more challenging. Audiences instantly recognize the cultural text of these dance forms and directly relate to the Munchkins because these dances are activities that we have in common with them. Audience members might well have done both of those dances themselves and read this cultural text with ease. The ballerinas are fully costumed in pink tutus with matching headdresses and pointe shoes and are instantly recognizable as ballet dancers. Although they evoke the refined and traditional world of ballet, they are not highly skilled in the dance. The dancers' turns are slightly awkward and are out of time with each other; executed with wide legs and bent knees. The dancers are not controlling their balance or momentum to a high standard. It is the awkwardness here, however, that adds to the warm appeal of the presentation and endears us to the ballerinas and in turn the people of Oz all the more. We can see that though the ensemble is not quite together, the dancers are doing their best in their performance to honor Dorothy. The cockney-style men from the Lollipop Guild are more obviously awkward and nervous. Their movement is deliberately rough and twitchy as they make their presentation. They have their hands in their pockets, evoking a cavalier attitude or perhaps nervousness shielded by bravado. The position of the thumbs out of the pockets comes from a gesture in the "Lambeth Walk," in which the dancers strutted with their thumbs either tucked in pockets or braces during the dance and finished the dance with a thumb over the shoulder gesture at the end. Their jaunty movement is endearing and evokes their unrefined, working-class background. They're very pleased with themselves for having done their piece as they exit with hands held high above their heads in self-congratulation.[9] The dancing in this scene allows the warm personalities of the Munchkins to come through while the Lambeth dance references contemporary culture. The two familiar dance styles hint to the viewer that we share many things in common with the Munchkins.

The presentation scene is the only scene in which the Munchkins execute detailed choreography. They also appear in the large chorus scenes in Oz and in the Emerald City and as a group execute uniform, general movement. At the announcement of the Witch's death, the Munchkins celebrate by skipping in pairs, circling about, in either a single or double handhold. The women's colored peasant skirts and layers of petticoats fan out and enhance the movement, adding to elated energy around the celebration. The dance formations show us the Munchkins responding as a bonded group, not as a series of individuals. A different community might just clap or cheer, but the Munchkins are a carefree people and will dance together, spontaneously, to express their relief and joy. During the Munchkin parade as Dorothy steps into the coach, pairs of Munchkin women form a snaking column, skipping and occasionally twirling as they parade, with the rest of the Munchkins watching and cheering on. Although Connolly's staging is complex, the movement of individuals is typically simple in these large scenes. Every carefully placed dancer contributes to the colorful pageant. Consequently, the unity of dance suggests unity of the people. The Munchkins are a close and happy community, as they celebrate together dancing as one.

The Scarecrow Comes to Life

The Scarecrow is the first character Dorothy meets on her journey, and Ray Bolger originally was to have had a longer dance number to introduce his character. The full number has been preserved and is available on the commercial DVD release. It's a solo jazz number combining tap-style shuffles and general dance movements such as kicks, turns, and leaps reflecting Bolger's vaudeville background. If any specific dance is represented here it may be "legomania," which was one of the "eccentric" dances/movements. Eccentric dancers were those who built their act using individual and exaggerated gestures incorporating the vocabulary of general jazz movement: shuffles, grinds, hops, kicks, and twists. It had its origins in the old medicine show entertainments in which there was no prescribed pattern or framework. Eccentric dance explored comic, exaggerated ways to capture attention, with dancers performing tricks or acrobatics or simply developing unusual and striking body movements, like "snake hips" or legomania. Also called "rubber legs," legomania specifically focused on fluid kicking and jumping movements such as "Kazotskys"—akin to the Hungarian style of kicking from a squatting or semi-squatting position.[10] According to historians Marshall and Jean Stearns, Bolger was taught rhythm dancing by Herbie Harper: "he knew his ballet but not his jazz toe and heel work. He had to come down out of air for this new blend."[11] If that was the case, Bolger soon mastered the art, for he was known for tap as well as eccentric dance including legomania. Bolger is present in the myth of the "Bill Robinson challenge," when three famous white dancers, including Bolger, are said to have competed against Bill Robinson in a tap contest. Whether the story is true or myth is not valid here. The point is that Bolger's name is put forward as one of the best (alongside the likes of Fred Astaire) to potentially out-dance the towering tap legend Bill Robinson. In the end, Bolger was a good tapper.[12]

In *The Wizard of Oz,* Ray Bolger was originally asked to play the part of the Tin Man, but he realized the Scarecrow had a solo number to be choreographed by guest artist Busby Berkeley, the hottest choreographic property in Hollywood. Bolger begged to take on the Scarecrow role and eventually won the day.[13] Ironically, while the majority of the Scarecrow solo was cut from the film, the Tin Man's dance was not (albeit probably shortened and not particularly featured). Regardless, the role of the Scarecrow still made Bolger's career. The extended Scarecrow number "If I Only Had a Brain" introduces the audience to the character. The number is designed to transition the Scarecrow from being a static object held on a post, to a fluid moving, humanized character. It is through the dance that the Scarecrow comes to life. The use of legomania makes sense with the Scarecrow as a character and Bolger as a dancer. A Scarecrow is made of straw, having no bones or muscles, so his body is indeed loose and floppy. As the routine starts, we see that the Scarecrow can barely support himself and needs assistance from Dorothy to stand. His body is weak and he cannot control his movement. Throughout the sequence, the moves portray a character that has no muscle tone, yet the viewer understands the deliberate irony here. Bolger was a well-known performer and his execution of the moves is complex and skilled. For instance, Bolger stands next to Dorothy and performs a corkscrew turn on the spot. Although the viewer cannot see his feet, he crosses his right foot in front of the left and he executes a controlled turn rotating in a downward spiral, to the left, finishing at Dorothy's feet. The move is done smoothly in a single action. The function of the move is to demonstrate the Scarecrow's weakness as he has dropped to the ground. What the audience sees, however, is the control of leg muscle, an unwavering center of balance and controlled, steady momentum as he turns and lowers, then rises again. In showing that the Scarecrow is weak, Bolger, the dancer, demonstrates that he is strong. We also see Bolger's balletic training as he executes a triple pirouette with a perfectly even axis on his lead foot—his left. The routine then gains energy, utilizing larger movements as it progresses. Each step flows easily into the next and as Bolger leaps, spins, falls to the ground, recovers, and "stumbles" around the set, kicking his way upstage or downstage, the disciplined control of movement creates the exaggerated comic effect of eccentric dance. Audiences of the time would have been familiar with eccentric dancing, including legomania, and would have appreciated the irony and context of this routine. They certainly understood the joke that it is via the skill of eccentric dance that the "out-of-control" Scarecrow is presented to the viewer.[14] Although the full dance was cut from the film, the essential message is still there, albeit in a brief shorthand, with spins and a stumbling fall executed with poise and control.

The Jitterbug in *The Wizard of Oz*

The word "jitterbug" has multiple meanings that change according to time and place. In the early days before the specific swing dances and current terminology had developed, "swing dancing" simply meant dancing to swing music, and the dancers did anything that they felt inspired to. The historical meaning of the word "jitterbug" is quite murky and still confusing. Karen Hubbard says it referred to "raucous swing music fans who typically danced the Shag."[15] It then quickly became a nickname for the Lindy Hop, perhaps after the Harvest Moon contest changed the title of the "Lindy Hop" event to "Jitterbug-Jive." Professional swing dancer Frankie Manning says it was always a nickname for Lindy Hop, although over time many people thought that jitterbug and Lindy Hop were totally different dances:

> Back in the 30's once the Lindy Hop got popular, many people started using the term "jitterbug." . . . It became my mission to let swing dancers know that jitterbug is just a nickname for the Lindy Hop.[16]

The Wizard of Oz was released just before the jitterbug dance craze took the world by storm, but the word itself was already in use due to Cab Callaway's popular swing number from 1934, "Call of the Jitterbug," and his short film of 1935, *Cab Calloway's Jitterbug Party* [17] The term referred to a person who had imbibed too much "jitter sauce" (illegal moonshine). In polite society, it had dubious overtones of illegal activities and black jazz music and sexual innuendo-laden dance cultures. It came from old juke joints and brothels and the more recent memory of speakeasies of the prohibition era. The terminology is important in relation to the setting within *The Wizard of Oz,* because the name "Lindy Hop" was lesser known and does not have the same illicit associations or edge to it. Perhaps that is exactly why contest organizers and film producers were attracted to the word jitterbug.

The narrative premise for the scene in the film is that the Wicked Witch of the West has sent a scary insect, the "jitterbug," to bite Dorothy and her friends, the effect of which sees victims dancing the jitterbug until they are exhausted. This allows the flying monkeys to swoop in and kidnap Dorothy. None of the original footage for the scene is extant except a piecemeal section filmed by the producer, mostly from the side, at a dress rehearsal.[18] The Wicked Witch of the West uses dance in this context as a device to bring about fear, control, and manipulation of the main characters. When *The Wizard of Oz* was made, the Lindy Hop or jitterbug was just becoming familiar to white audiences. Placement of the jitterbug as a friend and tool of the Witch makes sense; some social groups found jazz dance and the emerging Lindy Hop horrific and threatening because the illicit dance of the minority was now becoming a controversial dance at larger nightspots and ballrooms, where blacks and whites freely mingled.[19] It was still very much a working-class, black dance and, as the middle and upper classes saw it, reflected ribald African sexual tribal passions. The complex ancestry of Lindy Hop lies in the notorious jukes and honky-tonks, gilly tents (for a type of traveling show), and medicine shows. They, along with the more recent speakeasies, were venues for illegal gambling and drinking and were also most probably brothels. Hence the music and dance that took place there had a long association with illegal venues, prostitutes, and scandalous behavior. As jitterbug became more mainstream, it shocked and horrified just like the Waltz, Tango, and Charleston before it, another new cultural dance explosion. It was banned all over the world in the 1940s with the press reporting jitterbug "as a throwback to primitivism, and leading to sexual deviation" and concluding "jitterbugs won't live, it's so frenetic." One reader wrote to the American Medical association: "Isn't it possible that jitterbug dancing incorporates sufficient sex expression to create a minor perversion among adolescents who consciously or subconsciously form the habit of partial expression of sex to the accompaniment of 'hot' music?" [20] Jitterbug dancing was the parent of Rock and Roll dancing, similarly condemned a generation later in the 1950s and seen as being at the heart of the new "teenager" culture. If the dance culture of the teenager was born in the 1950s, it was conceived and grew in the womb of the jitterbug in the 1930s and '40s.

The cultural fear of the jitterbug at the time of *The Wizard of Oz* explains the placement of the number in the film, where the "jitterbug" insects are depicted as evil friends of the Witch. The effect of the jitterbugs on Dorothy and her party is reminiscent of the mysterious St. Vitus' dance of the eleventh to seventeenth centuries in Europe, where victims who were affected danced madly and uncontrollably to their death. In some regions, the phenomenon was thought to be due to the bite of the tarantula spider. In *The Wizard of Oz* the spider is now a bug, and the context of the illegal moonshine—jitter—couples with the bug and becomes the out-of-control fad dance that society feared at that time. The characters execute jazz steps as helpless victims of the dance, as they're taken over by the poison and lose control.

In the extant footage, the dance takes them nowhere but is simply a device of entrapment as they kick, do-si-do in circles, and change direction hither and thither. They are unhappy puppets to the movements and the Witch's spell. This scene sits in direct contrast to the optimistic, traveling, empowered motion of the skipping choreography of the Yellow Brick Road. The jitterbug scene evokes doubt, fear, and enslavement by the Witch as much as the skipping sequence evokes confidence, joy, friendship, and agency for the characters in moving forward emotionally and literally.

The extant fragments from the jitterbug scene display quite rough and poor choreography. We can see that the director wanted the negative effects of the spell to be evident to the viewer. Throughout the scene we see exaggerated, jerky, out-of-control movement rather than flowing, good dancing, which sets the dance perfectly within the story. The extant clip is obviously incomplete and quite possibly out of order. Although bits of choreography are repeated, it would be misleading to assume all the choreographic content is present. If the final performance footage existed, a more balanced and accurate assessment of the choreography and the scene as a whole could be made.

From what we see overall, the choreography is not complex and it is very difficult to see the intended finished product. This is amateur footage shot from the side and a mere snippet, with many cuts. It does not show us how the scene would have been presented in the film. It is unfair, therefore, to draw any sound conclusions about how the scene would have looked in a final version or worked as a choreographic piece. We do certainly understand, however, that the jitterbug here, executed with frantic, disjointed movement, is associated with losing physical control. The subtext is that if you do the jitterbug you'll be out of control and vulnerable to the evils of the dance. In our world, that's illicit activity leading to sexual downfall and shame; in the Land of Oz, that's being in danger, under the power of the Witch, of not seeing home or happiness again. Even from this tiny extant piece, the Witch's spell is visualized through the dance. It may look tame to our modern eye, but contemporary audiences would have known the political and racial context associated with these moves and the risqué, fashionable emerging dance. They could read the cultural text here; the jitterbug is dangerous and that's why the Witch is using it to control Dorothy and her friends.

At the time of *The Wizard of Oz*, the jitterbug was being demonstrated around the globe, and it was the recognition of this emerging popularity that was possibly the reason it was included in the film. In addition, Judy Garland's friend Ray Hirsch was an expert swing dancer and they had attended dances at Hollywood High School together. Was the inclusion of the jitterbug scene initially approved not only because it was the new dance of the time, a connector to current culture, but also because the leading lady could swing dance? [21]

The extant footage of the jitterbug scene in *The Wizard of Oz* is very early evidence of a cultural transition, with the dance moving from working-class black culture to white acceptance, as shown by the performance of the dance in a big commercial movie. It is a transition point, indicating that film professionals were aware of the current new dance craze and tried it out in the film, possibly to appeal to a youth audience and/or perhaps because the leading lady was already familiar with the dance. As the film went through savage content cuts to reduce its length, the jitterbug sequence was removed. Some sources suggest that the producers feared the sequence would date the film if it was a passing fad. Yet, had faddism been a concern, perhaps the same question might have also been raised regarding the use of the Lambeth Walk—an invention from a stage musical. The development of the jitterbug scene for *The Wizard of Oz* just preceded the widespread popularity of the dance; it was still too early for the jitterbug to be commercially reliable. It is interesting to consider that given the enormous popularity of the simple skipping sequence in *The Wizard of Oz*, now such an iconic facet of the film, one wonders what consequential impact the jitterbug scene might have had, had it been retained in the film (in fact the music was retained as the B side of the "Over the Rainbow" single). Would the style have been more accepted or the cultural impact been greater had it been shown in *The Wizard of Oz*, danced by one of America's most popular actresses, Judy Garland? Within five years of *The Wizard of Oz*, Dean Collins and Jean Veloz's work in films with the singing trio the Andrews Sisters was soon filling the cinemas with confident, exuberant, smooth, "white" swing dance scenes that remain a highlight of the 1940s films today. Filmmakers in the late 1930s were not to know of course that jitterbug was there to stay and that the dance would continue into the future. When dancer Dean Collins arrived in Los Angeles, his dance films with Jean Veloz and Jewel McGowan spread the jitterbug via the movie screen around the world. Beyond the beautiful dance work in films such as *Buck Privates, Springtime in the Rockies*, and *Swing Fever*, jitterbug would evolve into 1950s rock and roll and jive in the films *Blackboard Jungle* and *Rock around the Clock*, heralding a whole social identity for a generation and beyond. Swing would be seen and danced all over the world and then have another revival of its original form in the 1990s. Had *The Wizard of Oz* been made five years later, the jitterbug scene would have had a very different cultural context around it and it might have been read quite differently, even ironically. If the scene had been retained in the film, the dance would have been exposed to larger audiences earlier and may even have started a dance craze as so many films have at that time and since.[22]

There was no such controversy over faddism or cultural doubt around the Scarecrow's number, yet interestingly, it was also cut. In the end, the Scarecrow's dance did not contribute to the narrative of the film. It was overly long and the demonstration of technical features in it (film playing backward, the flying sequence, high camera shots looking down) give it a strange, experimental tone that did not fit with the rest of the film whatsoever. It is highly significant that the studio was prepared to cut the only two full dance numbers in the whole picture and in particular the dance sequence that had a specially hired, famous choreographer. That producers went to such great effort to reduce the overall length of the movie reduces the strength of the argument that the jitterbug scene was cut for cultural or racial reasons. If they were going to cut Busby Berkeley's work, anything was on the table for exclusion as was "Over the Rainbow," which was famously saved and retained. Of course, reasons for including or excluding a scene are not mutually exclusive and ought not to be reduced to a single, simplistic, common factor. While both the jitterbug scene and the Scarecrow's routine were cut for a common reason, in their own ways they were both misfits in the film. The removal of both of the featured dance numbers means that rather than song and dance standing hand in hand as culturally strong elements within the film, the cultural significance of dance is diluted.

Conclusion

The dancing planned for *The Wizard of Oz* is minimal and traditional. The jitterbug, skipping sequence, ballet piece, and the Lambeth Walk all reflect social day-to-day dance activities while the Scarecrow's routine draws on elements of a rich and complex jazz dance history. Save for the skipping sequence, they would all be realistic acts in a gilly show or vaudeville line-up. While professionals were employed to coordinate the staged scenes with large choruses, there was no overall choreographer for the film, as it was normal at the time for individual dancers to bring or create their own routines for film projects. Where bits of choreography were needed, such as the Yellow Brick Road skipping sequence, the writing was delegated to an assistant. The result is that the role of dance and its place across the whole project was unclear and inconsistent. The analysis of the deleted jitterbug routine and the Scarecrow's extended dance number demonstrates that significant dance components in the film had been planned originally but were ultimately not realized and their exclusion meant that the overall role of dance in the film was ultimately diminished. The dances that were included, however, serve as clear cultural text that we read as our own and share with the world of Oz. The familiarity and love we have for the dance strengthens the warmth that the audience feels for all the characters on the screen. Where dancing occurs, it is empowering and dynamic. The skipping sequence in particular has, over the decades, become one of the most popular, well-known, and loved elements in the whole film. The dancing in *The Wizard of Oz* deepens our empathy with the character's troubles, joys, and motivations. It contributes enormously to our love of film and our enduring fascination with it. Everyone wants to skip down the Yellow Brick Road.

Notes

1. See IMDb (Internet Movie Database) "Bobby Connolly" for a full list of film work credits, http://www.imdb.com/name/nm0175265/?ref_=nv_sr_1.
2. For all scene descriptions of *Sweet Adeline*, see "Irene Dunne Sings Lonely Feet," "You Were the Girl from over the Way," YouTube, https://www.youtube.com/results?search_query=lonely+feet, accessed December 8, 2017.
3. For all scene descriptions, see *Singalong Version of The Wizard of Oz*, 2 disk special edition DVD, Turner Entertainment, 2009.
4. See IMDb entry, *Broadway Melody of 1940*, http://www.imdb.com/title/tt0032284/?ref_=nv_sr_3, accessed December 8, 2017.
5. Cyd Charisse, Tony Martin, and Dick Kleiner, *The Two of Us* (New York: Mason/Charter, 1976), 120.

6. John Mueller, *Astaire Dancing—The Musical Films of Fred Astaire* (New York: Alfred A. Knopf, 1985), 40.

7. Mueller, *Astaire Dancing*, 162.

8. Dona Massin, interview in "Memories of Oz," 2001, YouTube, https://www.youtube.com/watch?v=oVsGo15aqok, accessed November 15, 2016.

9. For the Lambeth Walk see *Lambeth walk*, http://www.streetswing.com/histmain/z3lambth.htm, accessed May 18, 2017.

10. Marshall Stearns and Jean Stearns, *Jazz Dance* (New York: Macmillan, 1994), 232.

11. Stearns and Stearns, *Jazz Dance*, 166.

12. Stearns and Stearns, *Jazz Dance*, 186.

13. Ray Bolger, "Ray Bolger on God's Gifts," *Guideposts*, March 1982, posted online 2015, https://www.guideposts.org/better-living/entertainment/movies-and-tv/guideposts-classics-ray-bolger-on-gods-gifts, accessed September 8, 2017.

14. DVD *Wizard of Oz* extras; also see The Wizard of Oz—deleted scenes (lost footage of musical fantasy film; 1939), Lost Media Wikki, http://lostmediawiki.com/The_Wizard_of_Oz__deleted_scenes_(lost_footage_of_musical_fantasy_film;_1939), accessed May 18, 2017.

15. Karen Hubbard, "Social Dancing at the Savoy," *Ballroom, Boogie and Shimmy Sham Shake* (Chicago: University of Illinois Press, 2009), 145.

16. Frankie Manning and Cynthia R. Millman, *Frankie Manning: Ambassador of Lindy Hop* (Philadelphia: Temple University Press, 2007), 50.

17. Streetswing Dance History, http://www.streetswing.com/histmain/z3jtrbg.htm, accessed November 20, 2016. For an another in-depth origin of the jitterbug term, see Timme Rozenkrantz, "Harlem Jazz Adventures: A European Baron's Memoir 1934–1969," *Studies in Jazz* 65, 2012, 130–131.

18. Roger Clarke, "Story of the Scene: The Wizard of Oz; Victor Fleming (1939)," *Independent*, June 19, 2008, https://www.independent.co.uk/arts-entertainment/films/features/story-of-the-scene-the-wizard-of-oz-victor-fleming-1939-850746.html, accessed November 18, 2016.

19. Krin Gabbard, ed., *Representing Jazz* (Durham, NC: Duke University Press, 1995), 211.

20. Gabbard, *Representing Jazz*, 211.

21. Robert White, "RIP Ray Hirsch, Great So-Cal 'Swing' Dancer," *Swungover* blog. September 1, 2015, https://swungover.wordpress.com/2015/09/01/r-i-p-ray-hirsch-great-so-cal-swing-dancer/, accessed November 15, 2016.

22. Like the Hollywood swing films of the 1940s, more recent films such as *Saturday Night Fever, Grease, Strictly Ballroom, Swingers*, and *The Great Gatsby* have all started dance revivals or crazes.

6 "THE MERRY OLD LAND OF OZ"?

THE RECEPTION OF THE MGM FILM

Danielle Birkett

Following the release of Disney's critically acclaimed animated movie *Snow White and the Seven Dwarfs* in 1937, MGM set its sights on tapping into the fantasy market. Returning to L. Frank Baum's novel *The Wonderful Wizard of Oz* and taking its previous Broadway and screen adaptations as inspiration, the studio decided to create its own fantasy film. MGM went to great lengths to make this an exceptional project: a team of directors worked on the picture, a plethora of screenwriters contributed ideas (historian Aljean Harmetz suggests there were ten screenwriters), while E. Y. Harburg and Harold Arlen were invited to write the songs and Herbert Stothart to compose the underscore. A budget of approximately $2 million was provided for the project and MGM announced that the film would be shot in revolutionary Technicolor. Yet, as work began, the producers unexpectedly revealed that they were not anticipating "to make any money with the picture"; instead, according to Harburg, "once a year they did a loser for prestige."[1] MGM hoped the picture would break even, but, more importantly, strengthen their reputation by showing up heavily in the Academy Awards.

With such an extensive team working together to achieve these high expectations, the creative process was far from straightforward. As the film evolved it became evident that the budget was inadequate and ultimately the picture cost more and took longer than any other MGM film made the same year: the shooting schedule lasted twenty-two weeks and the final production cost was $2,777,000 (excluding advertising).[2] With pressure to recoup some of the financial expense, MGM quickly turned its attention to marketing. Initially, the aim was to release the film in time for Christmas 1938; but with the extended

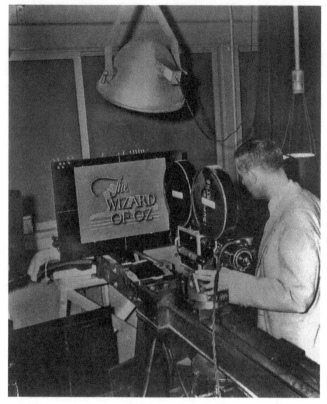

FIGURE 6.1. Technician shooting the title credit sequence. Credit: MGM/Photofest.

shooting schedule this deadline proved too optimistic. Next, the studio considered presenting the film as a roadshow attraction, but this too did not happen. Instead, MGM relied on an expensive promotional campaign to heighten anticipation. The marketing material celebrated the star cast (particularly Frank Morgan, Ray Bolger, Bert Lahr, and Jack Haley) and highlighted the movie's innovative visual style, but the publicity team also made sure *The Wizard of Oz* was advertised as a broad-based family movie, not just a fantasy for children. Advertisements appeared in newspapers and magazines and special postcards, posters, and other publicity materials were also issued. The sheet music for Harburg and Arlen's songs was published and an issue of Baum's original book was reprinted by the Bobbs-Merrill Company, with stills from the new film. Alongside this, a selection of memorabilia was also manufactured for children (including dolls, clothing, masks, and toy figures).

Following this elaborate marketing campaign, anticipation for the movie increased. One newspaper noted that the film was "backed by a terrifically high-powered exploitation campaign" and should therefore "find a ready-made audience practically everywhere."[3] Similarly, the *Variety* writer predicted that with "a sufficient period of pre-release showings in selected major spots" and "favourable word-of-mouth on the unique and highly entertaining features of the film" the movie should "perform some record-breaking feats of box office magic."[4] With considerable hype around the picture, many Americans were eager to watch MGM's latest production. On August 12, 1939, *The Wizard of Oz* began a five-day preview engagement in Oconomowoc (Wisconsin), before receiving a gala Hollywood premier at Grauman's Chinese Theatre in California on August 15. Two days later the movie had its premier run at the Capitol Theatre in New York where Judy Garland and Mickey Rooney sang and danced on stage between showings. With the presence of these stars, the film was an immediate hit and one writer described the audience as "a . . . friendly throng" who were "enthusiastic about the picture."[5] On August 25 the movie opened in theaters across the country. The film broke attendance records in many locales and was one of the top-grossing pictures of 1939: on opening day alone, 37,000 fans saw the film and hordes were turned away.[6]

Despite the extravagant publicity campaign and the favorable response in New York, as the picture opened across America, reviews were undeniably mixed. On the positive side, one of the most prestigious reviewers, Frank Nugent of the *New York Times,* praised the creative team as "wizards of Hollywood" and celebrated the new release: "*The Wizard of Oz* reached the Capitol's screen yesterday as a delightful piece of wonder-working which had the youngsters' eyes shining and brought a quietly amused gleam to the wiser ones of the oldsters."[7] Similarly, the *Cue Magazine* critic commended the "chuckleful" appeal of the film and approved it as "a solid hit—and . . . a pleasant evening's entertainment."[8] One critic went further to distinguish it as "an elaborate, magnificent and thoroughly beguiling screen treatment of *The Wizard of Oz*" and "an amazing achievement in entertainment as well as technical wizardry."[9] Another congratulated the writers for "elevat[ing] the artistic standards of musical extravaganza to a point unequalled in screen history."[10]

Others were more scathing of the movie, even some of those who had worked on the production. Noel Langley, who had been credited with adapting the script, bought a ticket to see the finished film "in a cinema on Hollywood Boulevard at noon" on August 25. He was distraught with the final product:[11]

> I sat and cried like a bloody child. I thought, "This is a year of my life." I loathed the picture. I thought it was dead. I thought it missed the boat all the way around. I had to wait for my tears to clear before I went out of the theatre.[12]

Langley was particularly outspoken in his dislike of the film (perhaps heightened by the tension that arose between him and the writing team toward the end of the production); others were more apathetic toward the final picture and certainly did not believe it had potential to become a hit. Jack Haley, who starred as the Tin Woodman, commented that it wasn't "a classic" but simply "a job [that] we were getting paid for,"[13] while Margaret Hamilton, who played the Wicked Witch of the West, noted that "some of the reviews were very pleasant, but they were not . . . 'money reviews.' "[14] Several newspapers were more disparaging of the picture. The *New Republic* dismissed it as full of "freak characters,"[15] while Russell Maloney of the *New Yorker* recounted his experience "cringing before MGM's Technicolor production of *The Wizard of Oz*, which displays no trace of imagination, good taste, or ingenuity"; ultimately he labeled the film "a stinkeroo."[16]

Following the apathetic reception in 1939, the movie was a financial disaster for MGM, but twenty years later it would earn its money back.[17] In 1949, the film was rereleased with a fresh publicity campaign; but it was the 1955 reissue that significantly transformed the reputation of the movie. Judy Garland had soared in fame after the success of *A Star Is Born* in 1954 and her burgeoning popularity attracted new audiences to the movie. Subsequently, twenty years after its original release, CBS entered a contract with MGM to broadcast the film annually on television.[18] New generations were introduced to the story, and watching *The Wizard of Oz* has since become a celebrated Christmas tradition for many Americans. One commentator notes:

> It was shown on television for the first time on November 3, 1956, and watched by 45 million people. And that, I guess, is where I came in. I'd been born the year before and I think I must have seen it every Christmas until I was 15. Always, at around 3pm in the afternoon, there it would be.[19]

These TV airings solidified the movie as part of American culture: as a result, the film was shown on numerous occasions and in 1980 it was made available on home video. Most recently, in 2013, the film was rereleased in 3D to celebrate its seventy-fifth anniversary.

Few movie musicals have experienced the long-term success of *The Wizard of Oz*. This chapter investigates its complex reception history to assess why this film has stood the test of time, despite the lukewarm response it received in 1939. In particular, five themes are central to this discussion: the adaptation of Baum's familiar text; the handling of the fantasy setting; the philosophy promoted within the story; the innovative filmic devices; and the star casting.[20] An array of archival documents from 1939 to the present day is used to address each of these points from both the writers' perspective and a critical viewpoint.[21] Additionally, the legacy of this iconic movie is explored to reveal the significance of *The Wizard of Oz* in American culture today.

"An Eagerness to Please Every Oz Fan": The Handling of Baum's Text

From the outset, one of the biggest challenges the production team faced was how to deal with the familiarity of the source material. Baum's novel was first published in 1900, and its widespread success led to a further sixteen fairy tales about the Land of Oz.[22] Just two years after the original book was first released, it was adapted for Broadway, followed by a second production for the silent cinema in 1910. Fifteen years later another feature-length film was released: directed by Larry Semon, this movie departed radically from Baum's novel, introducing new characters that brought a much darker tone. The popularity of the subject material provided MGM with an ideal foundation for a commercial film, but the familiarity of the book (and its adaptations) presented its own challenges. Director Victor Fleming summarized: "Millions of Oz lovers would be waiting for this picture and . . . would be offended if the story was juggled."[23] As a result, he concluded that the team must "approach the entire story with an eagerness to please every Oz fan."[24]

This difficult commission resulted in a lengthy adaptation process that involved an array of screenwriters: some worked on the project for a considerable length of time and made significant contributions; others were involved for very short stints. Florence Ryerson and Edgar Allen Woolf, who were ultimately credited with Noel Langley for writing the screenplay, summarized the complexities of this adaptation:

> No screen writer faces a more difficult task than the translation of a classic from the printed word into celluloid, and when the classic is for children, the difficulty is increased because many generations have read and loved that book. Of all children's books, *The Wizard of Oz* is most widely read, most dearly loved.[25]

Although, in most cases, one writer did not see what others had achieved, each tended to take a similar approach to adapting the book for the screen by "selecting the most important incidents and characters and telescoping or combining others."[26]

Ultimately, Ryerson and Woolf were thrilled with the accuracy of the final script and proclaimed: "We were amazed to realize how little had been left out. . . . We left in the most memorable incidents. Never altered the characters;

and we inserted most of the magic."[27] The film remained relatively faithful to Baum's novel and many critics commended its authenticity. One applauded the team for "add[ing] modern touches to the book, but not too many to spoil the sentiment for those of us who pored over the adventures."[28] Another commented that "the more fanatic Ozophiles may dispute MGM's remodelling of the story," but concluded that "the average movie-goer . . . will find it novel and richly satisfying."[29] Other critics, however, disputed these modern touches. Howard Barnes of the *New York Herald Tribune* argued that "the show misses a great many of the fabulous accents of the original."[30] Perhaps he was referring to subtle plot changes such as the adaptation of the poppy scene where a snowfall now freezes the flowers, the new importance of the Wicked Witch of the West, or the revelation that Dorothy's adventures in Oz are a dream. Alternatively, the more serious tone of this adaptation (which moves away from the dramatic sentimentality that ultimately dated the earlier stage musicals) could have been the problem. Overall, this apathetic response toward the retelling of Baum's classic story influenced this critic's wider appreciation and Barnes concluded that the movie "rarely has the power to bemuse one."[31]

The reception of the plot, however, shifted significantly in the years that followed. Rereleases of the film, the popularity of Garland, and traditional Christmas television broadcasts encouraged audiences to return repeatedly to the movie: *The Wizard of Oz* is now recognized by many Americans as "a timeless classic that most children know by heart by the age of four."[32] However, it is MGM's version of the story that has become the familiar narrative; in fact, many who watch the film today are unaware of the original novels. In 1939, the popularity of Baum's story concerned the writers as they deliberated on how to reimagine the classic tale, but as the reputation of the movie grew, MGM became the authority on the Land of Oz. As a result, one writer noted that "*The Wizard of Oz* . . . demonstrates how a film based on another medium can surpass its original source material and enhance, not degrade it."[33] New audiences now discover this much-loved fairy tale through the movie rather than the book; this approval is noteworthy in fueling the continuing success of MGM's film.[34]

"Injecting Reality into Fantasy": The Reimagined Land of Oz

Alongside the difficulties of adaptation, the writers also faced the challenge of dealing with the fantasy material. This subject had enjoyed popularity in literature since the early nineteenth century, but in films the genre had emerged more recently and received an ambiguous reception. Even by the 1930s, one critic still noted that "fantasies and fairy stories are way out of the groove of run-of-the-mill film entertainment."[35] Nevertheless, Disney had increased the prominence of fantasy through short feature animations and the genre had begun to manifest itself differently: fantasy musicals were now created to exist entirely in the imagination and required audiences to suspend broader ideas of reality.[36] Adopting this approach, the Disney studio created its first full-length fantasy movie in 1937 (*Snow White and the Seven Dwarfs*) and stimulated further experimentation with the genre.

Commencing work on *The Wizard of Oz*, MGM faced the challenge of bringing Baum's fantasy setting to life. Deliberating on the familiarity of the source material, producer Mervyn LeRoy recognized that many Americans had "an individual idea of what the characters and places looked like."[37] A successful reimagination of the Land of Oz would therefore require the writers to overcome audiences' preconceptions. Approaching this, the team aspired to incorporate real actors who would assume the parts of the fantasy characters as the story evolved.

> We had to make even a Scarecrow, a Tin Woodsman, a Cowardly Lion, a Witch, a Wizard and such strange people as Munchkins . . . seem like real personalities. Hence our chief problem was . . . making human beings out of characters that don't exist. . . . In other words we had to put realism into the fantastic.[38]

Familiarizing the characters was not only achieved through the writing process, but careful attention was also given to the costumes and makeup to ensure that "every . . . face is recognizable."[39] LeRoy concluded, "It was far from easy and it took months to achieve"; nonetheless, "all the work [would be] worth it, if our audiences really love[d] those characters."[40] Employing this strategy, the creative team aspired to "inject reality into fantasy" and juxtapose two opposite worlds: this ambition, however, would be contentious with the critics.[41]

On the film's release, the fantasy setting received the most mixed critical response as many reviewers drew comparisons with Disney's acclaimed adaptation of the Grimm fairy tale. The criticism was led by Otis Ferguson who satirically voiced his opinion in the *New Republic*.

> *The Wizard of Oz* was intended to hit the same audience as *Snow White* and won't fail for lack of trying. It has dwarfs, music, Technicolor, freak characters and Judy Garland. It can't be expected to have a sense of humor as well—and as for the light touch of fantasy, it weighs like a pound of fruitcake soaking wet.[42]

Although Ferguson acknowledged that "the story . . . has some lovely and wild ideas—men of straw and tin, a cowardly lion, a wizard who isn't a very good wizard," he chastised the writers for not "knowing what to do with them, except to be painfully literal and elaborate about everything."[43] Ferguson struggled to reconcile the inherent tension between the real and the fantasy: the presence of people in Oz meant the proceedings could not be dismissed as entirely supernatural phenomena; yet as they burst into song and existed in a make-believe world, it was also impossible to rationalize the unfolding events. MGM took a risk by blurring the distinction between reality and fairy tale, and for Ferguson this tension detracted from the imaginative plot.

Other critics also wrestled with the treatment of the fantasy subject. Russell Maloney of the *New Yorker* was altogether more scathing: "Fantasy is still Walt Disney's undisputed domain. Nobody else can tell a fairy tale with his clarity of imagination, his supple good taste, or his technical ingenuity."[44] Similarly, the *Variety* reviewer wrote that only "in some respects" did *The Wizard of Oz* "possess the same qualities of technical perfection and story appeal" as *Snow White*.[45] Although the *New York Herald Tribune* critic was more positive in his overall appraisal of the film (celebrating it as a "resplendent motion picture"), he criticized the writers for "never quite mak[ing] one accept . . . [the plot's] fantastic assumptions."[46] Again, the MGM musical was deemed to lack inventiveness in its manipulation of the fairy-tale story.

Of the few respected critics who were won over by MGM's handling of the fantasy, Frank Nugent was the most significant. Writing in the *New York Times* he acknowledged that "the circumstances of Dorothy's trip to Oz are so remarkable, indeed, that reason cannot deal with them at all."[47] Yet he was enthralled by the action:

> Not since Disney's *Snow White* has anything quite so fantastic succeeded half so well. A fairybook tale has been told in the fairybook style with witches, goblins, pixies, and other wondrous things drawn in the brightest colors. It is all so well-intentioned, so genial, and so gay that any reviewer who would look down his nose at the fun-making should be spanked and sent off, supperless, to bed."[48]

Another reviewer also made a positive comparison with the Disney movie and distinguished *The Wizard of Oz* as a classic: "It outshines any fantasy heretofore attempted, the only comparable picture in its class being *Snow White* with which it will compete for world grosses, critical and popular applause."[49] Many reviewers were captivated by the setting, with one writer particularly celebrating the "superlative treatment" of the fantasy subject throughout.[50]

Other critics were more specific in attributing the success of the film to the tension between fairy tale and reality. The writer in *Film Daily* admired the use of real actors and concluded, "for seldom if indeed ever has the screen been so successful in its approach to fantasy and extravaganza through the medium of flesh-and-blood."[51] Similarly, the *Time* reviewer argued that the film had the scope to "settle an old Hollywood controversy: whether fantasy can be presented on the screen as successfully with human actors as with cartoons." He simply concluded: "It can."[52] Of particular note, the *Boxoffice* critic provided a highly insightful assessment: he asserted that MGM had produced "a completely charming and wholly delightful film" but also acknowledged that the movie "went in a direction rarely attempted by Hollywood."[53] In particular, the writer was referring to the experimental use of real actors in a make-believe world, and he celebrated this innovative approach as it produced "a fantasy with all of its nostalgia, its escape and its appeal."[54] This critic recognized the ability of the device to allow audiences to empathize with the characters in the film while also offering them escapism from the everyday world.

In 1939, the reception toward the fantastical setting was mixed. As the years progressed, however, the genre became increasingly popular in musicals and the fantastical subject was less of a stumbling block for audiences. In 1943, MGM imposed a darker element on the fantasy genre with *Cabin in the Sky*, which introduced the warring armies of God and the Devil to the screen. The following year, Kurt Weill and Ira Gershwin employed Technicolor in their psychoanalytical musical, *Lady in the Dark,* which showcased the fantastical through three dream sequences.[55] At the same time on Broadway, Rodgers and Hammerstein worked alongside choreographer Agnes de Mille to draw on this new fashion in their extended dream sequence in *Oklahoma!* in 1943. Two years later, Billy Bigelow's ascent to Heaven and subsequent return to earth for redemption in *Carousel* expanded the theme, and in 1947 Lerner and Loewe's *Brigadoon* premiered: entirely based on fantasy, the action was set in and revolved around a Scottish village that appears only one day in every century. By the first rerelease of *The Wizard of Oz* in 1949, fantasy had become a common vehicle for addressing serious subject matter in musicals. Therefore, as audiences reengaged with *The Wizard of Oz* they were less critical of the imaginary setting and more concerned with the social message that lay beyond.

"Fairy Stories Must Teach Simple Truths": The Philosophy of Oz

Written in 1900 "amid the wreckage of the failed Populist movement," Baum's text is widely recognized as a "political allegory for grown-ups neatly encased within a fairy-tale for children."[56] One commentator argues that the utopia in the story grew from a desire to conceal populist ideals (with many of the events and characters in the book apparently resembling political images, such as the "Yellow Brick Road" representing the gold standard).[57] Although there is no indication that the creative team were aware of an underlying political message, which has been retrospectively applied to the novel, there were broader themes in the book to which the writers were acutely attuned. Many of the utopian ideals inherent in the story provided the opportunity to present a message of social reform. In her assessment of fantasy, Charlotte Burcher notes: "Classical themes such as honor, love, war, revenge, responsibility, otherness, obsession, and loyalty are explored in fantasy tales. Subjects such as bigotry, greed, religious extremism, politics, abuse, and addiction can be examined in fantasy contexts without offending cultural sensitivities."[58] Baum's text, therefore, provided an ideal foundation to make a profound comment on the essence of mankind.

As Harburg was asked to work on the film, it was this principle that encouraged him to accept the job:

> I was attracted to it because [of] the great basic truths. . . . *The Wizard of Oz* on the surface seems to be a childish fantasy, but it is far from that. It is the very basis of all our hopes and lives and things we live for. . . . [T]he three basic things in life are knowledge, love, and courage. . . . [T]hese three basic, elemental things are done with humour, with fun.[59]

When the Wizard gives the Scarecrow, Tin Woodman, and Lion their greatest desires, Harburg's ideals are prioritized: this scene establishes Oz as a symbol for utopia and epitomizes his optimistic longing for a better world. *The Wizard of Oz* therefore provided Harburg with a new lens through which he encouraged audiences to view his bold and often controversial socialist message. Nevertheless, the lyricist was deeply unsatisfied. He explained: "I got immediate reactions on the importance of *Finian['s Rainbow]* while *Wizard[of Oz]* was just for children."[60] Harburg's disappointment with the film was perhaps fueled by the creative team's mixed intentions: others had alternative ambitions for the film. LeRoy argued that "all the work [would be] worth it, if our audiences . . . absorb[ed] the wholesome philosophy which Baum put in his book forty years ago."[61] He believed that the central plot reflected a simpler, yet pertinent, message: "that what we often strive for so earnestly we ultimately find has been ours all the time, only we have been unable to see that."[62] This motivation to promote Baum's outlook was also supported by Ryerson and Woolf, who suggested they edited the ending to "point out Baum's philosophy" by "having Dorothy repeat the words, 'There's no place like home.'"[63]

Despite the mixed aspirations for the film, critics widely interpreted the musical within the tense political climate of the United States at that time. Faced with the prospect of a second world war, one writer noted that "fairy stories must teach simple truths" and concluded that *The Wizard of Oz* "has a message well timed to current events."[64] The social circumstances intensified Baum's yearning for a simple life, and an "underlying theme of conquest of fear" was also particularly relevant.[65] Peter Bradshaw of the *Guardian* recently noted that "this film did its noble bit to prepare Americans psychologically for their decisive intervention in the coming world war."[66] *The Wizard of Oz* presented a longing for a secure, better world and this resonated closely with the original audience. The contemporary political and social circumstances therefore had significant impact on the film's early reception: with a message that provided hope in an anxious political climate, audiences were more willing to accept this new adaptation and revisit it as a moral during the war years that followed. Even, as the film was rereleased, William Stillman (author of multiple *Oz* reference books) notes that "the film's all-American theme of solidarity, preservation of home and vanquishing of evil forces resonated with audiences in patriotic postwar 1949."[67]

As society continues to progress, however, the sentiments expressed in the film are received less favorably by some. In 2016, the *Telegraph* reviewer commented:

> I disliked Dorothy, a heroine who—in times of adversity—would either burst into song or, worse still, tears.... And ... I was disappointed by the film's less-than-stirring conclusion: "'If I ever go looking for my heart's desire again, I won't go further than my own back yard,' pouts Dorothy."[68]

His comments emphasize a significant change in social attitude: the simple message that original audiences valued in uncertain political circumstances is now understood as naive. Society's values have shifted and greater importance is now placed on adventure, exploring the world, and facing up to injustice. The message of *The Wizard of Oz* is therefore viewed as innocent and even repressive in a more liberal world.

"A Cinematic Masterpiece": Ambitious Special Effects

The fantastical setting not only allowed the writers to present a message of social reform, it also provided the opportunity to experiment with revolutionary cinematic devices. Director Victor Fleming had formerly worked as a cameraman; therefore, the pictorial composition and special effects were fundamental considerations in his representation of the story. This ambition, however, presented an overwhelming task and Fleming himself acknowledged that "the technical problems were so many."[69] He continued to summarize some of the most difficult concepts:

> First, there is the cyclone. . . . Next comes Munchkinland. It is the most colorful sequence, I believe, that has ever been screened. . . . Then, there is the magic. . . . Baum told us that all the straw was taken out of the Scarecrow and he lay flat on the ground, that the Witch melted away after being doused with water, that this Witch appeared and disappeared in a ball of fire, but there were monkeys which could fly and thousands of other things.[70]

Despite the financial and time pressures involved in realizing these effects, the technical accomplishment became one of the most prestigious elements of the movie. Fleming himself was delighted with the final product, remarking: "We obtained an excellent enactment of each strange event of Oz" and "were quite proud."[71] In particular he described the cyclone as "a great thrill to see . . . on the screen" and the magical moments as "a pleasure to see perfected."[72]

More decisively, many critics praised the movie as "one of the greatest technical feats the screen has to its credit."[73] The *Variety* writer, John Flinn, recognized the extensive resources required to produce such a film and proclaimed: "Nothing comparable has come out of Hollywood in the past few years to approximate the lavish scale of this filmusical [*sic*] extravaganza, in the making of which the ingenuity and inventiveness of technical forces were employed without stint of effort or cost."[74] Similarly, another reviewer attributed the success of the movie to "the technical trickery" suggesting the use of special effects "is perhaps even more impressive than the story itself."[75] The prestigious film magazine, *Hollywood Spectator*, concluded that the film explored such innovation that "motion picture appreciation classes will find it a valuable study in the technical possibilities of the screen as a medium of entertainment."[76] Others referred to more specific attributes that deemed *The Wizard of Oz* "a cinematic masterpiece."[77] In particular, one critic noted that the "creation of Munchkinland" was "one of the most remarkable achievements ever offered as entertainment by any medium."[78] Furthermore, he lavished "unbounded praise" for the "strangely original and highly picturesque settings" and noted "the special effects . . . are enough in themselves to make the picture remarkable, the Kansas tornado being one of the most wonderful things the screen has done."[79]

Nevertheless, some critics were less inspired. Despite his positive review of the fantastical plot, the *New York Times* writer was more scathing toward the special effects. He noted that "even great wizards . . . are often tripped in their flights of fancy" and even "with the best of will and ingenuity, they cannot make a Munchkin or a Flying Monkey that will not still suggest . . . a Singer's midget in a Jack Dawn masquerade. Nor can they, without a few betraying jolts and split-screen overlappings, bring down from the sky the great soap bubble in which the Good Witch rides and roll it smoothly into place."[80] Nugent was unconvinced by the execution of these fantastical proceedings, but this did not detract from his overall opinion as he ultimately labeled the movie "a delightful piece of wonder-working."[81]

The special effects were widely appreciated as revolutionary, and many critics applauded their function in heightening the storyline. Nevertheless, the writers were determined to produce an impressive movie that pushed the boundaries of cinematography, and thus they also filmed in relatively new Technicolor. This presented further complications as photographer Harold Rosson explained:

> [The] chief problems were in the characters. . . . Margaret Hamilton, as the Wicked Witch, wore black, with hands and face a bright green. . . . Jack Haley as the Tin Woodman, in shining metallic costume, had a tendency to go toward the blue, as light reflected from his outfit. . . . Judy Garland's ruby slippers, with their red sequins, tended to give off sparks of reflection. . . . Billie Burke's brilliant headdress as the Good Witch presented a similar problem. And Frank Morgan's accentuated make-up as the Wizard sometimes gave us shiny cheek bones to battle with. . . . Probably the most difficult set to photograph was Munchkinland. . . . [I]t contained dozens of shades of the primary colors.[82]

By framing each shot with care, the team addressed some of these concerns, but they also took the opportunity to showcase this filmic style by contrasting sepia Kansas scenes with the bright, colorful world of Oz. Many critics were awed by the color that appeared as Dorothy opened the door to Oz: one proclaimed that "the color sequences fascinate,"[83] while another described the Technicolor scenes as "a beautiful thing to behold."[84] Others were more enthralled by the "ever-changing panorama of scenic vesture"[85] and scenic passages, which were "so beautiful in design and composition as to stir audiences by their sheer enfoldment."[86]

Many reviews celebrated the use of "color and special effects [in] mak[ing] an elaborate fairy-tale" come to life on the screen; yet a few were a little more dismissive.[87] In his analysis of the movie, Maloney attributed "the vulgarity of . . . the film . . . [in] part [to] the raw, eye-straining Technicolor, applied with a complete lack of restraint."[88] More surprisingly, American filmmaker Pare Lorentz criticized the lack of filmic style. He identified the picture as "a Broadway musical comedy, unfortunately equipped with a score by Broadway musical-comedy writers."[89] Lorentz considered the special effects cumbersome and perhaps lacking in technical trickery; as a result, he failed to buy into the spectacular setting and denounced the musical as akin to a stage production.

Largely, however, in 1939 the film was widely celebrated as "an amazing achievement in . . . technical wizardry" and this drove its initial success.[90] As a result, *The Wizard of Oz* has since received a notable place in the history of cinematography and is often cited as one of the best fantasy films of all time. Consequently, for its seventy-fifth anniversary, the picture was again placed at the forefront of film innovation, "remastered and revived on giant Imax screens and in 3D."[91] One reviewer praised the success of this special version exclaiming: "The sugar-rush of that transformation from monochrome to color is now even more overwhelming, and the dream-fantasia of Oz even more dazzling."[92] The writer for the *Observer* admired the visual and special effects of the original as "eye-boggling" but disregarded the remastered version as "an entirely unnecessary ster-eoscopy upon images that never felt the least bit 'flat' in the first place"[93] Despite this ambiguity over the need for a new edition, the willingness of a studio to invest in such a project demonstrates the long-term appeal of this movie and the desire to rework this classic for new generations with different cinematographic expectations.

"Make Us Believe in This Land of Oz": The Commercial Significance of the Cast

Ultimately, one further element had a considerable impact on the reception of the movie: the casting. In particular, Dorothy's three friends were expected to drive the commercial appeal of the film. Bert Lahr was an acclaimed actor and come-dian who had previously starred in the musical comedy *Flying High* (1930), and alongside Beatrice Lillie in *The Show Is On* (1936). He was expected to introduce "some real broad comedy" into *The Wizard of Oz* as the Cowardly Lion. Casting the Scarecrow and Tin Man was more complex: initially, Ray Bolger (who had worked with Harburg on *Life Begins at 8:40*) and Buddy Ebsen (a dancer who had signed with MGM) were given these roles respectively. During rehearsals, how-ever, Ebsen was hospitalized after suffering a reaction to the aluminium dust used in his makeup; as a result, he was replaced by vaudeville star Jack Haley. Harburg, who noted that he was "in on casting," explains that there was some disagreement over which role these two actors should have; however, it was eventually decided that "Bolger was a much better dancer" and should play the role of the scare-crow.[94] The casting of Dorothy was also not straightforward. Initially, the creative team discussed the possibility of borrowing Shirley Temple from 20th Century Fox, but when that studio declined, MGM approached the Juvenile Academy

Award winner Deanna Durbin. Durbin, however, was unavailable, and as a result Judy Garland, who was under contract with MGM, was enlisted. Casting the Wizard also presented difficulties. Initially, the writers had hoped comedian W. C. Fields would accept $50,000 to play the role, but, wanting more money, he refused.[95] Next, Ed Wynn was considered for the part, but ultimately another MGM contract player, Frank Morgan, was given the role.

Nevertheless, the cast were largely well-received, with reviewers admiring the actors for "strike[ing] . . . a happy medium between humor and make-believe."[96] In particular many were thrilled by Garland's performance. Harburg described her as a star who "didn't even need to be directed," while critics were also impressed with her maturity.[97] The writer in *Scholastic* described her performance as entirely "believable"[98] and the *Variety* reviewer asserted that she was "an appealing figure as the wandering waif."[99] Other critics celebrated her naivety, in particular, Nugent of the *New York Times*: "Judy Garland's Dorothy is a pert and fresh-faced miss with the wonder-lit eyes of a believer in fairy tales."[100] Another observed that Garland plays the little Kansas girl "with charming simplicity,"[101] while the writer in the *Hollywood Spectator* exalted Garland as the star of the production:

> The story revolves around the adventures . . . of Judy Garland, and to me the outstanding feature of the production is the astonishingly clever performance of that youngster. . . . All through the picture moves the little Judy, holding it together, being always its motivating feature, and so natural is she, so perfectly cast, one scarcely becomes conscious of her contribution to the whole. I have read all the other local reviews of the picture and have not found in one of them the praise which in my opinion is due this accomplished child. . . . Her performance in *The Wizard of Oz* strengthens my conviction that in a few years she will be recognized as one of the screen's foremost emotional actresses.[102]

Even within more critical reviews of the film, Garland was celebrated as "wonderfully wide-eyed" and "the only one who could begin to make us believe in this Land of Oz."[103] Another critic was particularly captivated by her voice stating: "Judy Garland is perfectly cast as Dorothy. She is a clever little actress as she is a singer and her special style of vocalizing is ideally adapted to the music of the picture."[104] Many critics were thrilled by Garland's portrayal of Dorothy, and as a result she was given a Juvenile Academy Award.

Nevertheless, some were less enthusiastic: in particular, those who had struggled to appreciate the fantastical plot also found fault in the casting. In his satirical review, the *New Republic* critic gave a scathing response to Garland's performance: "It isn't that this little slip of a miss spoils the fantasy so much as that her thumping, overgrown gambols are characteristic of its treatment here. When she is merry the house shakes, and everybody gets wet when she is forlorn."[105] Dorothy was a five- or six-year-old in Baum's book, and perhaps her more mature depiction in the film influenced Ferguson's criticism of Garland's overly dramatic performance. Similarly, Maloney was also unconvinced by the acting and his only appreciation was given to Lahr, whom he acknowledged as "funny," yet still "out of place."[106] Lahr's performance caused the most controversy. Some applauded his humor and praised his ability to capture the whimsical charm of the original book "to its most beguiling end."[107] Yet for others, Lahr's characterization was particularly frustrating: "Unfortunately, the magic in this case never weaves its spell over the characters. . . . Bert Lahr's particular brand of comedy may be hilariously funny on a vaudeville program, over the radio, or in a straight comedy, but it completely spoils the illusion here."[108]

More generally, many critics widely congratulated the entire cast. One admired the performances given by all of Dorothy's friends and commented, "The Baum fantasy is at its best when the Scarecrow, the Woodman, and the Lion are on the move."[109] Another also offered extensive approval:

> Ray Bolger as the Strawman, Bert Lahr as the Lion, and Jack Haley as the Tin Man are such unique characterizations that they are liable to attract the most attention. Billie Burke as the lovely fairy queen and Margaret Hamilton as the witch also stand out in a manner which will attract much attention to them.[110]

One writer recognized that "the satire of the fable is not as cleverly pointed as . . . Disney's cartoon of *Snow White*" but believed this was rectified by the humor that particular characters brought to the screen: "The broad comedy of Bert Lahr's Cowardly Lion, Ray Bolger's Strawman, Jack Haley's Tin Woodman and Frank Morgan's Wizard, make up for those side-tickling subtle touches that made the Disney comedy a classic for the screen."[111]

The casting had a significant influence on the reception of the film in 1939, encouraging one critic to label the movie as the "highest form of entertainment for all ages, worthy to be seen many times."[112] However, the troupe also influenced the long-term popularity of the film. Although the vaudeville acting style of Lahr, Haley, and Bolger quickly dated (today these figures are best known for their roles in *The Wizard of Oz*), Garland went on to have an internationally respected career and her status retrospectively influenced the success of *The Wizard of Oz*. The re-release of the movie in widescreen format in 1955 was fueled by Garland's success in *A Star Is Born* and, subsequently, she now headlined the movie. As her fame continued to grow, Garland had a significant role in propelling the popularity of the film for future generations; yet, *The Wizard of Oz* is also noteworthy in Garland's career and has become the picture she is forevermore identified with.[113]

"Worthy to Be Seen Many Times": Closing Thoughts on the Legacy of Oz

As *The Wizard of Oz* appeared in 1939, the ephemeral film culture limited the immediate success of the movie: there were no TV airings or home videos to extend its life any further. Instead, it was the relevance of the political message and the appreciation of Baum's text that encouraged the first rerelease of the film in 1949. Six years later, Garland's rise in fame spurred another release in widescreen. The growing popularity of the movie then stimulated CBS to air the film on TV in 1956, where it began to gain iconic status. In this original broadcast, Lahr introduced the program, along with Garland's daughter, Liza Minnelli, and it was deemed "a huge success, drawing 45 million viewers."[114] However, it was a further three years before the network aired the film again. Hosted by Red Skelton and shown at an hour early enough for the very young to watch, this broadcast attracted even more viewers, and subsequently CBS and MGM negotiated a new contract for a third airing. *The Wizard of Oz* was established as "an annual 'special event'" and its audience grew exponentially.[115] Ever since, many Americans have watched the film religiously every year, and the popular appeal of *The Wizard of Oz* has held strong; consequently, Harmetz notes that the film continues to be "repeated each year *because* it has become part of American culture."[116]

Few movie musicals have had comparable success: in 2010 the Library of Congress named *The Wizard of Oz* the most widely viewed motion picture in television history, while various popular and critical polls across the years have ranked it among the "Top Ten Best Movies of All Time." The film has been released over a dozen times and many scholars have acknowledged its revolutionary approach to cinematography. For generations, film students have studied this picture as a classic. The technical achievements have continued to enhance the prestige of the film, but MGM's picture has also become the gateway to *The Wizard of Oz* narrative. Because of the film's towering status in popular culture, it has become the object of active hero worship: images and characters from the movie (including Dorothy and her three companions, the Yellow Brick Road, and the Emerald City) have become icons in both American and British culture, while the moral behind the story has been reinterpreted across generations. One writer attributes the long-term success of the film to this ability to affect viewers in new ways over time: "We come back to this film at various points in our lives, and we experience the story and its themes differently each time, but it is the viewer who changes, never the film."[117] Despite evolving social circumstances, political attitudes, and general tastes, *The Wizard of Oz* continues to appeal to both adults and children. When MGM created the film in 1939, the hope was to produce a prestigious picture at the expense of financial profit; they could never have imagined the influence this film would have in both the cinematic world and American culture.

Notes

1. Aljean Harmetz, *The Making of The Wizard of Oz* (London: Pavilion Books, 1989), 19.
2. Harmetz, *The Making of The Wizard of Oz*, 18–19.
3. *Film Bulletin*, August 26, 1939, 6; quoted in *Motion Picture Review Digest Volumes 4–5* (New York: H.W. Wilson Company, 1939), 94.
4. John C. Flinn Sr., "The Wizard of Oz," *Variety*, August 16, 1939, http://variety.com/1939/film/reviews/the-wizard-of-oz-3-1200412289/#!
5. Kate Cameron, "*The Wizard of Oz* Is an Instant Classic," *New York Daily News*, August 18, 1939, http://www.nydailynews.com/entertainment/movies/wizard-oz-instant-disney-classic-1939-review-article-1.2330990
6. Mark Evan Swartz, *Oz before the Rainbow: L. Frank Baum's The Wonderful Wizard of Oz on Stage and Screen to 1939* (Baltimore, MD: Johns Hopkins University Press, 2000), 254.
7. Frank S. Nugent, "The Screen in Review; *The Wizard of Oz*, Produced by the Wizards of Hollywood, Works Its Magic on the Capitol's Screen," *New York Times*, August 18, 1939, 16.
8. Jesse Zunser, *Cue*, August 19, 1939, 39.
9. *Variety (Hollywood)*, August 10, 1939, 3; quoted in *Motion Picture Review Digest Volumes 4–5* (New York: H.W. Wilson Company, 1939), 94.
10. Richard Sheridan Ames in *Rob Wagner's Script*, 22, no. 519, August 26, 1939, 16; quoted in Anthony Slide (ed.), *Selected Film Criticism 1931–1940* (Metuchen, N.J.: The Scarecrow Press, Inc, 1982), 272.
11. In the 1930s, writers and songwriters were not invited to previews or premiers of the pictures they worked on. Harmetz notes, "If the [songwriters] were curious about how well their songs would be arranged, orchestrated, and used, they could buy a ticket to see the finished film" (Harmetz, *The Making of The Wizard of Oz*, 59).
12. Harmetz, *The Making of The Wizard of Oz*, 59.
13. Jack Haley quoted in Harmetz, *The Making of The Wizard of Oz*, 20.
14. Margaret Hamilton quoted in Harmetz, *The Making of The Wizard of Oz*, 20.
15. Otis Ferguson, "*The Wizard of Oz* and *The Adventures of Sherlock Holmes* Reviewed," *New Republic*, September 24, 1939.
16. Harmetz, *The Making of The Wizard of Oz*, 21

17. Swartz, *Oz before the Rainbow*, 254.

18. In 1956, CBS tried to lease *Gone with the Wind* from MGM for $1 million. When MGM refused, CBS made a counteroffer of $225,000 for *The Wizard of Oz*. MGM accepted and as part of the deal also gave CBS an option to broadcast the film annually.

19. "L. Frank Baum: The Real Wizard of Oz," *Telegraph*, May 6, 2016, https://www.telegraph.co.uk/films/2016/05/06/l-frank-baum-the-real-wizard-of-oz/

20. Harburg and Arlen's songs, along with Stothart's musical underscoring, also had a significant role in the success of the movie. However, as these aspects of the film are considered in other chapters in this volume, they have been omitted from this discussion to avoid repetition.

21. E. Y. Harburg, "Interview with Aljean Harmetz," Yip Harburg Foundation Archives, New York City, Series 1: Transcripts (undated ca. early 1977), 4.

22. Baum's stories were all widely published and well received at the turn of the century.

23. Victor Fleming, quoted in "The Aims of the Makers" in *The Wizard of Oz: 70th Anniversary Deluxe Songbook* (Vocal Selections) (Van Nuys, CA: Alfred, October 13, 2009), 12.

24. Fleming, quoted in "The Aims of the Makers," 12.

25. Florence Ryerson and Edgar Allen Woolf, quoted in "The Aims of the Makers," 14.

26. Ryerson and Woolf, quoted in "The Aims of the Makers," 14.

27. Ryerson and Woolf, quoted in "The Aims of the Makers," 14.

28. Philip T. Hartung, *Commonwealth*, August 25, 1939, 421.

29. *Newsweek*, August 21, 1929, 21.

30. Howard Barnes, *New York Herald Tribune*, August 18, 1939, 8.

31. Barnes, *New York Herald Tribune*, 8.

32. Mark Kermode, "*The Wizard of Oz* 3D Review: Unnecessary Surgery to a Classic," *Observer*, September 14, 2014, https://www.theguardian.com/film/2014/sep/14/wizard-of-oz-3d-review-unnecessary-surgery-timeless-classic

33. "*The Wizard of Oz* and the Magic of Adaptation," *The Film 5000 Project*, http://film5000.com/my-100-favorite-films/the-wizard-of-oz/27.

34. It is worth noting that the songs in *The Wizard of Oz* are another reason the film is able to stand on its own and is not viewed as an inadequate version of Baum's novel.

35. Flinn, "The Wizard of Oz."

36. In the early 1930s, Disney created the concept of a short, animated feature film with *The Ugly Duckling* (1931) and *The Three Little Pigs* (1933).

37. Mervyn LeRoy, quoted in "The Aims of the Makers," 12.

38. LeRoy, quoted in "The Aims of the Makers," 12.

39. LeRoy, quoted in "The Aims of the Makers," 12.

40. LeRoy, quoted in "The Aims of the Makers," 12.

41. LeRoy, quoted in "The Aims of the Makers," 12.

42. Ferguson, "*The Wizard of Oz* and *The Adventures of Sherlock Holmes* Reviewed."

43. Ferguson, "*The Wizard of Oz* and *The Adventures of Sherlock Holmes* Reviewed."

44. Harmetz, *The Making of The Wizard of Oz*, 21.

45. Flinn, "The Wizard of Oz."

46. Barnes, *New York Herald Tribune*, 8.

47. Nugent, "The Screen in Review," 16.

48. Harmetz, *The Making of The Wizard of Oz*, 22.

49. *Variety (Hollywood)*, August 10, 1939, 3.

50. California Federation of Music Clubs; quoted in *Motion Picture Review Digest Volumes 4–5* (New York: H.W. Wilson Company, 1939), 93.

51. *Film Daily*, August 10, 1939, 6; quoted in *Motion Picture Review Digest Volumes 4–5* (New York: H.W. Wilson Company, 1939), 94.

52. *Time*, August 21, 1929, 41.

53. *Boxoffice*, August 19, 1939, 71; quoted in *Motion Picture Review Digest Volumes 4–5* (New York: H.W. Wilson Company, 1939), 94.

54. *Boxoffice*, August 19, 1939, 71.

55. *Lady in the Dark* appeared on Broadway in 1941.

56. Henry Littlefield, "The Wizard of Oz: Parable on Populism," *American Quarterly* 16, no. 1 (Spring 1964); quoted in Harold Meyerson and Ernie Harburg, *Who Put the Rainbow in The Wizard of Oz?* (Ann Arbor: University of Michigan Press, 1995), 9.

57. Littlefield, "The Wizard of Oz."

58. Charlotte Burcher, Neil Hollands, Andrew Smith, Barry Trott, and Jessica Zellers, eds., "Core Collections in Genre Studies: Fantasy Fiction 101," *Reference & User Services Quarterly* 48, no. 3 (Spring 2009): 227.

59. E. Y. Harburg, transcript of ' "Yip Harburg Interviewed by Studs Terkel,' " Yip Harburg Foundation Archives, New York City, Series 1: Transcripts (undated ca. early 1977), 26–27.

60. Harburg, "Interview with Aljean Harmetz," 7.

61. LeRoy, quoted in "The Aims of the Makers," 12.

62. LeRoy, quoted in "The Aims of the Makers," 12.

63. Ryerson and Woolf, quoted in "The Aims of the Makers," 14–15.

64. Flinn, "The Wizard of Oz."

65. Flinn, "The Wizard of Oz."

66. Peter Bradshaw, "*The Wizard of Oz* Review: A Dazzling Remastered Masterpiece," *Guardian*, September 11, 2014, https://www.theguardian.com/film/2014/sep/11/the-wizard-of-oz-review-remastered

67. William Stillman, quoted in Susan King, "How Did *Wizard of Oz* Fare on Its 1939 Release?" *Los Angeles Times*, March 11, 2013, http://articles.latimes.com/2013/mar/11/entertainment/la-et-mn-original-wizard-reaction-20130311

68. "L. Frank Baum: The Real Wizard of Oz," *Telegraph*, May 6, 2016, https://www.telegraph.co.uk/films/2016/05/06/l-frank-baum-the-real-wizard-of-oz/

69. Fleming, quoted in "The Aims of the Makers," 12.

70. Fleming, quoted in "The Aims of the Makers," 12.

71. Fleming, quoted in "The Aims of the Makers," 12.
72. Fleming, quoted in "The Aims of the Makers," 12.
73. Welford Beaton, *Hollywood Spectator,* 14, no. 10, September 2, 1939, 10.
74. Flinn, "The Wizard of Oz."
75. *Christian Science Monitor*, August 19, 1939, 17; quoted in *Motion Picture Review Digest Volumes 4–5* (New York: H.W. Wilson Company, 1939), 93.
76. Beaton, *Hollywood Spectator*, 10.
77. Beaton, *Hollywood Spectator*, 10.
78. Beaton, *Hollywood Spectator*, 10.
79. Beaton, *Hollywood Spectator*, 10.
80. Nugent, "The Screen in Review," 16. Jack Dawn was the makeup artist working on *The Wizard of Oz*.
81. Nugent, "The Screen in Review," 16.
82. Harold Rosson quoted in "The Aims of the Makers," 13.
83. *Fox W Coast Bulletin,* August 12, 1939; quoted in *Motion Picture Review Digest Volumes 4–5* (New York: H.W. Wilson Company, 1939), 93.
84. *Boxoffice*, August 19, 1939, 71.
85. Flinn, "The Wizard of Oz."
86. Flinn, "The Wizard of Oz."
87. *Weekly Guide*, August 19, 1939; quoted in *Motion Picture Review Digest Volumes 4–5* (New York: H.W. Wilson Company, 1939), 93.
88. Russell Maloney, *New Yorker*, August 19, 1939, 60.
89. Pare Lorentz, quoted in Harmetz, *The Making of The Wizard of Oz*, 19, 22.
90. *Variety (Hollywood)*, August 10, 1939, 3.
91. Bradshaw, "*The Wizard of Oz* Review: A Dazzling Remastered Masterpiece."
92. Bradshaw, "*The Wizard of Oz* Review: A Dazzling Remastered Masterpiece."
93. Kermode, "*The Wizard of Oz* 3D Review: Unnecessary Surgery to a Classic."
94. Harburg, "Interview with Aljean Harmetz," 5.
95. Harburg, "Interview with Aljean Harmetz," 5.
96. *Newsweek*, August 21, 1929, 21.
97. Harburg, "Interview with Aljean Harmetz," 7.
98. Harmetz, *The Making of The Wizard of Oz*, 22.
99. Flinn, "The Wizard of Oz."
100. Nugent, "The Screen in Review," 16.
101. Sheridan Ames, *Rob Wagner's Script*, 16.
102. Beaton, *Hollywood Spectator*, 10.
103. *Scholastic*, September 18, 1939, 32; quoted in *Motion Picture Review Digest Volumes 4–5* (New York: H.W. Wilson Company, 1939), 93.
104. Kate Cameron, "*The Wizard of Oz* Is an Instant Classic," *New York Daily News*, August 21, 2015, http://www.nydailynews.com/entertainment/movies/wizard-oz-instant-disney-classic-1939-review-article-1.2330990

105. Ferguson, "*The Wizard of Oz* and *The Adventures of Sherlock Holmes,* Reviewed."

106. Maloney, *New Yorker*, August 19, 1939, 60.

107. John Gibbons, *Boston Transcript*, August 18, 1939; quoted in *Motion Picture Review Digest Volumes 4–5* (New York: H.W. Wilson Company, 1939), 93.

108. *Scholastic,* September 18, 1939e, 32.

109. Nugent, "The Screen in Review," 16.

110. Beaton, *Hollywood Spectator*, 10.

111. Cameron, "*The Wizard of Oz* Is an Instant Classic."

112. *Fox W Coast Bulletin*, August 19, 1939.

113. Garland's status as a celebrated gay icon has also had a considerable impact on the success of the film, but this is not discussed here as it is the focus of a later chapter.

114. Stillman, quoted in Susan King, "How Did *Wizard of Oz* Fare."

115. Stillman, quoted in Susan King, "How Did *Wizard of Oz* Fare."

116. Swartz, *Oz before the Rainbow*, 256.

117. "*The Wizard of Oz* and the Magic of Adaptation," *The Film 5000 Project*.

7 "FRIENDS OF DOROTHY"

QUEERNESS IN AND BEYOND THE MGM FILM

Hannah Robbins

In Chapter 2 of L. Frank Baum's *The Wizard of Oz*, Dorothy stands transfixed in the doorway of her house, catching her first glimpse of a "country of marvellous beauty" she has been transported to.[1] While she takes in the vivid, exciting sights and sounds of this world so new "to a little girl who had lived so long on the dry, grey prairies," she observes an approaching group of "the queerest people she had ever seen."[2] As the Munchkins welcome her, Dorothy begins to embrace her new surroundings and the "odd" people she is about to become acquainted with. Baum's representation of discovering newness and otherness has been very convincingly translated to screen in the iconic sequence when Judy Garland's Dorothy opens a sepia-tinged front door to reveal the Technicolored Munchkinland beyond. There are few more recognizable works so intrinsically associated with popular American queer culture than MGM's *The Wizard of Oz*, and this specific cinematic moment provides a direct insight into much of the queer reception to this film. Although closely drawn from the source text, MGM's *Oz* has the impact of being tangible: a realized vision with specific aesthetic values. It is fantastically artificial and garish rather than whimsical and romantic. As such, this realization of Dorothy's arrival in a vivid and remarkable "other" place has become, for many, a metaphor for the possibility of escaping conformity and the ability to find a place where being different is not simply safe, but normal.

This reading of *Oz* is at the heart of numerous interpretations of the film. However, the crucial placement of and symbolism in Yip Harburg and Harold Arlen's "Over the Rainbow" as the focal point of the early Kansas scenes have also contributed to this "idyllic" approach. Furthermore, this song has also transcended its framing context in the film to become an anthem for many across the queer community. The immediacy of the association between the imagery in Harburg's lyrics and the Rainbow Flag, an international emblem for the lesbian, gay, bisexual, and transgender (LGBT+) community, has led to some belief that it inspired Gilbert Baker's original eight-striped design in 1978. An adaptation of Baker's flag (inspired by the "Flag of Race") was used by San Francisco's pride committee in the wake of the assassination of Harvey Milk,[3] leading to the eventual recognition of a six-striped flag by the International Congress of Flag Makers. It seems noteworthy that in the film bi-opic of Harvey Milk's life (2008), a sequence of a gay pride parade is underscored by a recording of Garland singing "Over the Rainbow." As such, this song, as performed by Garland, has taken on cultural status beyond, and yet because of, the film. It has become part of the soundtrack of hope and the fight for equality for many in the queer community.[4] Indeed, the use of "Over the Rainbow" in association with pride parades is made more significant because of the layers of celebration that permeate these events. As Mark Graham describes: "[The] *smorgasbord* of sexualities that gay pride parades display is meant for everyone, regardless of sexuality, it is not only meant to shock but also to attract and awaken desire."[5] As *The Wizard of Oz* showcases an abundance of "otherness" through the individualistic depictions of many of the film's central characters, its design, and also in some of its narrative themes, it seems fitting that "Over the Rainbow" should permeate this aspect of queer culture.

In addition to this, "Over the Rainbow" has become closely tied to Garland's performance legacy, especially her recognition as an influential figure in twentieth-century queer culture. The irony of Dorothy's wistful idealism in the film and the star's subsequently troubled life adds a complex symbiosis between the film and Garland's star persona, which is directly informed by the narrative themes of this adaptation. Therefore, there is a recurrent trend in popular and critical accounts of *The Wizard of Oz* that highlights the significance of Garland's performance of Dorothy (and of "Over the Rainbow") to the queer reception of the film. This has been extended by the proximity of Garland's death due to an accidental overdose in 1969 and the Stonewall riots in New York in July of the same year. The riots, which began at the Stonewall Inn in Greenwich Village, began as the result of a police raid on the bar that spiraled out of control. The demonstration of unified resistance shown by patrons against the police is seen as one of the most significant events to precede the gay liberation movement. In this way, Garland as an icon, "Over the Rainbow" as an anthem, and the aspiration to escape and find acceptance intersect in the reception to the MGM *Wizard of Oz*.

In addition to these aspects of reception, the expression "friends of Dorothy" reveals a potential further acknowledgment of the value of the film to queer culture. There are varied interpretations of how this phrase was first coined. Some suggest that it was developed specifically as a code phrase, used by soldiers serving in the American army (especially during the Vietnam war [1955–1975]) to identify other gay service personnel. After the Second World War, screening processes were introduced in army recruitment, meaning that potential soldiers were asked if they had experienced any homosexual feelings or acts as part of the induction physical checks. In 1950, President Harry S. Truman signed legislation, known as the Uniform Code of Military Justice (UCMJ), which labeled homosexual sex as "sodomy." The introduction of the UCMJ contributed to a considerable emphasis on unmasking and discharging gay service personnel who had entered the armed services.[6] The usage of "friends of Dorothy" seems to coincide with the resurgence of the MGM film as part of regular television programming in the United States. As this phrase seemingly allowed soldiers to identify themselves and others without detection, its likely derivation from MGM's film has potent significance. There is an obvious duality in the expression, which makes use of a popular and common woman's name but also subtly references the unusual personas of Dorothy's three companions—the Scarecrow, the Tin Man and the Lion—who accompany her on her journey to meet the Wizard. However, it also seems to link back to Garland's ability to deliver performances through a mask of glamour and positivity even as she struggled in her personal life.[7]

As highlighted by Steven Cohan in the introduction to *Incongruous Entertainment: Camp, Cultural Value, and the MGM Musical*, contemporary lexicology utilizes the terms "gay," "homosexual," and "queer" almost interchangeably.[8] In this essay, queer is taken to represent the pluralism Cohan outlines: "referring to people of any nonheterocentric sexual or gendered self-identification."[9] This distinction is important as it also encompasses asexuality, transgenderism, and gender fluidity. It is reactive to the nuances of this adaptation of *The Wizard of Oz* and its understandable potency as an example of universal culture that also speaks to many different members of the queer community. To some extent, this can be attributed to the novel's roots as a children's text in which the narrative themes are transmitted without the trappings of heterosexual romance. However, as Tison Pugh notes in his article about "queer utopianism" in Baum's novels, "Oddness cannot always be contained within hermetically sealed and ideologically approved interpretations after being so promiscuously unleashed in a world of fantasy and wonder."[10] As such, it is insufficient to reason that the absence of blatant heterosexuality in this adaptation and the film's "queer potential" can be exclusively interpreted as a result of the novel's intended audience. First, Pugh highlights the flux of heteronormative relationships and the use of gender fluidity that are featured in Baum's novels. This indicates a richness of possibilities that predates this version of *Oz*. Second, MGM's *The Wizard of Oz* conveys the semblance of otherness on textual levels far beyond the basic adventures and relationships that can be summarized in an overview of the plot. There is a thickness to the adaptation that allows queer spectators to take full ownership of the film without a substantial list of caveats.

Indeed, *The Wizard of Oz* remains unparalleled by any equivalently enduring film musical of the period for its lack of "conventional" romance, particularly tied into the transformative journey of a leading (frequently, female) character. (See *Easter Parade* [1948], *Singin' in the Rain* [1952], and *Gigi* [1958] for obvious examples.) In the context of "queer assimilation" with the narrative of MGM's *The Wizard of Oz* (as opposed to the camp aesthetics, which are also frequently noted), the lack of this central component is liberating. Importantly, queer spectators are not confronted with yet another cultural reinforcement that happiness, social equality, and self-actualization are intrinsically connected to heteronormativity. It is worth noting that for many generations of LGBT+ audiences, there were no flawlessly open representations of queer characters and relationships (that we take for granted today) on screen. Therefore, the absence of dominant heterosexual romance in the main plotline of *The Wizard of the Oz* is both striking and central to its popularity across generations of queer audiences.

Reading "queerness" in *The Wizard of Oz* (1939) is complicated by the layers of the film that lend themselves to this approach. As such, it is important to differentiate between (1) how we read different characters (specifically, Dorothy, the Scarecrow, the Tin Man, and the Lion), (2) how we interpret the friendships and polarities created in the film (after Baum's novel), and (3) how the "world of Oz" has been created in film with a potentially "queer aesthetic." Each of these aspects feeds into the cultural discourse that situates *The Wizard of Oz* as an important queer text, one that addresses identity, aspiration, belonging, escapism, and acceptance among other literary and fantastical themes. As a result, this chapter explores the complexity of queer ownership of *The Wizard of Oz*, analyzing details of the film, its popular and critical reception, and the iconic status of Judy Garland (as Dorothy) in order to understand the richness of the film in queer culture.

Expanding the Opening of *The Wizard of Oz*

The MGM adaptation adds substantially to the opening (and closing) pages set in Baum's Kansas (covered in only five pages of the novel). By expanding the framing environment, its writers created a richer, more complex context for Dorothy's visit to Oz. As Suzanne Rahn notes, this enabled the double-casting of actors as inhabitants of Kansas and as characters in Oz.[11] Rahn also suggests that this point of difference contributes to the film's individual identity from the novel as it illustrates Dorothy's influence over Oz, transforming the people she already knows into new personae and reacting to the bleakness of her home surroundings. Importantly, the extended Kansas scenes heighten the contrast between the set designs (and color palette) of Dorothy's two worlds. Furthermore, if we accept the symbolism that "Over the Rainbow" "expresses the yearning of every gay adolescent to find the location of the gay El Dorado,"[12] the suggestion that MGM's Dorothy *creates* Oz in her mind is all the more significant. She envisages a place of nonconformity, also shaped by the polarities of "good" and "evil," which remains a safe place for a spectrum of individuals.

In the novel, we have no sense of Dorothy's day-to-day life in Kansas beyond her feeling of entrapment in bland and unchanging scenery. The film rejects the nothingness outlined in Baum's first chapter in which Dorothy can "see nothing but grey prairie on every side," as the author succinctly characterizes the barren emptiness that has taken "the sparkle" from Aunt Em's eyes.[13] Whereas Baum provides a frame through which we can perceive the magic of Oz, the MGM Kansas creates a first opportunity for us to know, understand, and potentially assimilate it with Dorothy. Looking beyond the aesthetic shifts between the two worlds in the film, MGM's heroine seems to perpetually disrupt her companions in Kansas: she (by association with Toto) has antagonized Miss Gulch, she distracts Uncle Henry and Aunt Em while they are trying to count chickens, she distracts the farmhands from their work, and then she requires rescuing as she falls into the pigsty.

While none of these gestures are significant demonstrations of "otherness" in and of themselves, Dorothy is actively displaced from her community who are all trying to get on with "what they are supposed to be doing." This is made evident in Aunt Em's well-referenced instruction that frames Dorothy's performance "Over the Rainbow": "Now, you just help us out today and find yourself a place where you won't get into any trouble."[14] While scholars note the significance of Dorothy's evolution of Em's expression to somewhere "there isn't any trouble,"[15] her wistful vision of a world "over the rainbow," and her relocation to Oz a few minutes later, these authors make little of the fact that in establishing this song, Aunt Em asks Dorothy to "help" them by removing herself from their space. As such, it is not simply Dorothy's "journey," her character, or her potential agency as the creator of Oz that makes her a viable and appealing heroine, especially to a queer audience. This Dorothy is disconnected from the world around her and cannot seem to find a place where she can be both herself and in harmony with her surroundings.

When taken in the context of Garland's largely static, and gentle, performance of "Over the Rainbow," which is in complete contrast with much of the film, her Dorothy seems to need rescuing, or rather, to escape in order to break from the repressive surroundings she (and Toto) are trapped in. To some extent, this song moment also disconnects Garland from Dorothy as we hear her singing voice for the first time. The low rich, color of her voice, particularly in the opening passages, is noticeably mature, literally in a different register from the voice of the mildly hysterical little girl we see earlier in the scene. This tone contrasts with the costume and makeup intended to disguise Garland's extra years—"in a kind of drag, pretending to be a little girl despite that big voice and her tightly wrapped bosom"[16]—as well as with her subtle performance gestures, recognizably wistful but childlike. During the first half of the song, she plays with the hay bale she leans against and traces her fingers on a rusted wheel. These directions convey a youthfulness that is to some extent disconnected with Garland's more adult command of the song. Having traced her eyes rather abstractly back and forth across the sky (following the rainbow), Garland suddenly connects with Toto, staring into his eyes as she sings "Why then, oh why can't I?" in the first phrases of the last verse.[17] She strokes her dog's paw (presumably, a cue to the female dog playing the part) and "he" lifts it as though to comfort her. Immediately after this, she sees hears the bluebird sing and momentarily gives a wide, open smile that beams at a "ray of sunshine" appearing in the sky. As such, "Over the Rainbow" is simultaneously poignantly introspective, demonstrating Dorothy's isolation, and layered with imagery and metaphor that transcends the intimate moment. The parallelism of Dorothy and Garland as an actress brings a more adult meaning to a song built on innocent understanding.

In a film with so many iconic sequences, Garland's interpretation of "Over the Rainbow" is distinct as a moment of sincere, unfettered emotion. (This is made even clearer in her particularly emotive interpretation of the reprise of "Over the Rainbow" written for the time Dorothy is trapped in the Witch's castle. It was recorded but not included.)[18] In light of this, the expanded context of Kansas is central to this impact of the song. Harburg's lyrics, which embellish Dorothy's need and desire to leave or escape to some new, less burdensome place, and Garland's transmission of the song, take this sequence of the film beyond the narrative of a wide-eyed child, resisting order and authority. Dorothy's "unblemished innocence"[19] and psychological entrapment tied to the imagery of peaceful escape, which is built in the song's framing dialogue, the construction of the song, and Garland's performance, have undoubtedly framed some of the public sentiment toward Garland herself. The tragedy that "Dorothy" could end up so ill, addicted to drugs and alcohol, and near bankruptcy both contaminates Garland's image *as* Dorothy and reinforces the impression of strength and resilience that she continued to transmit through meaningful performances to her fans. Furthermore, it has become tied into a romantic mythology of Garland's life as both her "torch -" and her "swan song": it is reportedly the last piece she performed live onstage in the months before her death.

The cumulative effect of expanding the Kansas narrative establishes Dorothy as a richer, more complex heroine for all audiences. However, her sense of disconnect from her home and the people around who are not like her makes Dorothy a natural vessel for queer assimilation, especially in the context of enforced social repression. "Over the Rainbow" becomes an accent point of this narrative, adding to its potential as a stand-alone song away from the vehicle of the film. Similarly, this new introduction provides Dorothy with a "real-life" nemesis, Miss Gulch, who transforms into the Wicked Witch of the West during the cyclone. Raymond Knapp suggests that the linearity of the representation of the Wicked Witch in the film is "foundational to its appeal to gays."[20] If *The Wizard of Oz* represents "evil"—through the Wicked Witch—without any humanizing characteristics, the Wicked Witch becomes a surrogate for unprovoked marginalization and persecution. In this context, Knapp argues that queer spectators can "feel empowered through a complicated process of identification, by the image of Judy Garland on the brink of adulthood, playing a girl who gamely fights for her place in the world."[21]

From Monochrome to Technicolor: Queer Assimilation in the Land of Oz

The published screenplay for MGM's *The Wizard of Oz* reveals a deliberate vision for Oz—built on Baum's—which embellishes the imagery in the lyrics to "Over the Rainbow." (The melody of the song is reheard as it is quoted in the underscore when Dorothy steps out of the house into Munchkinland.) It is striking that, according to Aljean Harmetz's *The Making of The Wizard of Oz*, Herman J. Mankiewicz's first treatment for the film notes that the Oz scenes would be filmed in color to emphasize the "grey lifelessness" of Kansas.[22] It is clear, therefore, that the movement from monochromatic photography to deliberately colorful scenes was part of the earliest vision of the film, expanding the symbolism of dreary Kansas where a restless Dorothy struggles to conform to the environment around her. Whereas Baum was not engaged with creating a visually arresting spectacle (nor to respond to the imagery in Disney's *Snow White and the Seven Dwarfs* [1937]), MGM not only expanded the sense of Dorothy's displacement from her home environment but also developed a more complex picture of Kansas almost as a template from which their Oz then develops. Baum contrasts visual nothingness in Kansas with Dorothy's enraptured first impressions as she absorbs the lush and fertile color of his Oz. The MGM film expands this so the visual transition is tied more literally to Dorothy's actions: she seems not to belong among the ordinary rigor of this Kansas, moving frantically against the systems of the generic farm environment that contains her. By contrast, she is initially sedately enthralled by her first moments in Munchkinland.

The final description of Munchkinland in the published screenplay is detailed and of comparable length to Baum's. It explains how "the grass is spangled with daisies; flowers grow everywhere, three or four times life-size... The sky is bright blue with little white clouds; and a little stream runs near with huge lily pads on it."[23] This vision in the film reinterprets the exoticism of Baum's "banks of gorgeous flowers . . . and birds with rare and brilliant plumage," where Oz could be anywhere in the world (or in another world entirely), to create a heightened and garish companion to Kansas in the previous scenes.[24] In the context of passing reference to Oz's camp aesthetic made by nearly all scholars cited in this chapter, this aesthetic change from Kansas to Oz, which is both referential and distinct from the source material, is significant because of our theoretical associations between camp, the intensification of reality, and artificiality. Given the skill of the art department available to producer Mervyn LeRoy and director Victor Fleming, it is noticeable how fake Munchkinland appears. Arguably, this contributes to the suggestion that Dorothy has creative influence over it because there is deliberately emotive stylization of both Kansas and Oz, and Oz appears so unreal.

Salman Rushdie and Suzanne Rahn each highlight the cinematographic difference between the linear, square-edged aesthetic of sepia-toned Kansas and the nongeometric vividness of Oz, particularly in the opening scenes in Munchkinland.[25] Rushdie notes the use of vertical lines and simple geometry, suggesting that "with simple shapes and numbers, Dorothy's family erect their defences against the immense and maddening nothingness" of their home environment.[26] He suggests that Oz "bewilders" Dorothy with all its new shapes and "splits and forks every which way."[27] However, he posits that this is the beginning of Dorothy's spiritual journey. Raymond Knapp also explains how the color transition from Oz to Kansas similarly acts as one of many layers of doubleness in the film that is frequently found in fairy tales and is characteristic of queer coding in American popular culture.[28] He explains that it also demonstrates the hallucinatory, "mind-altering-drug dimension" to the transition from reality to the "make-believe" aspects of the film. Bringing these interpretations together, the aesthetic awakening Dorothy experiences as she enters Oz liberates her from the limitations of Kansas and allows her to adapt and grow. As a result, Dorothy can be seen to discover her own mental depths, to find her ability to conjure imagery she has no conscious awareness of, and to have characteristics that exceed the confines of her life in Kansas.

More than this, if Dorothy becomes the orchestrator of this environment (at least subconsciously), these details have further significance. In order to grow as a person, Dorothy has to break free of the mundane conformity of her home, and the transition from sepia to color symbolizes this journey. If Oz is a product of her imagination, it seems to react to her earlier imaginings of a "rainbow highway"—a vivid, colorful path of escape—during "Over the Rainbow" and leads her to create a place where she is surrounded by excitement and "otherness." Mark Graham interprets the cyclone as "nothing other than a cultural wormhole" that "decants [Dorothy's] house into a decidedly queer world."[29] However, we might question the validity of Oz as queer utopia and the viability of Dorothy as a queer heroine given the contradiction that she immediately wishes to leave the world she may have created.[30] Rushdie argues that "Over the Rainbow" and its prefacing dialogue establish *leaving* and *roots* as central to the levels of the film.[31] He also scorns the last section of dialogue in Oz, arguing that the "no place like home" concept is fundamentally at odds with the rest of the film.

To some extent, this lasting message seems to elevate Kansas above Oz and undermine the emotional significance of Dorothy's journey there. However, when Dorothy wakes at home, she is "changed for good": she recalls Oz and values what she discovered there. More abstractly, the message of finding "home" is not exclusively regressive. Just as the land over the rainbow is an escapist fantasy, "home" is *partially* abstract in MGM's *Oz* because change has taken place. Dorothy has grown as a result of her journey through the kingdom; she praises Oz as she tries to explain what she has experienced to her incredulous aunt, uncle, and the farmhands when she returns to Kansas. Importantly, she tells her companions that "some of it wasn't very nice—but most of it was beautiful."[32] Whether or not the emphasis on returning to "normal" (that is, normative) life damages *The Wizard of Oz* as a queer text, Dorothy's description of the kingdom is mature and realistic: it is a sophisticated evolution of the place "where there isn't any trouble."

Presenting Normative Romance in *The Wizard of Oz*

While it is easy to suggest that the utopian aspects of *The Wizard of Oz* do not relate exclusively "to the existence of being queer,"[33] several narrative themes of the film facilitate queer assimilation. For example, the film encompasses escaping conformity, creating or finding a community of one's own, and being accepted as an individual. Each of these themes is made more relevant because the MGM adaptation removes all heterosexual romantic relationships from Dorothy's experiences in Oz. Although Em and Henry are married, we receive no insights into their personal relationship with each other as they are not focal characters. Similarly, the film does not include the context from the novel that the Tin Man (or "Tin Woodman" as Baum named him) is seeking a heart in order to rediscover the love he previously felt for the Munchkin girl he was going to marry.[34] The absence of this theme throughout the film seems superficially to make the film asexual. Rushdie also argues that Garland's interpretation of Dorothy is colored by an "*unsexiness*" that makes her Dorothy powerful and appealing to audiences in contrast to a potentially coy and flirtatious performance as might have been delivered by Shirley Temple, who was also associated with the role.[35] It is perhaps noteworthy that *The Wizard of Oz* coincided with the release of the first major Garland and Mickey Rooney film *Babes in Arms* (1939). The actors had played against each other previously in *Thoroughbreds Don't Cry* (1937) and *Love Finds Andy Hardy* (1938) and developed a popular screen partnership in the years that followed. The teenage jealousy Garland portrays in *Babes in Arms* when she sees Rooney kiss another actress contrasts with the absence of romantic charge in *The Wizard of Oz*. Here, conventional romance is replaced with idealism, hope, and the quest to belong as well as by Dorothy's unconventional relationships with her three companions.

It is important to acknowledge that Baum incorporated unconventionally fluid representations of romance and gender identity in his series of novels; this is not unique to the MGM adaptation.[36] Furthermore, the absence of sex in MGM's *The Wizard of Oz* is understandable in the adaptation of a children's novel for a family audience. Indeed, there are few romantic details in the Garland/Rooney films, which are centered around a conventional "boy-girl" relationship. However, the lack of any trappings of heterosexual romance in *The Wizard of Oz* is significant because its utopianism is completely dissociated from heteronormative relationships. Mark Graham notes that many homosexuals experience childhood and some part of adolescence "by going through (most) of the motions of heterosexuality" and to some extent, *The Wizard of Oz* renders this unnecessary. The film is noticeably separate from the perpetual reinforcement of heterosexual romance and the achievement of happiness or self-actualization at the heart of most musicals.[37] As a result, queer spectators do not have to engage with or discard an oppressively exclusive narrative that reinforces the importance of heterosexual unions as part of an idyllic journey of personal identity. This is made still more significant by the fixed nature of film in contrast to stage works. *The Wizard of Oz* continues to provide the same "safe spaces" to contemporary audiences as it did in 1939.

In some ways, this absence of heteronormativity is reinforced by the MGM representation of Oz as "a land where difference and deviation from the norm *are* the norm."[38] For example, some of the characterization in the film (drawn from the novels) subtly subverts conventional gender roles and hierarchies. While Dorothy, Aunt Em, Glinda, and the Wicked Witch of the West have prominent characteristics that conform with specific female stereotypes—for example, innocence in youth or bossiness—they each exist in a different sphere from the male characters, especially in Oz. Although the Munchkins appear to maintain a masculine-led social structure, Glinda and the Wicked Witches evidently hold social status over the Mayor of Munchkin Town. Furthermore, the fabled Wizard has no magical ability while Glinda and the Wicked Witch are able to conjure spells, to steer the action from afar, and to appear at will. As such, the Wicked Witch, Glinda and Dorothy are all shown to have agency not granted to the male characters. As Rushdie emphasizes, the female characters have incomparable status in the film: "The power of men, it is suggested, is illusory; the power of women is real."[39]

The role of the Wizard highlights this difference in gender power in the film. In a conventional and normative representation of gender, a young girl (assisted by a pet dog, a camp lion, etc.) would not have the agency to undermine a flamboyant and (seemingly) powerful elder male. As such, the Wizard appears scary and powerful at first but is unmasked by Toto when Dorothy and her companions return from defeating the Wicked Witch. The Wizard is ultimately shown to be impotent in comparison to most of the other characters in Oz. This is reflected in the modern reimagining of *The Muppets' Wizard of Oz*, which moves the text away from queerness into the surreal. (It also reintroduces a love interest for the "Tin Thing" who hoped to marry a Muppet chicken.) In this version, "the Wizard" conjures ridiculous computer-generated images (e.g., a giant version of the puppet chicken, Camilla, for Tin Thing) to greet each of the visitors as they arrive to request their wishes. By contrast, the Wicked Witch (played by Miss Piggy) is a celebrity with an MTV-style reality show, a devoted boyfriend, and an entourage of henchmen. As such, the role of the Wizard is satirized in different ways just as his double, Professor Marvel, is depicted as a blatant fraud in the additional Kansas scenes at the beginning of the MGM adaptation.

This is not to argue that there is nothing normative about *The Wizard of Oz*. As noted above, the strength of the central female characters is perhaps diminished by their associations with uncomfortable (and largely, derogatory) female stereotypes. Not only is Munchkinland depicted as a conventionally patriarchal society, but it also appears to be an exclusively heterosexual community. Furthermore, the costumes and makeup largely reinforce normative gendering. Nonetheless, the excessiveness and artificiality of many of these details disrupt some of this normativity; they imply that this is partially performative. As with Garland's performance of "Over the Rainbow," this dimension of *The Wizard of Oz* both corresponds with a more adult understanding of the text and with the idea that parts of the film were created with "knowingness," arguably appreciating that audiences would acknowledge the artifice as they engaged with it.

Friends of Dorothy

Looking beyond the narrative and aesthetic details of *The Wizard of Oz* and Dorothy as the main protagonist of the film, her companions in Oz—the Scarecrow, Tin Man, and Lion—are frequently noted as part of the film's queer text. Whereas the Hollywood Production Code (1934–1968) advocated conjugal procreation as the only legitimate manifestation of sexuality in film, many scholars have demonstrated how queerness has been represented on screen since the beginning of cinema (e.g., through coded language, characterization, and the absence of heterosexual relationships). For example, there is some debate as to whether the "friends of Dorothy" in the film have been characterized as "connotative homosexuals,"[40] suggesting queerness through performance details such as vocal inflections and mannerisms. For some commentators, including Griffin Benshoff, there is absolutely no question that Lion—"a sissy"—was conceived as a queer character.[41]

The significance of the Cowardly Lion is most pointedly raised in the introduction to Alexander Doty's queer reading of *The Wizard of Oz* as a "Lesbian Fantasy." Doty describes the discomfort he experienced as a child, watching actor Bert Lahr's elaborate performance: "he [The Lion] seemed too out: flamboyant, effeminate, and self-oppressive."[42] Doty recalls how he struggled with the desire to be like Dorothy while actually identifying with the Lion. He then suggests that his growing appreciation for camp that developed as he came to understand his own sexuality ultimately helped him find peace with the Lion: "He was still "over-the-top," but no longer a total embarrassment. . . . He was more like a drag queen who just didn't give a fuck."[43] Through his chapter, Doty aims to reclaim *The Wizard of Oz* from heterocentrist readings in which any character whose sexual and romantic preferences are undisclosed is straight.[44] His anecdote about the Lion is vital here because it demonstrates the potential discomfort caused by *The Wizard of Oz* in which nonconformist characters are allowed to thrive in safe environments.

In his article about the underrepresentation and erasure of homosexuality in mainstream anthropology, Mark Graham uses the MGM *Wizard of Oz* to illustrate sections of his argument about "the assumption of universal heterosexuality."[45] Graham summarizes how the individual quests of Dorothy and her three companions each speak to queer experience: the search for a place to belong, the attempt to understand and recognize who we are, and the willingness to open our hearts to have them readily broken (Graham associates this with the loss and grief of AIDS victims and their loved ones).[46] Both of these accounts imply but do not articulately address the significance that each of these characters is bound up in the quest to live a richer life without seeking to achieve any obvious traits of performative masculinity. For example, Doty (and others) does not explore the nuance that the Lion begins his particular thread of the self-actualization theme in *The Wizard of Oz* at a point of shame that he does not present like a "proper" Lion. He has no instinctive affinity for what he understands to be normative behavior: of being brave, strong, and domineering. Superficially, Lahr's performance is arresting but the Cowardly Lion, like the Tin Man who is "torn apart" by his lack of ability to be "tender ... gentle / And awful sentimental," actually seeks a more complex characteristic.[47] The Lion does not need courage: he needs self-belief.

Knapp suggests that "the transformation of the three farmhands into Dorothy's Oz companions, all in elaborate costumes and makeup, and with more exaggerated mannerisms based on their Kansas personae, makes us even more acutely aware of the performers beneath, facilitating their transmutation into 'Friends of Dorothy' in all senses."[48] This is convincing in the context that Garland's vocal performance of "Over the Rainbow" seems to unmask her. It is important to note that this adaptation of *The Wizard of Oz* is not concerned with any lasting sense of naturalism (which would ultimately jar with the fantastical elements at its heart). Even in Kansas, the set design is noticeably artificial. However, it contains continued contrasts that draw our attention to its artifice. Knapp argues that Dorothy's companions' "elaborate drag and exaggerated modes of behaviour give them a distinctly gay aspect," which have been repetitively viewed by a growing queer community.[49] However, this exaggeration is also constructed through other details in the film: the Yellow Brick Road clashes with the gray and red brick paths next to it; it is not enough for the road to be yellow. More complexly, the Wicked Witch is not only ugly but also has vividly green skin framed by her all-black costume. The nature of this makeup both dehumanizes the Witch and also draws attention to the actress, Margaret Hamilton, underneath. In this context, the "drag" Knapp refers to is a knowing illusion that permeates Oz. Furthermore, the idea of "connotative" performance highlighted earlier permeates these layers and contrasts as many of the details of Garland's characterization of Dorothy, including posturing and gasping, have been directly linked to her status as a gay icon. Similarly, there is perceived ambiguity about Glinda, who travels by bubble and appears to know everything and nothing in her slightly-too-large crown and overblown gown that is seen to nod to an artificial performance of femininity found in drag performance (and for Doty in aspects of the femme Lesbian community).[50]

Both this emphasis on drag and the unique significance of Dorothy's companions, especially the Lion, intersect with the vague allusions to camp that saturate queer readings of Oz. To some extent, the identities and sympathies of the authors of these texts (and this essay) have led us to assume that the "camp" details of Oz are self-evident. A late-teenage actor has been disguised as a prepubescent child (but has a nearly adult singing voice). She is transported to an artificial and garish fantasyland full of misfit characters. There is undisclosed magic, the use of illusion, lavish costumes, and polarity among the scale of Munchkinland, the Emerald City, and the Witch's castle in this new place. As such, there is a cumulative effect of writing, design, and performance that enables largely unparalleled queer assimilation with this adaption of *The Wizard of Oz*. Normativity remains present without troubling the "queerer" aspects of the film so that the Lion can be flamboyant, the Tin Man can be emotional, and the Scarecrow can be more vulnerable than any other character without challenging any heterocentric perceptions of the film.

In this way, the cultural legacy of MGM's *The Wizard of Oz* is both unusual and complex. In a single example, its creators produced a musical adaptation of a well-loved children's story that has transcended generational tastes. Using (now) iconic cinematographic and visual techniques and including a range of catchy and potent musical numbers, this film has also taken on a unique status in modern queer culture. While the film does not explicitly explore queerness, MGM's adaptation has complex and important symbolism for queer spectators. This is partially indicated in recent reception through pervasive references to the film in gay TV shows such as *Queer as Folk* (2000–2005) and *Will and Grace* (1998–2006). *The Wizard of Oz* is also acknowledged repeatedly in the cult fantasy series *Buffy the Vampire Slayer* (1997–2003). (*Buffy* furthered the representation of lesbianism, including the first lesbian sex scene, on American network television.)[51] Similarly, it is interesting to note that certain gestures in *The Wizard of Oz* inspired the Transylvanian community in *The Rocky Horror Picture Show* (1975). Raymond Knapp notes the parallels between *Rocky Horror*'s "hero and heroine" Brad and Janet who end up displaced through a storm in a sort of alternative universe, and Oz's Dorothy.[52] Knapp also indicates that they considered emulating *The Wizard of Oz* by recording the opening sections of *Rocky Horror* in black and white and introducing color as Dr. Frank-N-Furter makes his first entrance. Given Frank-N-Furter's open transsexuality, his obsession with Rocky, and his affairs with Brad and Janet, this is a noteworthy progression, translating an "alternative" community into new terms that reacted to some contemporary manifestations of queerness.

In an additional example, the 2010 Broadway revival (a transfer production from London's West End) of the musical *La Cage Aux Folles* featured drag performer Albin (played by Douglas Hodge) in a Dorothy costume during one of the backstage scenes (including the song "With You on My Arm"). Throughout the performance, Hodge impersonated several iconic performers including Edith Piaf and Marlene Dietrich in his "onstage" scenes as Zaza. Here, this visual reference to Dorothy both acknowledged Garland and MGM's Oz in the context of other important cultural symbols within drag culture. In these isolated examples alone, it is clear that the queer reception to *The Wizard of Oz* is not just part of a discourse within the community but is also seen as part of the language of contemporary queer culture.

In the context of this legacy on screen and stage, the expression "friends of Dorothy" becomes saturated in meanings derived from culture outside the film itself. Nonetheless, *The Wizard of Oz* provided cleverly coded cover by which queer individuals could identify one another with a lasting joke on the blinkered heterosexual authorities who aimed to repress all LGBT+ society. MGM's film and its representation of Baum's heroine continue to offer considerable meaning to the queer community, even as we become increasingly aware of the limitations of other features of the film and its production process (e.g., the mistreatment of Garland on set or the alleged exploitation of the performers playing the Munchkins). Importantly, as the (almost) creator of this iteration of Oz, a luminous but complex place of escape, Dorothy learns that she cannot avoid trouble but that she can belong somewhere. Her innocent acceptance of her companions despite their perceived flaws and their reciprocal protection of her as a result of this friendship continue to be a vital allegory for queer individuals looking for cultural affirmation in a decisively heteronormative culture.

The prominence of Garland, her recordings of "Over the Rainbow," and the repeated presence of *The Wizard of Oz* on American screens has undeniably permeated the cultural meaning of the film. Garland constantly moved forward even as she aimed (and was forced) to maintain many of the qualities she was famous for in her youth. As "Over the Rainbow" has obtained new cultural status—it is frequently cited as the "greatest song of all time"—in addition to its importance in Western queer culture, this arguably loads "friends of Dorothy" with a still richer meaning. Rather than a simple identification with the Scarecrow, the Tin Man, or the Lion, there is also an implied allegiance with Dorothy herself; with the aspirations of a person who feels displaced from her surroundings; with a different energy and focus to her companions; and also with a character who empowers those around her as she grows. Rather than seeing Dorothy as a simple young girl who tumbles into an unexpected land, the film implies that she has shaped Oz in her mind and shows that she facilitates the personal quests of each of her friends. This Dorothy is a true ally.

Just as "Over the Rainbow" intersects with the real-life traumas of Judy Garland's adulthood, it also connects with the initial sense of hope and wonder Dorothy feels as she arrives in Munchkinland. Indeed, Dorothy's journey with her companions evolves as they move through the kingdom so that they encounter different challenges, sadness, and danger. However, they remain resilient together, finally realizing that each had the qualities they sought to find within themselves all along. The lack of articulated romance in the film, and therefore the insularity of this spiritual journey, is similarly significant to *The Wizard of Oz*'s place in queer reception. Not only does *Oz* provide a (limited) utopian ideology that suggests it is possible to belong, whoever you may be, but it also demonstrates that the journey of self-actualization of Dorothy and her companions is both individual and internal. In this way, the film frames a positive and hopeful message that is dissociated with "everyday" normativity. Furthermore, the complexity of this Dorothy and her open attitudes to newness, or even otherness, provide a simple but pointed image, which can be read as a vital expression of identity. As such, queer reception to MGM's *The Wizard of Oz* takes ownership of many of the film's central themes but also evolves its legacy, imbuing songs, characters, expressions, and even set and costume designs with meaning beyond the context of the original release. In facilitating the dreams of generations of audiences, *The Wizard of Oz* characterizes friendship, acceptance, and ultimately equality for those who wish to find it.

Notes

1. L. Frank Baum, *The Wizard of Oz* (Bungay, Suffolk: Armada, 1975), 9.
2. Baum, *The Wizard of Oz*, 9.
3. Milk was one of the first openly gay men to be elected to office in the United States. In 1977, he was appointed to the San Francisco Board of Supervisors in 1977 but was tragically assassinated within a year of taking his post. Milk campaigned for LGBT+ rights in a range of contexts including by standing in opposition to legislation that might have facilitated the dismissal of gay teachers from Californian public schools. Milk's status as a noted gay activist and the emergence of the Rainbow flag in the period after his death are easily linked with the idea of seeking acceptance as characterized in the imagery of the lyrics to "Over the Rainbow."
4. In addition to its use as an anthem at numerous pride celebrations, "Over the Rainbow" has been performed in numerous contexts as an emblem of hope and defiance against different types of trouble. For example, in June 2017, pop artist Arianna Grande closed her One Love Manchester benefit concert with a performance of "Over the Rainbow" (which she had previously covered) following a terrorist attack during one of her concerts in Manchester.
5. Mark Graham, "Follow the Yellow Brick Road: An Anthropological Outing in Queer Space," *Ethos* 63 (2010): 102–132, accessed August 14, 2017, doi: 10.1080/00141844.1998.9981566, 123.
6. Randy Shilts, *Conduct Unbecoming—Gays and Lesbians in the U.S. Military* (New York: St. Martin's Griffin, 1994).
7. Griffin Benshoff, *Queer Images: A History of Gay and Lesbian Film in America* (Lanham, MD: Rowman & Littlefield, 2006), 101.
8. Steven Cohan, *Incongruous Entertainment: Camp, Cultural Value, and the MGM Musical* (Durham, NC: Duke University Press, 2005), 4.
9. Cohan, *Incongruous Entertainment*, 4.

10. Tison Pugh, "'There Lived in the Land of Oz Two Queerly Made Men': Queer Utopianism and Antisocial Eroticism in L. Frank Baum's Oz Series," *Marvels & Tales* 22 (2008): 217–239, 21, http://www.jstor.org.sheffield.idm.oclc.org/stable/41388876.

11. Suzanne Rahn, *The Wizard of Oz—Shaping an Imaginary World* (New York: Twain, 1998), 111.

12. Mark Graham, "Follow the Yellow Brick Road," 102.

13. Baum, *The Wizard of Oz*, 5–6.

14. Noel Langley, Florence Ryerson, Edgar Allan Woolf, L. Frank Baum, and Michael Patrick Hearn, *The Wizard of Oz* [screenplay] (London: Faber & Faber, 2001), 8.

15. For example, Harvey R. Greenberg, "*The Wizard of Oz*—Little Girl Lost—And Found," in *The Movies on Your Mind* (New York: Saturday Review Press, 1975), 18; Alexander Doty, "'My Beautiful Wickedness': *The Wizard of Oz* as Lesbian Fantasy," in *Flaming Classics: Queering the Canon* (New York: Routledge, 2000), 59.

16. Raymond Knapp, *The American Musical and the Performance of Personal Identity* (Princeton, NJ: Princeton University Press, 2006), 133.

17. Langley et al., *The Wizard of Oz* [screenplay], 9.

18. The audio recording of the reprise is available on the extended film soundtrack. Garland sounds sincerely and profoundly distressed as she performs the new lyrics: "Someday, I'll wake and rub my eyes / And in that land beyond the skies / You'll find me."

19. Cohan, *Incongruous Entertainment*, 319.

20. Knapp, *The American Musical and the Performance of Personal Identity*, 140.

21. Knapp, *The American Musical and the Performance of Personal Identity*, 140.

22. Aljean Harmetz, *The Making of The Wizard of Oz* (New York: Delta, 1989), 27–28.

23. Langley et al., *The Wizard of Oz* [screenplay], 23.

24. Baum, *The Wizard of Oz*, 9.

25. Salman Rushdie, *The Wizard of Oz* (London: British Film Institute, 1992), 22.

26. Rushdie, *The Wizard of Oz*, 21–22.

27. Rushdie, *The Wizard of Oz*, 21–22.

28. Knapp, *The American Musical and the Performance of Personal Identity*, 134.

29. Graham, "Follow the Yellow Brick Road," 105.

30. Dorothy tells Glinda "Oh I'd do anything to get out of Oz altogether" when Glinda says she had better leave to escape the Wicked Witch. Langley et al., *The Wizard of Oz* [screenplay], 34.

31. Rushdie, *The Wizard of Oz*, 23.

32. Langley et al., *The Wizard of Oz* [screenplay], 109.

33. Benshoff, *Queer Images*, 67.

34. The Tin Woodman is cursed by the Wicked Witch of the East to prevent the marriage. L. Frank Baum, *The Wizard of Oz*, 32–33.

35. Rushdie, *The Wizard of Oz*, 27.

36. Please see Pugh's article for a rich discussion of this aspect of Baum's novels. Tison Pugh, "'There Lived in the Land of Oz Two Queerly Made Men': Queer Utopianism and Antisocial Eroticism in L. Frank Baum's Oz Series."

37. Mark Graham, "Follow the Yellow Brick Road," 108.

38. Benshoff, *Queer Images*, 68.

39. Rushdie, *The Wizard of Oz*, 42.

40. Benshoff, *Queer Images*, 9.

41. Benshoff, *Queer Images*, 68.

42. Doty, "'My Beautiful Wickedness,'" 50.

43. Doty, "'My Beautiful Wickedness,'" 50.

44. Doty, "'My Beautiful Wickedness,'" 50.

45. Graham, "Follow the Yellow Brick Road," 102.

46. Graham, "Follow the Yellow Brick Road," 103.

47. These quotes are derived from the lyrics of "If I Only Had a Heart." Langley et al., *The Wizard of Oz* [screenplay], 47.

48. Knapp, *The American Musical and the Performance of Personal Identity*, 133.

49. Knapp, *The American Musical and the Performance of Personal Identity*, 133.

50. Doty, "'My Beautiful Wickedness,'" 50.

51. *Buffy* included considerable layers of coding, metaphor and references to other popular culture of which *The Wizard of Oz* formed a small part.

52. Knapp, *The American Musical and the Performance of Personal Identity*, 245.

8 "WE'RE NOT IN KANSAS ANY MORE"

THREE STAGE ADAPTATIONS OF THE MGM FILM

Dominic McHugh

After the success of MGM's *The Wizard of Oz* (1939), it was perhaps inevitable that the material would be further exploited in the form of a stage adaptation, although stage musicals based on films were not yet common in the early 1940s. Yet there were numerous problems. The contrasting nature of the two media and the impact of having put this particular story on the screen to such spectacular effect meant that simply transferring the film's screenplay and score to the stage would be difficult. There was also the question of length and format: stage musicals tend to be longer than films, and a two-act form needed to be created to incorporate an intermission. As Jonas Westover explained in Chapter 1, Baum himself had made drastic changes to the book for the very first Oz stage show in 1902, acknowledging that his evocative prose needed to be replaced by new characters, dialogue, and plot points in a theatrical version. To do a new adaptation of the movie—itself an adaptation of another source—was even more difficult.

Some aspects of the film could never be realized like-for-like on the stage. The twister, for example, was such a cinematic moment that a stage version could never quite match it. The impact of moving from black and white in the Kansas sequence to color on Dorothy's arrival in Oz was particular to film. The sheer scale of some of the movie sets would never be the same in a stage version. Another challenge was to re-create the star power of the movie's cast: Judy Garland, Ray Bolger, Jack Haley, Bert Lahr, and Margaret Hamilton each contributed in personal ways to the film's magic, and to give lesser actors the same lines and songs could be underwhelming. The reconception of the casting of the Munchkins also needed careful and sensitive thought. There were other problems too. For one, there are not nearly as many musical numbers in the movie as is conventional in a stage musical—the last third of the film has little music, due to the excision of "The Jitterbug" and the reprises of "Over the Rainbow" and "Ding-Dong! The Witch Is Dead." Also, the film had made some drastic changes to Baum's book, notably the film's implication that Dorothy's adventures in Oz were all a dream (Baum makes it clear that she actually visits Oz). Should such changes be retained in a stage version, especially when fantasy is generally considered to be more acceptable on the stage than in the more realistic medium of film?

In this chapter, I consider three distinct attempts to adapt the MGM movie into a stage musical: the St. Louis Municipal Opera adaptation (the "Muny" version) from 1942, adapted by Frank Gabrielson; the Royal Shakespeare Company (RSC) version of 1987, adapted by John Kane; and the Andrew Lloyd Webber version of 2011, adapted by Lloyd Webber and Jeremy Sams. Each had a different philosophy and approach to adaptation; each used most of the songs from the movie; each was commercially successful; and none was nearly as successful as the movie. My discussion examines topics such as the treatment of the story and screenplay, the adaptation of the score, issues of staging and casting, and the overall success and reception of each adaptation. What emerges is not only an important aspect of the reception of *The Wizard of Oz* after the MGM film but also a useful case study of the nature of adapting a musical from the screen to the stage.

Devising Three Adaptations

The earliest stage adaptation that used material from the movie was created by Frank Gabrielson in 1942 for the St. Louis Municipal Opera (the Muny). America's largest and oldest outdoor theater, the Muny was founded in 1919 and has presented an annual summer season in its large arena (of over 10,000 seats) ever since. For his version of *Oz*, Gabrielson created a completely new script—presumably the rights to MGM's screenplay were unavailable, or perhaps no attempt was made to acquire such a cinematic property—and worked many of the movie's songs into it. Yet even a cursory glance at his new book reveals a completely different approach to the presentation of the story. The opening scene in Kansas is a good example of the change of emphasis. Toto is gone, which not only means that Dorothy has no companion throughout her journey but more importantly that there is no conflict to act as a catalyst for her desire to escape her current, mundane life: Miss Gulch is removed, as are two of the three farmhands and Professor Marvel, so the nuances of the various threats in Kansas (Gulch's capture of Toto, Dorothy's fall in the pig pen, Marvel's mysteriousness) are all removed. Instead, Gabrielson's opening scene jumps straight to the impending twister, with Aunt Em looking for Dorothy so that she can find safety in the storm cellar. When Dorothy returns to the house to collect flowers she has gathered for Uncle Henry's birthday, she is caught in the cyclone and carried to Oz.

Self-evidently, the story is simplified in Gabrielson's retelling, which dispenses with the details in favor of eight basic scenes (five in Act 1, three in Act 2). This renders the musical easier to stage, and the intimacy of the screenplay, with its vibrant depiction of Dorothy's intense inner life and imagination, is replaced by stock dialogue to move the characters from one situation to the next as economically as possible. The dialogue revolves entirely around the musical numbers, which are expanded in several cases to become the centerpieces of the new musical comedy-style scenes. For example, Dorothy's "Over the Rainbow" is followed immediately by a choral arrangement of the refrain for the villagers and farmhands, cashing in on the impact of the theatrical presentation of a popular song at the expense of dramatic nuance.

A particular shift in style is the depiction of the Witches. Glinda is now called the Sorceress of the North, and when she is introduced to Dorothy she does not identify herself as a witch. This seems to be so that she can be distanced from the pantomimic exaggerations of the characterization of the Witch of the West: because Miss Gulch is trimmed from the story, the Witch of the West is a more conventional creation rather than a figment of Dorothy's anxious psyche, rendering it necessary to recategorize Glinda as a beneficent sorceress. When the Wicked Witch arrives, the script notes: "She is a regular old-fashioned, Halloween style witch, broomstick and all. She laughs evilly."[1] In a new scene, the Witch casts a spell over a bridge that Dorothy and the Scarecrow are trying to cross on their journey (Act 1, Scene 3). Every time they try to cross, the bridge revolves and takes them back to where they started. After a few attempts, they manage to outsmart the Witch, who leaves in disgust (1-3-33). The scene is incredibly tame compared to anything that happens in the film—the friends are scarcely in any peril, they're merely inconvenienced—and it is clear that this is a light-hearted family spectacle rather than the kind of psychological drama provided by the MGM film.[2]

Gabrielson's numerous other alterations to the story include the omission of the ruby slippers—the ownership of which is the focus of so much dramatic tension in the film—leading to a new denouement in which the Wizard takes Dorothy home to Kansas in his rocket ship; the creation of the Jitterbugs scene, which presents a new stumbling block on the friends' journey to Oz; some pantomime business involving the Ozian Army at the start of Act 2; and the new characters of Lord Growlie and his daughter Gloria, who lead "The Merry Old Land of Oz" and advise Dorothy and her companions on what to expect from the Wizard. The Witches' Castle sequence is played for laughs rather than providing genuine darkness in the story. For example, the Witch plays host to two Visiting

Witches around a cauldron, from which she offers them a cup of babies' blood or a bat's wing.[3] The Witches also have a dance number and the climax of the scene is a comedy chase, at the height of which the Witch of the West is dropped into her own cauldron by Dorothy, Lion, Tinman, and Scarecrow; in this version, there are no ruby slippers to acquire so the Witch is simply aiming to destroy Dorothy, and Dorothy does not cause her to melt.

Conflict and danger are averted in the Muny version, and the softening of the presence of peril weakens the depth of the story. Nevertheless, it became a favorite stage show in America and beyond, and the simplicity of the structure meant it could be easily adapted to new circumstances. For instance, the published script and score (which derive from a British production in the 1940s) reflect an English perspective (the Witch's assistance, Tibia, speaks in a manner that is described as "very 'Jeeves'"), while at least one production in Denver in the 1940s added "Someday My Prince Will Come" from Disney's *Snow White*. The rental version also contains some small differences in the dialogue, incidental music, and dance music compared to the British published version, but the structure and overall content is common to both, illustrating again how flexible Gabrielson's vision was. Tams-Witmark, the company that hires out the show, describes the Muny version as "theatrically conservative," explaining that it "employs its stage, actors, singers, dancers and musicians in traditional ways."[4] Though it takes material from the film, it imposes pantomime conventions on the story and score to create what Tams-Witmark generously calls "a classic stage musical." (The website is wrong, however, in stating that Baum's book was the primary source for Gabrielson's script.)

The Muny version regularly returned to its original venue over the next four decades. But in the mid-1980s, the Royal Shakespeare Company decided to commission a brand new version, as its adapter John Kane explains:

> When Terry Hands, Director of the Royal Shakespeare Company approached Ian Judge with a view to creating a new Musical for the Barbican Theatre, there was no hesitation. It had to be the Wizard of Oz but the starting point for the adaptation had to be the version created by MGM in 1939. Apart from a magnificent score by Harburg and Arlen, the basic novel by Frank L. Baum [*sic*] was filtered through the creative sieve of at least ten top screenwriters before it reached the screen. The result is a dramatic structure which could hardly be bettered.
>
> As a result adapting the film for the stage was one of the easiest and happiest jobs I've ever done. Whenever a scene needed to be enlarged or elaborated, we returned to the original book and always found material that fitted perfectly, (which again demonstrates how true the original screenwriters had been to the spirit of Frank L. Baum).[5]

The RSC version aimed to put the movie on the stage more directly than the Muny version had. It kept the score intact, including a lot of Stothart's work on the underscore, and, like the Muny version, added "The Jitterbug" (discussed in more detail below). This new version was marketed as a "faithful" adaptation, and it certainly diverged from the Muny rendition in treating the material "straight and without parody," as a promotional article at the time of the RSC premiere revealed. The production's Dorothy, Imelda Staunton, similarly commented: "It's not worth doing if you're going to send it up."[6]

Yet neither Kane's adaptation nor director Ian Judge's production was a simple transcription of the film. Quite the reverse, in fact. Judge was clear: "Our catastrophe would be to go about the movie and try and repeat everything as it was onstage." He added that the screenplay had been expanded: "We've just fattened it out a little bit because you need a few more words in the theater than you need in the movies."[7] A good example of this is the opening scene, which—in stark contrast to the Muny version—not only retains nearly every word from the movie (though the pig sty moment, impractical in a stage version, is cut) but also adds several extra lines. When Aunt Em offers the farmhands some cookies (changed from crullers in the movie), she adds: "You don't have to sit down to eat them."[8] This makes her slightly more brusque even than in the movie. Kane's version also gives her a line, "A farm's no place for fun. You want fun, go join a circus," which further increases her austere attitude. Yet this strength of character becomes more effective in the encounter with Miss Gulch, when Aunt Em has extra lines in which she offers Miss Gulch cookies to try to calm her down, reassures Miss Gulch that Dorothy will be glad to apologize in any way she can, and emphasizes how sorry Dorothy is. She sticks up for her niece in a way that is not the case in the movie's more passive characterization of Aunt Em, an example of Kane's making an enhancement through a subtle shift of focus in his adaptation.

In another respect, the RSC version was completely unfaithful to the movie. Though the script and score were familiar, the production itself offered a completely fresh experience, as is apparent from the photographs in the booklet accompanying the CD release, as well as several clips on YouTube.com. For example, the "Poppies" scene was staged in the style of a Ziegfeld Follies or Busby Berkeley production number, with extrovert stylized choreography performed on a revolving stage, creating a suitably rousing end to the first act.[9] Mark Thompson's Olivier Award–nominated set and costume designs nodded to the movie by using monochrome in the Kansas scenes and full color in Oz, but on the whole he created an entirely new visual world, including edgier, contemporary costumes that were sometimes closer in style to *The Wiz* (or even *Starlight Express*) than the MGM *Wizard of Oz*. Another significant change was that the Witch was played by a man in drag. In other words, the RSC version retained the underlying strengths of the film—the score and script—but devised a completely new visual conceptualization (which was employed almost as an interpretative lens). This meant that it could function as an entity distinct from the film rather than becoming a pale imitation of it.

Kane's adaptation was so convincing that it quickly became the standard rental version (though the Muny version also remains available); it satisfied people's expectations from the movie but also offered a new experience. Yet twenty years on, a new attempt was made to adapt the movie for the stage. In 2010, Andrew Lloyd Webber, by far the most commercially successful composer in the history of musical theater, decided to mount a new production of *The Wizard of Oz*. One impetus for the production was to provide the focus of his latest reality TV project, following on from BBC series devoted to casting the lead roles in revivals of *The Sound of Music* (2006), *Joseph and His Amazing Technicolor Dreamcoat* (2007) and *Oliver!* (2008). Yet Lloyd Webber also decided to revisit and revise the material rather than remounting the RSC version, and he acted both as co-adapter (with director Jeremy Sams) and as composer for a group of new songs to expand the score. As well as casting Dorothy via a television series in which viewers could vote for their favorite actress to play the role, Lloyd Webber chose Michael Crawford, who originated the title role in his greatest hit *The Phantom of the Opera* (1986) as well as Count Fosco in *The Woman in White* (2004), to star as Marvel/Wizard. Lloyd Webber spoke extensively about his approach to the adaptation of *Oz* and the general challenges of the project:

> Around 1996 I bought an option to produce *A Star is Born* on stage and I got as far as doing a workshop of it. But a stage musical is totally different to a movie. For a start, *A Star is Born* does not have enough songs for a stage show, hence the problem with stage versions of *The Wizard of Oz* so far. There is nothing in the movie for Professor Marvel/The Wizard, The Wicked Witch, or anything to set up Dorothy and her background in Kansas.
>
> So when the opportunity came for me to produce a new version of *Oz* on stage I said I could only do it if I was allowed by the rights holders to try and fill in the gaps.
>
> *Oz* contains some of the greatest songs ever written including, some say, the greatest song ever written. So I have tried to be a servant of Harold Arlen and E. Y. Harburg and have only added what I guess they might have done if they were to compose *Oz* for the theatre.[10]

Lloyd Webber's comments neatly summarize his approach: he acknowledges the quality of the raw material but also recognizes the dilemma of storytelling in a stage musical versus a film musical. He also tried to face the difficulties of any audience's strong expectations of such a production, based on the enduring popularity of the movie.

Among the safer aspects of the Lloyd Webber production were Robert Jones's costume designs, which were much more traditional than Thompson's for the RSC production. For example, the Witch looked much more (if not wholly) like her MGM counterpart, thereby satisfying expectations from the movie. Jones's set designs also brought a cinematic style to the production—photographs of the Kansas scene in the booklet accompanying the cast album depict a large brooding sky and gloomy farmyard—but the lengthy journey to Oz sequence was performed on a simple circular yellow brick road set that was arguably too gaudy and colorful to indicate the vicissitudes of the four friends' adventures. As with the Muny version, the Witch's sequence in Act 2 was the most altered part of the script (i.e., compared to the film), with an extended set piece depicting the character's jealousy and frustration about Dorothy (though it essentially operates as a broad tableau of stage evilness in the vein of a melodramatic Witches' Sabbath or Walpurgisnacht). Another change was the position of the interval (intermission): in the previous versions, the first act ends with the characters surviving their journey and preparing to enter the Emerald City in Act 2, but Lloyd Webber's version moved the interval to the moment when the Wizard sends the friends off to collect the broomstick of the Witch of the West, thus creating a new cliffhanger.

Adapting the Score

Of particular importance to the subject of this chapter is the use of music in the three versions. Although each has a completely different list of musical numbers, at the heart of all three is the collection of songs by Arlen and Harburg. Almost all of the movie's songs were retained in each case, with a few variations: it is as if the cultural impact of the movie renders the songs inseparable from the story since 1939. (Indeed, the Muny adaptation is almost more liberal with the story than with the score, as we have seen above.) All these versions include "Over the Rainbow," "If I Only Had a Brain/a Heart/the Nerve," "Munchkinland," "Ding-Dong! The Witch Is Dead," "We're Off to See the Wizard," and "The Merry Old Land of Oz"; the Muny and RSC versions use "The Jitterbug," cut from the movie; and the Lloyd Webber and RSC versions use "Optimistic Voices." This adoption of the Arlen-Harburg score seems to have been a natural consequence of the musical comedy style that many of the movie's original reviewers perceived (one reviewer had called the film "a Broadway spectacle").[11]

At the same time, common to all three, but particularly the Muny and Lloyd Webber versions, is a sense that the songs from the film would not be enough for a stage musical. The adaptation to another medium meant that expansion was inevitable. In light of this, it is curious that the Muny version does not include either "If I Were King of the Forest" or "Optimistic Voices," both of which would have helped to beef up the score, but other additions were made. Indeed, the Muny adaptation itself has a number of different versions in which certain numbers were varied, replaced, or rearranged. Table 8.1 reveals two permutations of it: the rental version available from Tams-Witmark and the version published in London in 1964 (in italics). Although there are various differences between these, the basic structure is the same and the general treatment of the score is similar, with two particularly noticeable changes from the film.

First, "The Jitterbug" was repurposed and put back into the story: it was written for the movie as part of the sequence just before the Witch's castle in the latter half of the film but in the Muny version it becomes the climactic number of Act 1. The jazziness of the song facilitates a lively scenario in which Dorothy and her friends sing in close harmonies and are then attacked by the Jitterbugs during a dance sequence. Second, a new ballad was added for Dorothy in the second act: "Evening Star" by Mitchell Parish and Peter de Rose. This gave the female lead of the show a second big number to perform, satisfying musical theater conventions. (As noted above, in at least one production this was replaced by "Someday My Prince Will Come" from *Snow White*, further emphasizing the flexibility of the text.) Yet much of the music in the score is functional, covering entrances, exits, and scene changes, and numerous opportunities for dancing were added. For the rental version, some of the dance music is based on favorite classical works such as *Dance Macabre, Swan Lake*, and *The Sleeping Beauty*, while the published score (the London version) includes a "Skeleton Dance" by the British composer and conductor Ronald Hanmer, who worked on a number of British stage musicals (including a stage adaptation of *Calamity Jane*). As in the film, the second half has less music and focuses on wrapping up the plot, with only one song in the final stretch of Act 2 (the reprise of "Ding, Dong! The Witch Is Dead").

For his version, Andrew Lloyd Webber similarly approached the score as needing an expansion of the basic set of Harburg-Arlen songs, but in this case he decided to write the new songs himself (see Table 8.3). Joining forces with his celebrated collaborator Tim Rice, Lloyd Webber identified what he perceived to be the gaps in the score in terms of telling the story:

[W]e realized that there's a problem with it in the theatre as it stood—in that there are no songs for either of the witches, there's nothing at all for

Table 8.1. Musical Synopsis for the Muny Version

Act 1	Act 2
Overture [Orchestra]	March: Changing of the Guard
Opening Melos [Orchestra] [a]	[Orchestra]*
Over the Rainbow [Dorothy and	*Opening: Act 2, Military Parade [Orchestra]*
Chorus]	March [Orchestra]*
Cyclone [Orchestra]	*Exit of Army and Rumpus [Orchestra]*
Over the Rainbow – Scene Change	**The Merry Old Land of Oz** [Gloria]
[Orchestra]*[b]	*[1964 version: with Growlie and Chorus]*
Sorceress of the North [Orchestra]*	Funeral March of a Marionette [Dance for
Entrance of the Sorceress of the North	Scarecrow] [Orchestra]*
[Orchestra]	*Exit of Men [Orchestra]*
Opening Music [Orchestra]	**Evening Star**[d] [Dorothy] *[1964*
Munchkinland [Sorceress, Munchkins	*version: with Gloria and Girls Chorus]*
and Dorothy]	***Encore: Evening Star** [Dorothy, Gloria,*
Exit: Sorceress of the North	*and Girls]*
[Orchestra]*	Entrance: Wizard [Orchestra]*
Sorceress of the North Exit [Orchestra]	*Entrance of Wizard [Orchestra]*
Witch of the West Entrance [Orchestra]	Exit: Wizard [Orchestra*
If I Only Had a Brain [Scarecrow]	*End of Scene 5 [Orchestra]*
Reprise: Ding, Dong, the Witch Is	Wicked Witch Music [Orchestra]*
Dead**[c] **[Ensemble]	*The Witch's Castle [Orchestra]*
Opening: Second Interlude	*Witch's Castle Scene Change [Orchestra]*
Wicked Witch Music [Orchestra]*	Ghost Dance [Saint-Saens' *Danse*
Witch of the West Entrance	*Macabre*] [Orchestra]
Entrance of the Sorceress of the North	*Skeleton Dance [Music by Ronald Hanmer]*
Exit of Witch and Sorceress	**Ding, Dong, the Witch Is Dead**
Opening: Scene 3	[Dorothy, Tinman, Scarecrow, and
End of Scene 3	Lion]
If I Only Had a Heart [Tinman]	**Reprise: Ding, Dong, the Witch Is**
We're Off to See the Wizard	**Dead** [Dorothy, Tinman, Scarecrow,
[Dorothy, Tinman, Scarecrow,	and Lion]*
Munchkins]	Ballet: Change of Scene [Dance for
We're Off to See the Wizard	Sorceress] [from Tchaikovsky's *Swan*
[Dorothy, Tinman, Scarecrow]	*Lake*] [Orchestra]*
Scene Change Music	*Opening: Fourth Interlude [Orchestra]*
If I Only Had the Nerve [Lion]	**Reprise: Merry Old Land of Oz**
The Jitterbug [Dorothy, with Tinman,	*[Ensemble]*
Scarecrow, Lion]	Entrance of Wizard [Orchestra]*
	Second Entrance of Wizard [Orchestra]

(continued)

Table 8.1. Continued

Act 1	Act 2
Entrance: Sorceress of the North [Orchestra]	**Finale: Act 2** [Ensemble] *[1964 version has solo for Dorothy]*
Entrance of the Sorceress of the North, and Melos [Orchestra]	*Play Out [Orchestra]*
Reprise: Jitterbug – Dance [Orchestra]*	
Ballet [Tchaikovsky's *Sleeping Beauty Waltz*] [Orchestra]*	
Finale Act 1: **We're Off to See the Wizard** [Sorceress, Dorothy, Tinman, Scarecrow and Lion]	
Ballet, and Finale Act 1 [Orchestra and Ensemble]	

Source: Based on the rental vocal score. Numbers in bold are songs.

ᵃ Numbers in italics represent additional numbers found in the published vocal score from 1964 that are not in the current version.

ᵇ An asterisk indicates numbers in the current version that were not in the 1964 published score.

ᶜ In each stage version, the punctuation of this song is changed. These figures reproduce this difference and the main text also adopts them.

ᵈ In a 1947 Detroit production, "Someday My Prince Will Come" was added in place of "Evening Star." https://www.newspapers.com/newspage/98323302/, accessed July 12, 2017.

the Wizard, there's nothing for Glinda and Dorothy to close the thing up, and there's obviously a massive cut in the movie where there used to be the Jitterbug.[12]

His solution was to write "four-and-a-half new songs, but also quite a lot of new music throughout. For example, the tornado scene has been conceived for the theater—we can't really do what's in the movie, so I've come in and done some of the linking." He also explained: "One of the things that [director and co-adapter] Jeremy [Sams] and I felt very strongly about is that previously onstage—and, in a way, in the film—there's nothing that really sets up Kansas; you're suddenly into 'Over the Rainbow.' But Tim [Rice] is very good at storytelling, so we've taken the dialogue of the movie and written not an opening number but something that I think sets the scene and takes you to 'Over the Rainbow,' and does it quite concisely, and I think with a lot of wit as well."

Table 8.2. Musical Synopsis for the RSC Version

Act 1	Act 2
Overture [Orchestra with Girls Chorus]	Entr'acte and **Optimistic Voices**
Trouble in School – Dorothy's Entrance [Orchestra]	[Orchestra with Girls Chorus]
More Trouble – Scene Change [Scene Change]	Guard Entrance [Orchestra]
Over the Rainbow [Dorothy]	**The Merry Old Land of Oz** [Dorothy, Tinman, Scarecrow, Lion, Guard, and Ozians]
Miss Gulch – Scene Change [Orchestra]	**Reprise: The Merry Old Land of Oz**
Incidental – Scene Change [Orchestra]	[Dorothy, Tinman, Scarecrow, Lion, Guard, and Ozians]
The Cyclone [Orchestra]	Guard Exit
Munchkinland – Incidental [Orchestra with Girls Chorus]	**If I Were King of the Forest** [Lion with Dorothy, Tinman, and Scarecrow]
I Am Not a Witch – Incidental [Orchestra]	Guard Entrance [Orchestra]
Munchkinland Musical Sequence & Ding Dong! The Witch Is Dead [Glinda, Dorothy and Munchkins]	Guard Exit [Orchestra]
	At the Great Door to the Wizard's Chamber [Orchestra]
Incidental – Witch Appears [Orchestra]	Magic Smoke Chords [Orchestra]
Incidental [Orchestra]	Lion's Running Exit [Orchestra]
Incidental – Slippers [Orchestra]	Guard Entrance [Orchestra]
Incidental [Orchestra]	**March of the Winkies** [Winkies]
Incidental – Witch Disappears [Orchestra]	**Winkies Exit** [Winkies]
	Monkeys Exit [Orchestra]
Leaving Munchkinland – Underscore [Orchestra]	The Haunted Forest [Orchestra]
Yellow Brick Road [Munchkins]	**The Jitterbug** [Dorothy, Tinman, Scarecrow, Lion, and Jitterbugs]
Scarecrow Fall [Orchestra]	Reprise: Jitterbug [Jitterbugs]
If I Only Had a Brain [Scarecrow, Dorothy, and Crows]	The Witch's Castle – Scene Change [Orchestra]
We're Off to See the Wizard – Duet [Dorothy and Scarecrow]	Incidental – Toto's Escape [Orchestra]
Apple Throwing [Orchestra]	Incidental – Hour Glass [Orchestra]
Tinman/Trees – If I Only Had a Heart [Tinman, Dorothy, and Trees]	Reprise: Winkies March [Winkies]
	Winkies March with Friends & Reprise: Over the Rainbow [Dorothy, Tinman, Scarecrow, Lion, and Winkies]
Witch on Roof [Orchestra	
We're Off to See the Wizard – Trio [Dorothy, Tinman, and Scarecrow]	Incidental – Witch Returns [Orchestra]
	Witchmelt [Orchestra]

(continued)

Table 8.2. Continued

Act 1	Act 2
Lions, Tigers, and Bears [Dorothy, Tinman, and Scarecrow]	**Reprise: Ding Dong! The Witch Is Dead** [Winkies]
If I Only Had the Nerve [Lion with Dorothy, Tinman, and Scarecrow]	Magic Smoke Chords [optional number] [Orchestra]
We're Off to See the Wizard – Quartet [Dorothy, Tinman, Scarecrow, and Lion]	Graduation Exercise – Scarecrow [Orchestra]
	Graduation Exercise – Lion [Orchestra]
Poppies [Glinda, Dorothy, Tinman, Scarecrow, Lion, and Chorus]	Graduation Exercise – Tinman [Orchestra]
	Incidental – March [Orchestra]
	Balloon Descent [Orchestra]
	Balloon Ascension No. 1 [Orchestra]
	Incidental – Scene Change [Orchestra]
	Balloon Ascension No. 2 [Orchestra]
	Incidental – Scene Change [Orchestra]
	Incidental – Underscore [Orchestra]
	Finale Act Two [Orchestra]
	Bows and Playout Music [Orchestra]

Source: Based on the rental vocal score. Numbers in bold are songs.

Abandoning "If I Were King of the Forest" and declining to use "The Jittterbug," Lloyd Webber and Rice found new moments where the story could be told through song. In a way, they were reflecting contemporary taste (and Broadway practice); through-sung scores are more common and there tends to be less dialogue in new musicals. The first scene now featured an establishing number in which Dorothy sings of how she does not fit in with her surroundings: "Nobody Understands Me." The song is in alternating sections of 12/8 and 4/4 time and Dorothy's sections feature extensive use of open fifths, reflecting not only the mid-West locale but also Dorothy's hollow existence. This number then sets up "Over the Rainbow," her "I want" song—a demonstration of how the Lloyd Webber-Rice score extends the Arlen-Harburg original. Their next contribution also came early in the show. The Professor Marvel/Wizard duality is important to the Lloyd Webber/Sams version and this character was to be played by a recognizable star (Michael Crawford), so theater convention dictated that he needed to be given several songs. As Marvel, he was allocated a patter song (picking up on the wordplay of Harburg's originals), "Wonders of the World," in

Table 8.3. Musical Synopsis for the Lloyd Webber Version

Act 1	Act 2
Overture [Orchestra and Ensemble]	Entr'acte [Orchestra]
Nobody Understands Me [Dorothy, Aunt Em, Uncle Henry, Hunk, Hickory, Zeke, and Miss Gulch]*a	**The Haunted Forest: We Went to See the Wizard** [Dorothy, Scarecrow, Tin Man, and Lion]*
Over the Rainbow [Dorothy]	**March of the Winkies** [Ensemble]
The Wonders of the World [Professor Marvel]*	**Red Shoes Blues**b [Wicked Witch of the West and Winkies]*
The Twister [Orchestra]*	Bacchanalia [Orchestra]*
Arrival in Munchkinland [Orchestra]	**Red Shoes Blues: reprise** [Witch]*
Munchkinland/Ding-Dong! The Witch Is Dead [Glinda, Dorothy, and Munchkins]	**Over the Rainbow: reprise** [Dorothy]**c
Follow the Yellow Brick Road [Glinda, Dorothy, and Munchkins]	**If We Only Had a Plan** [Lion, Tin Man, and Scarecrow]*
If I Only Had a Brain [Scarecrow and Dorothy]	**March of the Winkies: reprise** [Ensemble, Tin Man, Scarecrow, and Lion]
We're Off to See the Wizard [Dorothy and Scarecrow]	**The Rescue** [Orchestra]*
If I Only Had a Heart [Tin Man]	**Hail-Hail! The Witch Is Dead**** [Ensemble]
We're Off to See the Wizard [Dorothy, Tin Man, and Scarecrow]	**You Went to See the Wizard** [Wizard]
If I Only Had the Nerve [Lion]	Farewell to Oz [Wizard]*
We're Off to See the Wizard [Dorothy, Tin Man, Scarecrow, and Lion]	**Already Home** [Glinda, Dorothy, and Ensemble]*
We're Outta the Woods [Optimistic Voices] [Dorothy, Lion, Scarecrow, Tin Man, and Ensemble]	**Finale** [Dorothy and Company]
The Merry Old Land of Oz [Ensemble]	
Bring Me the Broomstick [Wizard]*	

Source: Based on the program, cast album, and www.timrice.co.uk/wizs.html. Numbers in bold are songs.

a An asterisk indicates a new number written for this version.

b Originally called "Red Shoes Waltz."

c Two asterisks indicate material cut from the original movie but added into this version.

which he explains to Dorothy that she does not need to leave Kansas to see "the unabridged assembled wonders of the world."

Lloyd Webber also provided new music for the twister, but the next part of the score was left roughly intact, reflecting Arlen and Harburg's tight sequence of musical storytelling with "Come Out, Come Out," "Munchkinland," and "Ding-Dong! The Witch Is Dead" upon Dorothy's arrival in Oz; the Munchkins' instruction to "Follow the Yellow Brick Road"; and Dorothy's discovery of her new friends with "If I Only Had a Brain/a Heart/the Nerve," each of which was followed by "We're Off to See the Wizard." The "Optimistic Voices" number was also retained though retitled "We're Outta the Woods," and "The Merry Old Land of Oz" was also kept intact. However, to create a more traditional musical theater cliffhanger-style Act 1 finale, Lloyd Webber and Rice wrote a new number for the Wizard, in which he instructs Dorothy and her friends to "Bring Me the Broomstick of the Witch of the West." As the curtain falls, the fate of the four principal characters is left unknown.

As previously noted, the second act was an obvious challenge in adapting the film for the stage due to the lack of songs in the second half of the film, partly because MGM had cut so many numbers late in production. Therefore, just as the Muny version added "Evening Star," Lloyd Webber and Rice created several pieces of new material for Act 2. The centerpiece became "Red Shoes Blues," a waltz number in which the Witch of the West sings of how she wants to overcome Dorothy and take control of the ruby slippers. A big production number ensues, with a "Bacchanalia" in the middle in which Dorothy and her friends lose control and collapse on the ground; this takes the same function as "The Jitterbug" in the Muny version. Here, Lloyd Webber intervenes in a much more dominating way in the general style of the score, and the decision to reject a jazz-based Arlen song for Dorothy in favor of a new, musical theater–style song for the Witch (thereby giving her more status and stage time) is an interesting gesture of adaptation. Lloyd Webber and Rice also created a new eleven o'clock number, the ballad "Already Home," again applying Broadway convention as a tool of adaptation. Elsewhere in the second act, Rice provides new lyrics for several reprises of Arlen-Harburg songs: "If We Only Had a Plan," "We Went to See the Wizard," and "You Went to See the Wizard." Versions of "Over the Rainbow" and "Hail-Hail! The Witch Is Dead" that were cut from the movie were also used. In this way, a balance is maintained between the familiar and the new, which sums up the approach to adaptation in this version of the show: it goes far beyond the Muny version in adding new material and sets up a new dynamic because of the stature of the new composer and lyricist, but the movie's score is still at the heart of the property.

The RSC version approached the score with an entirely different philosophy. Though the physical production was fresh and new, the score adhered closely to the movie, including retaining much of Stothart's memorable underscoring. This time, all the songs from the film were incorporated, including "Optimistic Voices" and "If I Were King of the Forest," and to round off the second act, "The Jitterbug" was reinstated along with the cut reprises of "Over the Rainbow" and "Ding-Dong! The Witch Is Dead" from the movie that Lloyd Webber's version would later use. Nonetheless, the end of the Oz scene and the denouement in Kansas are both devoid of song in the RSC version. As is clear from Table 8.2, there were numerous musical cues and fragments, many of which were adapted by orchestrator Larry Wilcox and dance and vocal arranger Peter Howard from Stothart's work, helping to give the impression of putting the film on the stage, complete with underscore; Fiona Ford has written usefully about the potent psychological impact of the nonsong musical moments in the film and it applies equally to the RSC's stage adaptation.[13] Although there are dozens of musical differences in terms of figures, instrumentation, and the deployment of vocal lines, plus the additions mentioned above, the approach to adapting the score in the RSC version was to give the *impression* of being faithful, in contrast to the looseness of the score of the Muny version that preceded it. In turn, Lloyd Webber's approach was to promote the creativity of his version, choosing to explain how he "fixed" the musical by filling in the gaps in the story through song.

The Stage Adaptations in Performance

While the 1939 movie has continued to endure over the years, the fates of the three stage adaptations of it have varied. The Muny production was first seen in 1942 and was revived there in 1946, 1951, 1957, 1962, 1968, and 1975.[14] Of note, Margaret Hamilton appeared in her original role of the Wicked Witch from the movie in the 1957, 1962, and 1975 revivals.[15] The 1975 production featured the rock group, the Hudson Brothers, as Dorothy's three friends. An article at the time of the opening of that revival noted:

> The Hudson Brothers don't pretend to be the coward lion Bert Lahr or scarecrow Ray Bolger or tinman Jack Haley. . . . "Who could go out there and be Ray Bolger?" asked Mark Hudson, who has portrayed the fearful lion in a theatre production of the beloved story to near-capacity audiences. . . . "We've got to be us," said Mark with the nodding approval of brothers Brett, the scarecrow, and Bill, the tinman, all experienced rock performers doing theatre for the first time. Being "us" means ad-libbing in their roles, says Bill, often to the chagrin of the producers and director. It means such antics as Mark imitating the MGM lion when the Wicked Witch of the West sees them and Dorothy in her crystal ball. Or scarecrow

Brett quipping "It's three o'clock" when tapping Bill's tin chest to see if he has a heart.[16]

It is obvious from these comments that little care and attention was paid to the presentation of the story in this production—a natural consequence of the loose nature of the Muny version, which invites a liberal approach in performance.

Along similar lines, film historian John Fricke notes that the Muny's early productions encouraged star-led revivals across America:

As such, it was The Muny that started a major trend, as the box office potential of a stage OZ with MGM songs was quickly noted by many other major stock and regional theaters. From the 1950s into the 1980s, audiences elsewhere in the country enjoyed (or at least saw) such stars as Dorothy Collins (bravo!), Connie Stevens, Andrea McArdle, or Cathy Rigby as Dorothy; Buddy Ebsen (at last playing his originally assigned 1938 MGM role of The Scarecrow); Stubby Kaye as The Cowardly Lion; and Phyllis Diller or Nancy Kulp ("Miss Jane" Hathaway of THE BEVERLY HILLBILLIES) as The Wicked Witch.[17]

In other words, by the 1980s, *The Wizard of Oz* on stage meant a commercial, family-oriented experience led by familiar names (whether they were appropriate casting or not). The basic storytelling and light-hearted script allowed star performers to take roles in the show and use them as vehicles for their celebrity personas. The pantomime-style dialogue noted earlier in this chapter seems to have regularly encouraged performers to do what they wanted to, since all the delicacy of the movie was ignored in Garbrielson's broad adaptation for the large Muny auditorium.

No wonder the RSC production seemed so welcome when it opened in London in 1987. The time was right for a new approach, and the reviews were positive. For example, the *Times* remarked that it "is a show that is literate, logical, brimful of spirit and on several occasions brings wholesome tears to the eyes." In the *Evening Standard*, critic Milton Shulman reported: "This is as sure-fire, gilt-edged a hit as anything seen this year." Another critic, Gregory Jensen, wrote that the RSC's approach "not only has theatrical equivalents for movie magic but adds up to a subtle tribute to the whole tradition of the Hollywood musical," continuing:

Thus the castle of the Wicked Witch of the West becomes a stage-girdling, Busby Berkeley-style staircase—the witch simply melts into it when Dorothy flings the famous glass of water.

The movie's poppies and apple trees become chorus girls in spectacular headgear and Mae West sheath dresses. At the center of the Munchkins' charming toy town is a studio arch labelled "Munchkin Pictures."

The Munchkins themselves are children, not midgets—two dozen kids, some of them so tiny they make even Imelda Staunton's 5-foot-nothing Dorothy seem tall. . . .

In Mark Thompson's superb designs, this stage "Wizard" opens with a black and gray Kansas, like the movie's initial monochrome scenes.

But once Dorothy and Toto are whirled away by the twister—here a choreographed dance in dense clouds—a neon rainbow arches over the stage and each scene becomes splashed with a distinctive primary color.[18]

Jensen brings home perhaps the key reason the RSC production was so successful: its post-modern approach to the film. Without trying to literally reproduce the movie in its entirety, it embraced the need to *acknowledge* it in a stage adaptation rather than compete with it. Thus, everything in the RSC version was carefully chosen, presented, and styled: the familiar songs and dialogue were mostly carried over, but the staging often inverted what happens in the film by employing theatrical language instead (e.g., choreography rather than cinematic effects to represent the twister). Indeed, in most cases, the realistic language of the cinema was replaced by the symbolic and expressive language of the stage. The only way to take on such a layered cultural object as the movie *The Wizard of Oz* was to find equivalent but not identical techniques for a stage adaptation.

Yet the Lloyd Webber version took a third approach, one that was more narrative-focused than the Muny version and employed more musical theater conventions than the RSC version. It also brought a contemporary perspective on the property, for example, by adding new songs in order to be able to tell more of the story in song. But after the success of the RSC version, the bar had been raised high, and the critical reception of the Lloyd Webber version was quite mixed. For example, in the *Guardian*, Michael Billington wrote:

Although this adaptation of the Frank Baum book and the 1939 movie, with additional songs by Andrew Lloyd Webber and Tim Rice, is quite an eyeful, it's somewhat lacking in humanity. I came out feeling blitzkrieged rather than charmed. . . . [T]he story and the people get swamped. . . .

Of course, there are the songs; it's good to be reminded of such classics as Over The Rainbow, We're Off To See The Wizard, and Follow The Yellow Brick Road. The additions by Lloyd Webber and Rice are also perfectly acceptable. Dorothy is given a good plaintive opening number, and

Red Shoes Blues, sung by the Wicked Witch, has a pounding intensity. But, as a film scholar remarked to me, the movie was a story with songs rather than a full-blown musical. That delicate balance has been changed, and an essentially simple fable about the importance of individual worth seems overblown. . . .

[T]he paradox of the evening is that it suffers the same dilemma as the Tin Man: it might have been so much more if it only had a heart.[19]

Billington and other critics found this version "overblown," apparently feeling that so much had been added to the show—and so many resources had been used to stage it—that it had lost its heart. Nonetheless, some of the other critics were more positive (the *Independent* and *Evening Standard* both awarded it four stars out of five) and, like the RSC version, the production was nominated for an Olivier Award for Best Musical Revival. Having taken in more than £10 million before it opened[20] and run for more than 500 performances, the production was a commercial success (if not overwhelmingly so). It opened in Canada in December 2012, went on a North American tour from 2013 to 2014, and opened in Australia in late 2017.

Conclusion: Three Models for Adapting a Movie Musical Classic to the Stage

When Gabrielson made his adaptation of *The Wizard of Oz* in 1942, it was unusual to think of turning film musicals into stage shows. For that matter, there had not been a particularly large number of stage-to-screen adaptations by that point either, since the early days of Hollywood represented a rapid peak for original screen musicals (with notable examples including most of the Fred Astaire-Ginger Rogers series and the celebrated movies made by Busby Berkeley for Warner Bros). But more than seventy-five years later, the influence of the screen on the stage has never been more potent, and many of the major landmark film musicals have now been adapted to the stage, including *Meet Me in St. Louis, Singin' in the Rain, Calamity Jane, Gigi, Seven Brides for Seven Brothers, Top Hat, White Christmas, High Society, State Fair, 42nd Street, Mary Poppins, Victor/Victoria, Holiday Inn,* and *An American in Paris*. Indeed, the availability of these films on DVD/Blu-ray, coupled with frequent television screenings, has perhaps led to some of them being more commercially viable in stage incarnations today (because they are still well known) than many less-familiar shows written for the Broadway stage in the same era (i.e., the 1940s and 1950s) that were not turned into movies. Yet most of the stage versions of these films have struggled, including two short-lived attempts at a Broadway *Gigi* (1973 and 2015), an eight-month run of *Meet Me in St. Louis* (1989), a troubled stage rendition of *State Fair* (110 performances, 1996), and the 144-performance run of *High Society* on Broadway (1998).[21]

The Wizard of Oz was perhaps the first major property to pave the way for this trend of screen-to-stage musical adaptations, and its three principal adaptations have shown different ways of thinking about the subject. The Muny version, with its pantomime-esque style, focuses more on humor and the opportunity for star performances than it does on doing justice to MGM (and Baum); the Lloyd Webber version imposes musical theater conventions on the movie material and fleshes out the story, as well as adding a contemporary flavor with new songs; and the RSC version pays tribute to the movie by being faithful to its text but showing freedom in its presentation. There have been other permutations of these three versions too, for which there has been insufficient room for discussion in this chapter: the Lloyd Webber production was revised for the North American tour, simplifying the staging of the Yellow Brick Road, for instance; the RSC version was staged with more of the film's style in a 1988 production starring Cathy Rigby at the Long Beach Civic Light Opera; a lavishly cast TV version (produced for charity) called *The Wizard of Oz in Concert* was largely based on the RSC version, with pop singer Jewel as Dorothy and Broadway veteran Nathan Lane as the Lion; and a new, trimmed-down adaptation of the RSC version by the Paper Mill Playhouse was adopted by Madison Square Garden in New York for a popular production in 1997 (its revival the following year featured Eartha Kitt as the Witch and Mickey Rooney as the Wizard), which then toured America in 1998. The proliferation of stage adaptations serves as a reminder of how firmly established the *Oz* legend is in American culture, yet none of them has matched the impact of the film. It would take two completely new versions of the myth, *The Wiz* (see Chapter 9) and *Wicked* (see Chapter 10), both of which acknowledge but are firmly liberated from the movie, for *The Wizard of Oz* to become a truly successful property on the Broadway stage.

Notes

1. Muny script, 1-2-21. Available from Tams-Witmark Theater Library.
2. A British rendition of the Muny version was published (both script and vocal score). Although broadly similar to the American version, there are some extra speeches for the two Witches. The two have several encounters and in one of them, the British version notes that the Witch of the West "gives the speech the full Disney-Witch treatment." In a retort to the Sorceress's caution, she declares: "That 'mark-on-the-brow stuff is quite a good gimmick / But I've magic, too—even more pantomimic!" These additions emphasize the pantomime flavor of the Muny

version, an exaggeration that presumably suited the British audience for whom the genre is particularly familiar. Published script (1964), 36 and 75.

3. Published script (1964), 75.

4. "The Wizard of Oz," Tams-Witmark website, http://www.tamswitmark.com/shows/the-wizard-of-oz-muny-version/, accessed July 12, 2017.

5. John Kane, liner notes, *The Wizard of Oz* London Cast Recording, TER/Jay Productions (CDTER 1165).

6. Matt Wolf, "Royal Shakespeare Company to Have a Go at 'Wizard of Oz,'" *Los Angeles Times*, December 17, 1987, http://articles.latimes.com/1987-12-17/entertainment/ca-29444_1_wizard, accessed July 12, 2017.

7. Wolf, "Royal Shakespeare Company to Have a Go."

8. RSC rental script, 11. Available from Tams-Witmark Theatre Library.

9. The cast's performance on the Olivier Awards in 1988 is captured in the following YouTube video: https://www.youtube.com/watch?v=3gGF9-ZlIVg, accessed July 12, 2017.

10. Liner notes, CD release of the London Palladium production.

11. Aljean Harmetz, in *The Making of The Wizard of Oz* (Chicago: Chicago Review Press, 1977), emphasizes this aspect of the movie's early reception; for example, Harmetz quotes McCalls as calling it "not a fantasy but a Broadway musical comedy, unfortunately equipped with a score by Broadway musical comedy writers" (p. 22).

12. Mark Shenton, "Andrew Lloyd Webber Talks of 'Wizard of Oz, Evita, Love Never Dies,' His Health, His Next Show and More," Playbill.com, March 1, 2011, https://www.yahoo.com/news/andrew-lloyd-webber-talks-wizard-oz-evita-love-20110301-142957-477.html, accessed July 12, 2017.

13. Fiona Ford, "Be It [N]ever So Humble? The Narrating Voice in the Underscore of *The Wizard of Oz* (1939)," in *Melodramatic Voices: Understanding Music Drama*, edited by S. Hibberd (London: Ashgate, 2011), 197–214.

14. Subsequent revivals of the musical, in 1992, 1997, 2001, and 2006, appear to have used the RSC version.

15. John Fricke, "Meet Me in St. Lou-Oz! Another Op'nin! An Ozzy Show!," Oz Museum Blog, June 3, 2016, https://ozmuseum.com/blogs/news/118068036-meet-me-in-st-lou-oz-another-op-nin-an-ozzy-show, accessed August 29, 2017.

16. "Hudson Brothers talk of Wizard of Oz," *Manhattan Mercury*, August 17, 1975, 7, https://www.newspapers.com/newspage/11976789/, accessed August 29, 2017.

17. See https://ozmuseum.com/blogs/news/118068036-meet-me-in-st-lou-oz-another-op-nin-an-ozzy-show, accessed April 25, 2018.

18. This and the other quotations from reviews of the RSC production are from Gregory Jensen, "'Wizard' Stage Production Recaptures 'Wonderful,'" *UPI* archives, http://www.upi.com/Archives/1988/01/08/Wizard-stage-production-recaptures-wonderful/7342568616400/, accessed August 29, 2017.

19. Michael Billington, "*The Wizard of Oz*—Review," *Guardian*, March 2, 2011, https://www.theguardian.com/stage/2011/mar/02/the-wizard-of-oz-review. accessed August 29, 2017.

20. Lizzie Catt, Lisa Higgins, and Jack Teague, "Andrew Lloyd Webber and Sir Tim Rice: Creative Differences," *Express Online*, June 20, 2011, http://www.express. co.uk/dayandnight/251788/Andrew-Lloyd-Webber-and-Sir-Tim-Rice-Creative-differences, accessed August 29, 2017.

21. Admittedly, other productions of these musicals have fared better, including the 1987 London production of *High Society* that ran for 420 performances; my observation here is focused on Broadway productions, most of which have struggled to succeed. Many thanks to Geoffrey Block for his comments on this point and on the chapter as a whole.

9 "EASE ON DOWN THE ROAD"

BLACK ROUTES AND THE SOUL OF *THE WIZ*

Ryan Bunch

When *The Wiz* opened on Broadway in 1975, its manifest intention was to be an African American version of *The Wizard of Oz*. Subsequently, in both its stage and screen versions, it has become one of the most successful adaptations of the familiar story, as well as one of the most popular and culturally significant African American musicals. Although the film version of 1978 has been critically disparaged, it nonetheless acquired canonical status as a classic film musical in the African American community, and the stage show continues to be popular with regional, community, and school theaters. Of the recent series of live musicals broadcast annually on NBC, *The Wiz Live!* (2015) was second only to *The Sound of Music Live!* (2013) in its critical and popular success.[1]

Entering into a tradition of musical adaptions of *The Wizard of Oz* that performatively express American identity and community formation, *The Wiz* recasts both America and its most influential "fairy tale," to include the experiences of African Americans.[2] Whereas the famous MGM film is an agrarian myth of white America, emphasizing rootedness in a stable idea of home, *The Wiz* calls on the performance aesthetic and philosophy of soul to transform *The Wizard of Oz* into a contemporary story evoking the migratory history of African Americans. Because of this experience and its expression through the cultural practice of soul, the concept of home, while still of utmost importance in *The Wiz*, takes on a significance that is different from what it had in L. Frank Baum's book or the MGM film. Traveling along its own version of the Yellow Brick Road, *The Wiz* leads us to an understanding of home not merely as a place to which one returns but as a metaphor for self-understanding, soulfully confessed in song.

In this chapter, I look at the ways in which *The Wiz* celebrates a particular set of cultural representations of black difference and cohesion that defined soul in the 1970s. By taking account of the particulars of the performance text and the moment in which it was produced, I hope to mitigate what Guthrie Ramsey describes as the "appearance of reifying or 'essentializing' cultural expressions" in the study of black culture. In this way, we can see *The Wiz*'s performance of black America as both historically situated and intersectional with many categories of identity, including those of gender, age, sexuality, and class in different contexts over time.[3] To achieve a soul aesthetic, the creators of *The Wiz* revised the MGM film's songs and other elements in black terms, and as my analysis of documents relating to the musical's development and reception shows, those terms were influenced by the Black Arts, Black Theater, and Black Power movements. In addition, audiences and critics embraced or rejected the show based on their knowledge of black pride signifiers that were common in the 1970s and were expressed, among other ways, through styles of music related to soul. Prompted by the perspective of critics who saw allegories of slavery and migration in *The Wiz*, I will essay a close reading of the musical inspired by these responses while also attempting to keep that reading open to differing experiences. The Yellow Brick Road thereby becomes a metaphor for the geographical and temporal meanderings of the black migratory experience and its encounters, as Dorothy embarks on a journey to discover her own black soul.

Signifying on the Yellow Brick Road: Soul Music and *The Wiz*'s Black Difference

The original cast album promoted *The Wiz* as the "Super Soul Musical 'Wonderful Wizard of Oz.'"[4] As this tagline suggests, the essence of blackness in *The Wiz* was understood to be in its use of contemporary soul music. There is a relationship among soul, the migratory experience, and the concept of home as understood in *The Wiz*. The "souls of Black folks," to invoke W. E. B. Du Bois, have been a matter of some urgency in American culture and racial politics.[5] Questions about the existence and nature of black souls informed debates about slavery and the status of African Americans within Christianity, eventually influencing the formation of distinct African American churches, spiritual practices, and musical traditions. By the 1960s and 1970s, arising from the civil rights, Black Power, and Black Pride movements, soul became a powerful black pride signifier with special cultural currency. Soul food, soul music, and soulful ways of dressing, talking, and performing served as automatic markers of black cultural identity.[6]

To inject some soul into its version of *The Wizard of Oz, The Wiz* executes an elaborate act of signifying. As an African American expressive tradition, signifying may involve double-voiced or indirect cunning to outwit an opponent or to comment on dominant power structures. Examples include "signifying the dozens," in which competitors alternately insult each other (typically by insults to each other's mother) until one gives up, or the toasting tradition exemplified by the Signifying Monkey tales, in which the Monkey in some way tricks the Lion into insulting the Elephant, who summarily trounces the Lion. In each case, the repetition of the story pattern or of the form of the insult (your mama's so . . .) serves as a trope that may be repeated with variation. According to Henry Louis Gates Jr., signifying can also include the revision of white texts "'authentically,' with a Black difference . . . based on the Black vernacular" in order to comment simultaneously on black and dominant cultural realities.[7]

The Wizard of Oz, a mainstream text regarded as cultural myth of the United States, was readily available for this kind of revision.[8] The MGM film's depiction of both Dorothy's home in Kansas and the American fantasyland of Oz includes no people of color, and the music by Harold Arlen, with lyrics by Yip Harburg, reinforces this cultural whiteness by consisting largely of light-hearted songs (Arlen called them "lemon drop" numbers)[9] and Gilbert and Sullivan–inspired operetta pieces. When Dorothy embarks on her journey to seek the Wizard's help in returning home, the Munchkins urge her along the Yellow Brick Road in song, repeating the lyrical hook "Follow the Yellow Brick Road" on a musical phrase that "walks" up and down the first four notes of a major scale in straight rhythm and melodic direction. (Example 9.1). Then the song breaks into a bouncy jig in 6/8 time, typical of the folk traditions of Anglo-American song and dance, as Dorothy takes her first steps on the road. When she reaches the border of Munchkinland, the song transitions into "You're Off to See the Wizard," which is reprised at each leg of the journey to the Emerald City after Dorothy's encounters with the Scarecrow, Tin Man, and Cowardly Lion. Munchkin fiddlers play her off, scratching on the strings of their instruments in a manner evocative of a hoedown as she breaks into a skip-like dance down the road. Whether heard as European or Anglo-American, this music is coded white.

In *The Wiz,* Dorothy and her traveling companions are motivated down the Yellow Brick Road to the beat of a new song (Example 9.2). "Ease on Down the Road" exhibits textbook traits of black music. It opens assertively with an instrumental motive that appears to reconfigure the ascending and descending four-note

EXAMPLE 9.1. "Follow the Yellow Brick Road" from MGM's *The Wizard of Oz* (1939).

EXAMPLE 9.2. "Ease on Down the Road" from Universal's *The Wiz* (1978).

scale from MGM's "Follow the Yellow Brick Road," recasting it in the notes of a blues scale with flatted thirds and sevenths (B flat and F natural in the key of G), strong syncopation, and expressive changes of direction. This musical flourish serves as a clarion call to hit the road with a distinctly soulful attitude. The song's melody proper is composed predominantly on the notes of the pentatonic scale— a basis of black music from the traditional folk spirituals to the runs improvised by contemporary rhythm-and-blues (R&B) singers—with blue notes added for flavor (B flats again). The lyric similarly signifies on the MGM version. Whereas Judy Garland's Dorothy "follows" the Yellow Brick Road, the listener is here instructed to "ease on down"—a motion whose manifest coolness is emphasized by setting the word "ease" on the syncopated blue note at the beginning of the sung melody's first full measure.[10] All of this is supported by Motown-style backup vocals and a funky instrumental texture with a syncopated bass line, layered polyrhythms, and percussive effects characteristic of black popular music in the 1970s. As advertised, the essence of blackness in *The Wiz* lay in its use of soul music. The lyrical and musical composition of "Ease on Down the Road" seems to refer to, and deliberately revise, the analogous song from the MGM film. On a larger scale, *The Wiz* in its entirety is a signifying performance, using soul music to make a black commentary on a white text. Even the title of the show signifies on the original— *The Wizard of Oz* is revised to the shorter, hipper *The Wiz.*

Making the Super Soul Musical

The signifying strategies employed in *The Wiz* can further be understood in relation to the context and aesthetic values of the Afrocentric, Black Nationalist, and Black Arts movements of the 1960s and early 1970s, which influenced the show's collaborators. The initial idea for *The Wiz* came from black aspiring producer Ken Harper, a New York City radio station administrator who initially envisioned a series of adaptations of familiar stories, including *The Wizard of Oz*, for television, but eventually settled on the idea of making *The Wiz* into a Broadway musical instead.[11] Harper lacked theater credentials, but his letters to potential collaborators and investors reveal a man with remarkable ambition and audacity who solicited the assistance of some of the biggest names in the industry. In these correspondences, he described *The Wiz* as the newest entry in the recently emergent subgenre of the rock musical—one that would bring soul music to Broadway in the same way that shows like *Hair* (1968) and *Pippin* (1972) had introduced rock and pop styles. He expressed a consciously Afrocentric vision:

> We're going to do a new version of *The Wizard of Oz* with a contemporary score and an all-black cast. It will be fun, and it will be spectacular, with the music expressing every phase of the various rhythms associated with black culture, including West Indian, Afro-Cuban, blues, jazz, rock and even gospel.[12]

The soulful music and lyrics to fit this bill were composed by Charlie Smalls, a prodigious Juilliard graduate who had performed with Harry Belafonte and South African jazz musician Hugh Masakela, as well as with his own band in New York City nightclubs.[13] Initially, Harper had conceived of a score compiled from contributions by numerous songwriters in different styles, but in the end, Smalls emerged as essentially the sole composer of *The Wiz*'s score (only one song by another composer, Luther Vandross's "Everybody Rejoice/Brand New Day," discussed later, remained in the score). Smalls's resume hints at diverse African, Caribbean, Latin, and European influences, as does his appearance in an episode of the television program *The Monkees*, in which he explains to Davy Jones the differences among white, black, and Latin forms of soul.[14] The black musical traditions suggested by Smalls's songs received their final gloss from Harold Wheeler's orchestrations, which added rich instrumental timbres evocative of both Broadway and Motown. More than any other element of the show, Smalls's heartfelt songs, vibrantly performed by the actors, expressed the soulful philosophy at the core of *The Wiz*.

Librettist William F. Brown, the only white member of the creative team, supplied a script suffused with black vernacular dialogue:

> LION: Don't hit me no more!
> TINMAN: Will you dig that?
> LION: Don't you know you could hurt a person that way?
> SCARECROW: And you call yourself the king of the jungle?
> LION: You don't see no other cat begging for the gig, do you?[15]

This dialogue performs a celebratory style of black difference that would have been familiar to audiences from blaxploitation films and 1970s sitcoms like

Good Times (1974–1979) and *The Jeffersons* (1975–1985), whose first season was heavily advertised in the *Amsterdam News,* New York's popular black newspaper, alongside the reviews and commentaries on *The Wiz.* Although they were not big stars at the time, many of the cast members of *The Wiz* went on to appear in other iconic black musicals and television programs, suggesting their participation in a certain moment's optimism about the visibility of black life in popular culture.[16]

The stage production evinced a flair for visual, ritual pageantry and high-energy performances from the combination of Geoffrey Holder's direction and costume design, George Faison's choreography, and Gilbert Moses's direction in the early stages of production. Holder was initially slated to both direct and play the title character, but investors were concerned that his responsibilities would be spread too thin, so Holder's primary contribution for a time was the design of colorful costumes that evoked African mask art and the Carnival traditions of his native Trinidad, lending the show a pan-African flavor (Figure 9.1). Moses, who took over direction, had participated in the Black Theater Movement, having founded the Free Southern Theater (1963), directed Amiri Baraka's ritual pageant play *Slave Ship* (1967), and made his Broadway debut directing the black musical *Ain't Supposed to Die a Natural Death* (1971). During disastrous out-of-town tryouts, direction was given back to Holder, who received final credit for the job, but much of the work done under Moses remained in the show, including

FIGURE 9.1. Geoffrey Holder's costumes from the original Broadway production of *The Wiz* (1975). Photo by Martha Swope. ©Billy Rose Theatre Division, New York Public Library for the Performing Arts.

FIGURE 9.2. The Yellow Brick road from the touring production of *The Wiz* (1978). Photo by Martha Swope. ©Billy Rose Theatre Division, New York Public Library for the Performing Arts.

set designer Tom H. John's invention of a group of men in yellow tuxedoes, representing the Yellow Brick Road, who guided Dorothy and her companions along their journey (Figure 9.2).[17] Faison had danced with the Alvin Ailey American Dance Theater, and his choreography for *The Wiz* included such bold gestures as an elaborate tornado ballet featuring an enormous band of black fabric that emerged from a dancer's costume to swirl around the stage.

The appealing theatricality of the stage show was largely abandoned in the film version produced by Universal Studios, but the soul of the show, the songs, remained. Under the direction of Sidney Lumet, whose work was known for its urban realism, Oz locations appeared as New York City landmarks in phantasmagorical transformation. The World Trade Center became the Emerald City, and the Chrysler Building, in stylish repetition, formed part of the skyline in a darkly fantastical yet familiar cityscape (Figure 9.3). The Yellow Brick Road meandered through this city like a roller coaster track (Figure 9.4). These visual evocations of the city reinforced the cultural work of the soul music, which was rearranged under the supervision of Quincy Jones with a more lustrous sheen and pronounced disco pulse than Wheeler's orchestrations for the Broadway version. The luminous score combined with the mostly bleak and grungy visuals to celebrate both the grit and the glamor of the city in a film that Jacqueline Warwick describes as a "tamer and more accessible" variant of the blaxploitation film.[18] The

FIGURE 9.3. Chrysler Buildings in the cityscape of the Universal film production *The Wiz* (1978).

FIGURE 9.4. The Yellow Brick Road from the Universal film production *The Wiz*.

casting of iconic singers and actors like Diana Ross, Michael Jackson, and Lena Horne helped cement the film's importance in black community reception. Like the libretto of the musical, the screenplay of the movie was written by a white man, Joel Schumacher, whose gay identity and attraction to contemporary self-help philosophy might have helped shape significant narrative changes from the Broadway production, putting even more emphasis on the idea of home as self-knowledge rather than a place of geographical origin.

Jumpin' Jivernacular: The Soul Musical and the Critics

All of these elements contributed to a musical and theatrical experience resonant with black artistic movements of the time, but especially revealing of contemporaneous perceptions of race and African American culture are the critical responses in the popular press. Some critics expressed displeasure with a perceived loss of innocence in the updating and recasting of the classic children's story in black style, drawing unfavorable comparisons to the MGM film and Judy Garland. These complaints were sometimes tinged with racial bias, as in Rex Reed's vitriolic review for the *New York Daily News*. Imagining himself the persecuted party in "this all-black sacrilege," he complained:

> One has nightmare visions of being denounced as an Archie Bunker, then chased through the streets of Harlem by the Furies with their Afros on fire. . . . Next to bombing the White House, I can't imagine a better way to start a race war than to denigrate *The Wizard of Oz* and everything it stands for in the minds and hearts of children of all ages.[19]

Clive Barnes's assessment in the *New York Times* was more ambivalent:

> It has obvious vitality and a very evident and gorgeous sense of style. I found myself unmoved for much of the evening, but I was respectfully unmoved, not insultingly unmoved. . . . There are many things to enjoy in *The Wiz*, but, with apologies, this critic noticed them without actually enjoying them.[20]

The Broadway show's initially mixed reception, as some commentators in the black community noted, might be blamed partially on an inability of white Broadway critics to properly evaluate a piece of black theater.[21] If *The Wiz* is a signifying parody on *The Wizard of Oz*, allowing black expression to bypass dominant culture power brokers, it was the white theater critics who, like the lion tricked by the signifying monkey in traditional African American lore, bore the brunt of the signifying act. They just didn't get it. After tepid reviews, *The Wiz* seemed destined for a short run, and a closing date notice was reportedly posted on opening night.[22] However, an invigorated promotional push by 20th Century Fox, which had invested in the show, along with black community advocacy, saved *The Wiz*. A series of supportive reviews appeared in the black press, notably the *Amsterdam News*, which also ran opinion pieces asserting that mainstream critics had misunderstood *The Wiz*'s black style of parody. The newspaper urged black theatregoers to actively attend the show, while church groups and black theater parties helped fill the seats. Also helpful was 20th Century Fox's decision to pursue a television advertising campaign. Ultimately, *The Wiz* ran for four years from January 5, 1975, to January 28, 1979, and won seven Tony awards.[23]

Critics who did like the show were entranced by its black vernacular style and demonstrated their enthusiasm by using soul language and imagery in their reviews.

> The show . . . is saucy with black urban humor. Its talk is jumping jivernacular, its walk is a big-city strut, its dances have a blowtorch frenzy, and its songs range from a warm gospel glow to the rock beat of a riveter mining asphalt.[24]

What T. E. Kalem of *Time* here refers to as the show's "jivernacular" was fully embraced by Patrick Pacheco of *After Dark*.

> All-black, bright and sassy, Motown seemed to have come to Broadway in this production. . . . *The Wiz* is a big, splashy, soulful rock happening that should attract many diverse groups to the Majestic Theatre. Hallelujah, baby, and right on![25]

More than one reviewer described the music and the performance by Stephanie Mills, who played Dorothy, as "dynamite," perhaps recalling the popular catchphrase from Jimmie Walker's character J. J. on the sitcom *Good Times*, which had begun airing in 1974.[26] The concept of soul, whether specifically referenced or suggested through similar ideas such as vitality and spirit, surfaces often in these and other reviews.

Several months after *The Wiz* had become a success, an article by African American columnist Bryant Rollins appeared in the *New York Times*. Suggesting that the newspaper's original review might have missed something, it was entitled "Does *The Wiz* Say Something Extra to Blacks?" Rollins treats Dorothy's journey as a metaphor for black migration and hardship in the United States, saying, "The main themes running through the show are slavery and emancipation, the black church and religion, the great black migration from rural south to urban north."[27] Jack Kroll in *Newseek*, had also picked up on these themes:

> American blacks have been moving down a yellow brick road (badly in need of repair) for a long time, looking for Oz or the Emerald City or some other dream deferred, so the idea of an all-black version of *The Wizard of Oz* makes perfect sense.

He further described the show's "blazing high spirits" and "its piping hot servings of soul."[28] What emerges from these commentaries is the view that there was something good in *The Wiz* for those who were hip enough to get it. Using the materials of its time, *The Wiz* emphasized racial difference in a positive way.

Moreover, the show might be understood as an allegory for the entire African American experience, including the hardships that resulted in the waves of migration from the rural South to the urban North that were themselves repercussions of an earlier displacement from Africa in the transatlantic slave trade. It is this idea of *The Wiz* as an allegory of black migration that I would like to take up in the closer reading of *The Wiz* that follows, but I would like to keep this reading open to many twists and turns. Paul Gilroy makes a distinction between the *roots* and *routes* of black Atlantic culture and proposes the ship as an icon of black migration capable of navigating between essentialist and constructionist positions.[29] We might similarly take *The Wiz*'s Yellow Brick Road as a route along which musical journeys can be traced metaphorically—not a linear route leading from a singular source to a fixed destination, but one that, like the curling, twisting, meandering highway in Lumet's film adaptation, circles back on and intersects with itself on a journey through an urban landscape with no end in sight (Figure 9.4). Just as the influences of the creative team—stemming from Africa, Europe, the Caribbean, and North America—suggest the multiple experiences of blackness, *The Wiz*'s black fantasyland is a decentered one, whose Yellow Brick Road leads not only back to these *roots* but also across, through, over, and under the many *routes* of black life. The intersections with those routes, particularly those constructed by gender, sexuality, class, and stage of life in addition to race, become important nodes of comingling identities, in what bell hooks calls postmodern blackness—the "multiple experiences of black identity that are the lived conditions which make diverse cultural production possible."[30]

Ease on Down the Road: Black Soul and Migration in *The Wiz*

In *The Wiz*, Dorothy's journey is a journey to find her soul—and soulfulness. This imperative is linked both to the African American migratory experience and to the particular notions of home that result from that history. In the stage show, Dorothy lives on a Kansas farm with her aunt and uncle, far from the urban environment that encodes black life in the popular imagination. Listless, Dorothy acknowledges that she isn't much help to Aunt Em and Uncle Henry on the farm. In response, Aunt Em sings "Don't Lose the Feeling That We Have," which immediately sets the tone for the musical's soulful philosophy. The notion of a feeling—the search for it and the fear of losing it—runs through *The Wiz* and is something with which Dorothy seems to struggle. Her difficulty connecting with soulful feelings is even more pronounced in the movie, in which Dorothy is portrayed as a twenty-four-year-old assimilated Harlem schoolteacher, played by a thirty-three-year-old Diana Ross. As Aunt Em sings the same song in the movie, we see a warm scene of love and family at a holiday gathering with food and fellowship at the dinner table. Dorothy is painfully shy and out of place in this scene. Hiding in the kitchen, she sings "Can I Go On," expressing her inability to understand the feeling everyone else seems to thrive on.

What Dorothy is missing, according to Tommy J. Curry, is "that old tyme feeling of race," in which self-knowledge is dependent on knowledge of black family, community, and culture. In Curry's reading, Dorothy's inability to respond to Aunt Em's song, which expresses an understanding of race *as* family, results from Dorothy's failure to know her racial self and her interdependent relationship to the family of her race.[31] Taken together, the openings of the stage show and the movie demonstrate Dorothy inhabiting two different settings in the black experience—the country and the city. In either setting, and wherever black people find themselves on the road, the nurturing of the soul is necessary for survival. When Aunt Em sings "don't lose the feeling that we have," she is speaking to the entire community and its need for cohesion as well as to Dorothy about the cohesion of the family. Dorothy doesn't quite get this yet, and so is in some way not fully at home. This soulful sense of home is the object of her quest in Oz.

After being dropped in Oz by cyclone (as expected), Dorothy is surrounded by characters who express themselves in black vernacular styles of speech, music, dance, and dress. As written by Brown for the stage show, Dorothy plays "straight" to the other characters' comedy, and especially as played by Ross in the film, she lacks the "jivernacular" confidence of her new friends.[32] In this way, she might serve as a figure of identification for both black and white audiences (much like Ross's role as a Motown artist) as witness to a performance of black difference which serves as a lesson in the virtues soul.

Dorothy's latent soulfulness begins to show as opportunities arise for her to sing about her new experiences in Oz. Like the new friends she encounters, who don't know they already have brains, heart, and courage, Dorothy perhaps unknowingly reveals to us in song that she really does have "the feeling." These soulful moments were possible in the stage musical because of the youthful Stephanie Mills's "dynamite" performance and embodiment of the character. While the other characters get mostly funky up-tempo numbers with a strong physical impulse, most of Dorothy's songs are ballads, which imply her authentic selfhood, even as she seems to still be searching for "the feeling." The narrative tells us Dorothy lacks soul, but the songs and vocal performances suggest otherwise.

However, Dorothy's expressions of soul are initially uncertain. In the stage show, Dorothy doesn't sing until after she has landed in Oz, been greeted by the Munchkins, met the Good Witch of the North, and been instructed to follow the Yellow Brick Road to see the Wiz. "Soon as I Get Home" expresses her uncertainty and fear in a strange new world. It begins with an introductory verse set as a disorienting waltz suggesting the sound of a carousel calliope. As the lyric indicates, she has begun to have the feeling that she lacked, but is confused and frightened by it: "There's a feeling here inside that I cannot hide, and I know I've tried / But it's turning me around." As Dorothy thinks about home and musters the courage to face a new world, the music transitions into a more confident and soulful 4/4 time and modulates to a new key as it builds to the refrain: "I'm gonna be alright, soon as I get home / Soon as I get home." This transition is complete on the word "home," where the harmony finally lands squarely on the tonic chord (what would also be thought of as the "home" chord in the key of the refrain).

"Soon as I Get Home" evokes the experience of displacement as well as of the racial double-consciousness it produces in its bifurcation between European waltz and black soul.[33] Dorothy is further divided because she embodies multiple identities, notably the marginalized categories of black, female, and child. The waltz also evokes childhood ("I'm acting just like a baby"), while the encoding of authentic feeling in soul music anticipates the state of maturity Dorothy will achieve at the end of the musical. Dorothy must now embark on what Stacy Wolf describes as a "spiritual journey in a hostile environment."[34] Like African Americans uprooted from their ancestral lands and cultures, Dorothy has only her body, her voice, and her internal resources—along with the collective memory of racial, family, and community feelings—with which to reinvent herself in this "new world."

On the road, Dorothy learns about the feeling Aunt Em sang about as she accumulates a community of friends who are also in search of their soulful interiors, symbolized by brains, heart, and courage (just as Dorothy's soulfulness is connected to the concept of home).[35] In the formation of this community, the music signifies on the MGM film as described before but also on black musical traditions themselves. As noted by Samuel Floyd Jr., black music signifies on African musical traditions that can be traced to the circle dance and the ring shout of the black church, with their dialogical and communal dynamics, including call and response forms and layered rhythmic musical textures.[36] *The Wiz* follows this participatory tradition, building on the tropes of both Oz and black music and inviting each character into the center of the circle as he or she has the opportunity to solo in a musical number. In contrast to the MGM film, in which they share the same song ("If I Only had a Brain/a Heart/the Nerve"), in *The Wiz,* each of Dorothy's companions gets his own unique song, and even the Wicked Witch of the West gets a rousing gospel solo, "No Bad News." Much as Dorothy's soulful moment in her first ballad betrays her latent feelings of racial authenticity, her friends' performances of songs in gospel, soul, funk, vaudeville, blues, Dixieland, and soul styles give evidence of their own soulful essences, despite their perceived physical deficiencies.

These embodied expressions of black soul, however, are multifaceted. Dorothy's relationship to soul is important specifically because she's a black girl in circumstances that make particular demands on her role in the community. In discussing the stage version, Stacy Wolf describes Dorothy as the head of an "assembled family" in which she stands in for black women as heads of households and African American community leaders in the 1970s.[37] Similarly, Rhonda Williams, discussing the movie, sees *The Wiz's* black women, including Dorothy and the witches, as occupying positions of power in the community. As one of these women in training, Dorothy has to "rescue, re-educate, support, encourage and uplift the Black man in order to reestablish the Black family unit and community."[38] These black men are represented by her three traveling companions and the Wizard who all need her help in realizing their potential. While Wolf and Williams's readings bring welcome attention to the valued role of black women, they may also remind us of the pressure under which black girls may be expected to "grow up" quickly in order to assume this role. The urgency of this process is especially pronounced in the movie, in which Aunt Em is eager for Dorothy to leave her job teaching young children to take a better-paying one working with high school students. If Dorothy's journey centers on her black girlhood and the demands of taking up black womanhood, her companions might be seen as embodying anxieties about black masculinity and appropriate expressions of intelligence, compassion, and courage.[39]

The Wiz's gender and race dynamics have the potential to radically de-center the concepts that impose these constraints. The musical queers both gender and the color line, suggesting that racial identity is multiple, diffuse, and spiraling like the Yellow Brick Road. When the foursome arrive in the Emerald City, they meet the Wiz, a James Brown–like showman variously described as a pimp, drug dealer, and preacher.[40] Played in the original production by Andre de Shields, who was known in New York circles for his cabaret act with a strong queer sensibility, the Wiz's chameleon-like changes of costume, personality, and musical language run a gamut of musical styles from funk to glitzy seventies pop. These playfully embodied black and queer performances were a specialty of de Shields. The Wiz sends Dorothy and her friends to defeat the Wicked Witch Evillene, a slave driver and "Big Mama" of a gospel shouter.[41] After successfully melting the Witch, Dorothy, her friends, and a chorus of the Witch's former slaves sing "Everybody Rejoice/Brand New Day" in celebration of the freedom from oppression that the *New York Times'* Bryant Rollins saw at the heart of *The Wiz*. In the film, this number throbs to a strong disco beat and includes an extended dance sequence, a liberation ballet, in which the slaves unzip their cumbersome, puppet-like costumes, revealing their naked bodies and suggesting that their dance of freedom is also sexually liberating. The disco sound, with its significance in black, queer, Latino, and women's communities, suggests the optimism felt by these marginalized groups in an era of civil rights advances and growing visibility. Written by a young up-and-coming Luther Vandross, whose gay identity has more recently come to light, the song is led by Diana Ross, a black diva who is an icon of both the African American and gay communities. She is accompanied by the androgynous and sexually ambiguous Michael Jackson, whose performance in the film, according to Jacqueline Warwick, negotiates liminal embodiments of gender, race, and age during Jackson's transition from child star to mature artist.[42] The intersection of queer and black aesthetics in a text based on *The Wizard of Oz* also reminds us that *The Wizard of Oz* itself was an important myth of the American gay community in the mid-twentieth century, with gay men referred to as "friends of Dorothy" and the journey to the Emerald City serving as a metaphor for leaving home to join the gay communities of New York and San Francisco.[43] Ambivalence about home and the destination of the city have formed vital narratives for many people.

The route taken through *The Wiz*'s cityscape, then, would seem convoluted. In reviewing the movie, Pauline Kael complained about the lack of geographical logic to the Yellow Brick Road's meanderings.

> Although Oz is meant to be in Manhattan, it includes locations in Queens, the Bronx, and Brooklyn, and after Dorothy accumulates her traveling companions, they have to go over a couple of bridges to get to the Emerald City (the capital of Oz), in lower Manhattan. Geographically, we're thoroughly dislocated.[44]

Such literalness may be missing the point. *The Wiz*'s imaginary city is a global and geographically ambiguous one, encompassing the multiple urban spaces and musical cultures. The songs emerge at the intersection of musical routes traversing the rural South, the urban North, and the black Atlantic from New York to Detroit, New Orleans, Memphis, and Chicago. Dorothy's journey from Kansas to the Emerald city retraces, if not any singular direct line, then the panorama, of black migration.

Love Overflowing: Feeling Home

Upon returning to the Emerald City, Dorothy and her friends discover that the Wiz is a humbug. As in the book and the MGM film, he nonetheless gives Dorothy's friends symbols of their brains, heart, and courage. In the Broadway version of *The Wiz*, in an expression of the American ideal of self-invention, he sings "Believe in Yourself," before taking off in his balloon, leaving Dorothy still without a way to get home. At this moment, Glinda, the Good Witch of the South, comes to the rescue, singing "A Rested Body Is a Rested Mind," a song about reaching journey's end. This song suggests that the hard work done by African Americans is a strain on both the body and the soul. When one is rested, the other is restored. At the end of her journey, Dorothy demonstrates her new-found competency in black culture by declaring, "Nobody knows the trouble I've seen!" in reference to the well-known spiritual.[45]

In a reprise of "Believe in Yourself," Glinda explains that Dorothy has always had the power to go home with her magic shoes. The movie is even more emphatic about the importance of this theme of self-sufficiency, turning "home" into an explicit metaphor of self-knowledge. The Wiz, played by nonsinging Richard Pryor, is a pathetic figure, unlike the stage show's more charismatic portrayal. In the film, it is Dorothy instead of the Wiz who sings "Believe in Yourself," revealing to her friends that they have had brains, heart, and courage all along. When the Wiz asks if she can help him, her response is "I don't know what's in you. You'll have to find that out for yourself. But I do know one thing. You'll never find it in the safety of this room. I tried that all my life. It doesn't work. There's a whole world out there. And you'll have to begin by letting people see who you really are."[46] Glinda, played in the movie by no less an authoritative diva than Lena Horne, gives Dorothy some of her own advice, saying that home, too, is a matter of the soul, and that she has always had the power to find it: "Home is a place we all must find, child. It's not just a place where you eat or sleep. Home is knowing. Knowing your mind, knowing your heart, knowing your courage. If we know ourselves, we're always home anywhere."[47] This lesson is a shade different from the one expressed by Dorothy in the MGM film: "If I ever go looking for my heart's desire again, I won't look any farther than my own backyard; because if it isn't there, I never really lost it to begin with!"[48] Something along these lines might be true for African Americans, but it necessarily has a different meaning in the context of the migratory experience. Instead of returning to the place of one's backyard, one must find the feeling of home wherever one is.

This sentiment is communicated in one last soulful number. Facing out to the audience (the camera in the movie), Dorothy sings "Home," a transformed rendition of the song in which she initially expressed her disorientation on arriving in Oz. This time, the verse, with its child-like waltz, makes no appearance. The song is a fully soulful and mature anthem of self-knowledge. The lyric indicates that, having learned to love others and believe in herself, Dorothy has finally found that "feeling" about which Aunt Em sang.

> Living here in this brand new world
> Might be a fantasy,
> But it's taught me to love,
> So it's real to me
> And I learned that we must look
> Inside our hearts to find
> A world full of love
> Like yours, like mine
> Like home.[49]

In Gates's theory of signifying on established tropes, this is a repetition of the original theme from the MGM film with a difference, and the difference is soul. Dorothy's final performance is a testimony to the feelings of the race, with roots in the gospel music of the black church. Here she expresses her black interior, which according to Elizabeth Alexander allows African Americans to envision their power and complexity in the "metaphysical space beyond the black public everyday."[50] Dorothy clicks her heels and we are left with a brief final image of her returning home—to Kansas in the stage show and to Harlem in the movie. It is brief because the place is now incidental. Indeed, as Kael has pointed out, Dorothy has hardly seemed to leave her geographical home in Oz, where New York represents both home and the dream-world.[51] The ambiguity about which is the real and which is the alternate world in the film version of *The Wiz* makes the inner transformation the solely important matter of Dorothy's journey. Dorothy returns from Oz not to remain content staying with Aunt Em and Uncle Henry, but to embark on her own new adventures of self-discovery.

Keep on Keepin' on the Road That You Choose: Where Next?

The Wiz stands at something of a crossroads. Allen Woll notes that the stage version had dispensed with the explicit treatment of social and political concerns addressed by black musicals earlier in the1970s.[52] The film version marked the end of the era of blaxploitation and similar film genres that, along with black popular music, had expressed the optimism of black difference in the 1960s and 1970s. Shortly after the film flopped, disco died and Motown faded. After their work on *The Wiz*, Michael Jackson and Quincy Jones teamed up to redefine the sound of popular music in the 1980s, hybridizing soul with rock and other styles. Thus, *The Wiz* represents both a high watermark of soul and the beginning of a transition to a less political post-soul moment characterized by an individualistic self-help culture and suggestive of the dawning of the 1980s, with the Reagan presidency, the Huxtables, Oprah Winfrey, and the displacement of soul music by the adult contemporary radio format.[53] Although *The Wiz* is also about community, its emphasis on individualism might be seen as offering a self-centered aesthetic that distracts from political action—especially in the movie, which was influenced by Schumacher and Ross's interest in Werner Erhard's self-help philosophy.[54]

Perhaps in part because it nostalgically represents the optimism of the soul era, *The Wiz* remains important in the black community, where there is a strong sense of ownership of its vision of Oz. Nonblack and multi-ethnic productions, which seem to challenge the notion of *The Wiz* as an essentially black musical rooted in a stable racial identity, raise questions about just how far the routes of *The Wiz* should be allowed to wander. In Chicago, the first professional production to feature white actors in minor roles met with controversy in the 1980s, but a recent production in San Diego barely raised eyebrows when it included a multi-ethnic cast and revised music with more explicit Latin, urban dance, and hip-hop elements.[55] School and community productions are often multi-ethnic or even all-white. Perhaps in part because *The Wiz* does not address race explicitly, these performances have been relatively accepted within their communities, which may or may not be racially conscious ones and where the sound of soul, familiar from "oldies" radio play, seems to have been assimilated into the larger landscape of American music where it only vaguely signifies the 1970s. Meanwhile, recently successful European productions featuring both black and nonblack casts in Britain and the Netherlands suggest the show's transatlantic appeal, while NBC's highly rated live television broadcast in 2015 helps to ensure that *The Wiz* will continue to have a prominent place in the theatrical repertoire. Indeed, the broadcast was not only well received on television but also reinvigorated the conversation over the significance of *The Wiz* as a black musical online, with strong emotional responses from the community of African American social media users loosely known as Black Twitter live tweeting the event in conversation with overlapping fandoms in the theater and LGBTQ communities.[56]

The Wiz stakes a claim on the American fairy tale in a bold assertion of African American access to American mythology, not by assimilating or accommodating the mainstream, but by bending a mainstream text to accommodate black difference. As it continues its own journey through changing times and places, *The Wiz* traverses infinite spaces, musical cultures, and historical moments populated by mobile subjects who are constantly participating in their own soulful creation.

Notes

1. John Koblin, *"The Wiz Live!* Scores Strong Ratings," *New York Times*, December 4, 2015. For a history of the black musical and *The Wiz's* place within it, see Allen Woll, *Black Musical Theatre: From* Coontown *to* Dreamgirls (1989; reprint, New York: Da Capo Press, 1991). On the significance of *The Wiz* as a black film, see Tommy J. Curry, "When *The Wiz* Goes Black, Does It Ever Go Back?" in *The Wizard of Oz and Philosophy: Wicked Wisdom of the West,* edited by Randall E. Auxier and Phillip S. Seng (Chicago: Open Court, 2008), 63.

2. For more on Oz musicals and the performances of American identity, see Ryan Bunch, "Oz and the Musical: The American Art Form and the Reinvention of the American Fairy Tale," *Studies in Musical Theatre* 9 (2015): 53–69.

3. Guthrie Ramsey, *Race Music: Black Cultures from Bebop to Hip-Hop* (Berkeley: University of California Press, 2003), 21.

4. Charlie Smalls, *The Wiz: The Super Soul Musical "Wonderful Wizard of Oz,"* Atlantic SD 18137, 1975, LP.

5. W. E. B. Du Bois, *The Souls of Black Folk* (1903; New York: Dover, 1994).

6. On the aesthetics of soul music in this historical and social context, see Portia K. Maultsby, "Soul," in *African American Music: An Introduction*, edited by Mellonee V. Burnim and Portia K. Maultsby (New York: Routledge, 2006), 271–289.

7. Henry Louis Gates Jr., *The Signifying Monkey* (New York: Oxford University Press, 1988), xxii. For more on signifying, see Gena Dagel Caponi, *Signifyin(g), Sanctifyin', and Slam Dunking: A Reader in African American Expressive Culture* (Amherst: University of Massachusetts Press, 1999), 27–30; see also, in the same volume, Claudia Mitchell-Kernan, "Signifying, Loud-Talking, and Marking," 309–330.

8. On Oz as American myth, see, for example, Jack Zipes, *Fairy Tale as Myth/Myth as Fairy Tale* (Lexington: University Press of Kentucky, 1994), 119–138; and Alissa Burger, *The Wizard of Oz as American Myth: A Critical Study of Six Versions of the Story, 1900–2007* (Jefferson, NC: McFarland, 2012), 10–29.

9. Edward Jablonski, *Harold Arlen: Rhythm, Rainbows, and Blues* (Boston: Northeastern University Press, 1996), 130.

10. See also Stacy Wolf's analysis of "the 'cool,' relaxed hipness of black vernacular in the music, lyrics, and choreography of "Ease on Down the Road" in *Changed for Good: A Feminist History of the Broadway Musical* (New York: Oxford University Press, 2011), 116.

11. The Ken Harper Papers, Billy Rose Theatre Division, New York Public Library for the Performing Arts. In addition to the Harper Papers, details on the production and reception history of *The Wiz* have been gathered from *The Wiz* Collection, Manuscripts, Archives, and Rare Books Division, Schomburg Center for Research in Black Culture, New York Public Library; Mance Williams, *Black Theatre in the 1960s and 1970s: A Historical-Critical Analysis of the Movement* (Westport, CT: Greenwood Press, 1985), 101–102; Stanley Green, *The World of Musical Comedy*, 4th ed. (New York: Da Capo Press, 1980), 366–367; and Wolf, *Changed for Good*, 113.

12. Letter to Clive Richards, August 4, 1972, Harper Papers. Ultimately, Charlie Smalls's music was based on contemporary black pop and was less influenced by Afro-Caribbean characteristics than were other elements such as Geoffrey Holder's costume designs.

13. Charlie Smalls resume, Harper Papers. For more on Smalls, see Stanley Richards, ed., *Great Rock Musicals* (New York: Stein and Day, 1979), 4–5; and Green, *The World of Musical Comedy*, 367.

14. "Some Like It Lukewarm," Episode No. 56 of *The Monkees,* NBC, March 4, 1968.

15. William F. Brown and Charlie Smalls, *The Wiz,* libretto (1974; revised and rewritten, New York: Samuel French, 1979), 34.

16. Ted Ross (the Cowardly Lion) had been in the cast of *Raisin* (1973) and appeared on *The Jeffersons* (one episode in 1978); Andre De Shields (the Wiz) starred in *Ain't Misbehavin'* (1978); Mabel King (Evillene) starred in *What's Happening!* (1976–1978), and appeared on *The Jeffersons* (one episode in 1984); and Clarice Taylor (Addaperle) appeared on *Sanford and Son* (one episode in 1974) and *Sesame Street* (1977–1989).

17. Green, *The World of Musical Comedy*, 367.

18. Jacqueline Warwick, "You Can't Win, Child, but You Can't Get Out of the Game: Michael Jackson's Transition from Child Star to Superstar," *Popular Music and Society* 35 (2012): 25.

19. Rex Reed, "The Wiz," *New York Sunday News,* January 12, 1975, 6.

20. Clive Barnes, "Stage: The Wiz (of Oz): Black Musical Shows Vitality and Style," *New York Times,* January 6, 1975, 32.

21. "Special Editorial Part II: Now, It's the Drama Critics," *New Amsterdam News,* January 11, 1975.

22. Green, *The World of Musical Comedy*, 366; Wolf, *Changed for Good,* 114.

23. Woll, *Black Musical Theatre,* 263–265; Wolf, *Changed for Good,* 114–115.

24. T. E. Kalem, "The Theatre: Jumping Jivernacular," *Time*, January 20, 1975, 92.

25. Patrick Pacheco, "The Wiz," *After Dark,* March 1975. Note also the possible reference to the 1967 musical *Hallelujah, Baby!*

26. Pacheco, "The Wiz"; Marilyn Stasio, "Witty Wiz," *Cue Magazine*, 1975.

27. Bryant Rollins, "Does 'The Wiz' Say Something Extra to Blacks?" *New York Times*, December 28, 1975.

28. Jack Kroll, "*Oz* with Soul," *Newsweek*, January 20, 1975, 82.

29. Paul Gilroy, *The Black Atlantic: Modernity and Double Consciousness* (Cambridge, MA: Harvard University Press, 1993), 4, 19.

30. bell hooks, "Postmodern Blackness," *Postmodern Culture* 1, no.1 (1990).

31. Curry, "When *The Wiz* Goes Black," 64–68.

32. Harper Papers.

33. Du Bois, *The Souls of Black Folk*, 2; Gates, *The Signifying Monkey*, xxiii.

34. Wolf, *Changed for Good*, 113.

35. See Wolf, *Changed for Good*, 115, on *The Wiz* as the formation of a community.

36. Samuel A. Floyd Jr., *The Power of Black Music: Interpreting Its History from Africa to the United States* (New York: Oxford University Press, 1995), 7.

37. Wolf, *Changed for Good*, 111–112.

38. Rhonda Williams, "*The Wiz*: American Culture at Its Best," in *The Universe of Oz: Essays on Baum's Series and Its Progeny* (Jefferson, NC: McFarland, 2010), 195.

39. For one such perspective, see Jesse Scott, "The Black Interior, Reparations and African American Masculinity in *The Wiz*," in *Pimps, Wimps, Studs, Thugs and Gentlemen*, edited by Elwood Watson, Kindle edition (Jefferson, NC: McFarland, 2009).

40. Jack Kroll, "Under the Rainbow," *Newsweek*, October 30, 1978, 89.

41. Douglas Watt, "Fine Cast and Splendid Look in 'Wiz,'" *New York Daily News*, January 6, 1975.

42. Warwick, "You Can't Win, Child," 251–253.

43. For more on the significance of Judy Garland and *The Wizard of Oz* in this history, see Ronald Zank, "'Come Out, Come Out, Wherever You Are': How Tina Landau's *1969* Stages a Queer Reading of *The Wizard of Oz*," in *The Universe of Oz: Essays on Baum's Series and Its Progeny*, edited by Kevin K. Durand and Mary K. Leigh (Jefferson, NC: McFarland, 2010), 61–76.

44. Pauline Kael, "Saint Dorothy," *New Yorker*, September 30, 1978.

45. Brown and Smalls, *The Wiz*, libretto, 87.

46. *The Wiz*, Blu-ray, directed by Sidney Lumet (1978; Universal City, CA: Universal Studios Home Entertainment, 2010).

47. *The Wiz,* Blu-ray, directed by Sidney Lumet.

48. Noel Langley, Florence Ryerson, and Edgar Allan Woolf, *The Wizard of Oz: The Screenplay*, edited by Michael Patrick Hearn (New York: Delta, 1989), 128.

49. Brown and Smalls, *The Wiz*, libretto, 89–90.

50. Elizabeth Alexander, *The Black Interior* (St. Paul, MN: Graywolf, 2004), x.

51. Kael, "Saint Dorothy," 138.

52. Woll, *Black Musical Theatre*, 263, 265–266.

53. On the post-soul turn in black music and popular culture, see Mark Anthony Neal, *Soul Babies: Black Popular Culture and the Post-Soul Aesthetic* (New York: Routledge, 2002).

54. J. Randy Taraborrelli, *Diana Ross: A Biography* (New York: Citadel Press, 2007), 313. See also Neil Earle, The Wonderful Wizard of Oz *in American Popular Culture: Uneasy in Eden* (Lewiston, NY: Edwin Mellen Press, 1993), 165, on many of these issues, including the "1970s pop psychological uplift."

55. Sid Smith, "'The Wiz' Works Wonders to Put Its Controversy Aside," *Chicago Tribune*, January 29, 1987; Bob Verini, "Review: 'The Wiz,'" *Variety*, October 12, 2006.

56. For more on social media participation and the live broadcast of *The Wiz*, see my "You Can't Stop the Tweet: Social Media and Networks of Participation in the Live Television Musical," in *iBroadway: Musical Theatre in the Digital Age*, edited by Jessica Hillman (New York: Palgrave Macmillan, forthcoming).

10

"*THE WIZARD OF OZ* AND *WICKED*"

RESONANCES, LEGAL ISSUES, AND THE APPROPRIATION OF A CLASSIC

Paul R. Laird

Introduction

Stephen Schwartz lives to write musicals, and he has reported that whenever he hears a good idea for a show, a bell goes off in his brain.[1] Such was his experience when he learned of the novel *Wicked* by Gregory Maguire while on a snorkeling trip to Hawaii in 1997. Given that the show that he helped derive from this cerebral tome has run on Broadway since October 2003 and proven popular in several other countries, one must acknowledge the accuracy of his first impression. The idea's germ came from Maguire's ingenious treatment of *The Wizard of Oz*, probably the most famous literary fantasy in the history of the United States. It seems inevitable in these post-modern times that somebody would turn L. Frank Baum's tale on its head, casting the Wizard as the bad guy and the Wicked Witch of the West as a misunderstood loner, but in the process Maguire created in Elphaba a memorable character, perhaps as distinctive as any personality that Baum conceived in his many *Oz* stories. What Schwartz understood is that Elphaba's passionate embrace of life and epic battle with the Wizard rendered her a character who could fulfill one of the most important measures involving musical theater: she needs to sing! This was one of his most important arguments in convincing Marc Platt of Universal Studios to mothball the film of *Wicked* that they were developing in favor of a musical treatment for Broadway.[2] Schwartz used a similar argument to convince novelist Gregory Maguire to grant the rights for a musical, telling him: "You've written a story with a lot of strong emotion, and it can stand being sung directly to an audience."[3]

Success is never a given in the creation of a Broadway musical, and an extraordinary number of steps had to work out before *Wicked* became a hit. The creative team started with solid advantages, including the popularity of *The Wizard of Oz* and Maguire's striking reversal of the story, but it was Schwartz, book writer Winnie Holzman, producer Platt, director Joe Mantello, and several others who guided the good ship *Wicked* through the treacherous waters of writing, workshops, rewriting, designing, and multiple rounds of revisions before it became a show that has "defied gravity."

Schwartz was determined from the outset to make as much use as possible of the iconic 1939 film, *The Wizard of Oz*. For example, he wanted the audience to witness the emergence of the Wicked Witch of the West with the black dress and cape, carrying and riding on a broom.[4] Such concern for the film's images was important because Maguire tells a very different story in his novel, recognizably based on Baum's characters, but with new developments and situations that are potentially upsetting for *Oz* fans. The film is far better known. As Schwartz later discovered, however, lawyers at Universal Studios believed that images and lines from the famous film were part of MGM's copyrighted approach to the story, and they wished to avoid lawsuits for appropriating those images. This led to a frustrating juncture in the creation of *Wicked* for Schwartz and Holzman, as is considered below. First, however, we must appreciate what the show's creators took from Maguire's novel and the version told in the iconic film starring Judy Garland.

Maguire's Model: A "Novel" Challenge

Gregory Maguire (b. 1954) is a writer of children's books who resolved to pen an adult novel in which he explored the concept of evil, a project that concluded with the publication of *Wicked: The Life and Times of the Wicked Witch of the West* in 1995.[5] It is an engrossing tale told with stylish prose, rich description, and considerable aplomb, with fascinating exploration of the inner workings of Elphaba's mind. Maguire divided the novel into a short prologue and four longer sections: "Munchkinlanders," "Gillikin," "City of Emeralds," and "In the Vinkus." Elphaba hails from Munchkinland, and in the first segment we learn about her birth, family, youth, and "Otherness." Galinda (the name with which Glinda starts the story)[6] is from Gillikin, and in the second section the reader meets her as she travels to Shiz University for the first time, a supremely confident young woman and the antithesis of Elphaba in just about every way possible. Most of this segment informs the reader of life at school with Galinda, Elphaba, and their other friends. By the end of "Gillikin," Galinda and Elphaba have experienced a disastrous audience with the Wizard, causing Elphaba to join the underground struggle against his rule. "City of Emeralds" is a description of these activities and an affair that Elphaba has with Fiyero, a Winkie prince and college friend. She joins a convent, where she lives for the seven years that transpire before "In the Vinkus," where Elphaba goes to live with Fiyero's family. Dorothy arrives in Oz and familiar events occur, but Maguire tells the story from a different perspective and sometimes with contrasting versions of the events. Synopses of each section provide necessary details from Maguire's story, helping to demonstrate how Schwartz and Holzman adapted the story.

The "Prologue" begins late in the tale. Elphaba flies over the Yellow Brick Road looking for Dorothy and her three famous companions. She finds them sitting under a tree, gossiping about the Wicked Witch. A storm breaks up the encounter and Elphaba must hide lest she become wet, but she resolves to confront Dorothy about the shoes.

"Munchkinlanders" presents Elphaba's life through early childhood. Her parents are Frex, a pastor, and Melena, granddaughter of the leader of Munchkinland. Elphaba is born with green skin and sharp teeth; through her Nanny we learn that the baby's father was a tinker who used a green liquid to have his way with Melena. Frex and his wife reluctantly accept this unusual child. Melena has another affair that brings about the conception of Nessarose, born without arms because Frex prevailed upon his wife to ingest dangerous medicine that would keep this child from being born green. Frex dotes on Nessarose although he knows she is not his biological daughter, and almost ignores Elphaba. Melena later dies in childbirth while bearing a son.

"Gillikin" opens years later. Galinda is on the train to Shiz, a city in her home province, where she will attend university. She converses with Doctor Dillamond, a goat that serves as a science professor at the school. Upon arrival, Galinda meets headmistress Madame Morrible and learns that her roommate will be Elphaba. They do not get along at first, but eventually become part of a large cadre of friends. Madame Morrible holds a poetry reading and shows her bias by reciting a verse opposing Talking Animals; meanwhile Elphaba, her friend Boq (another Munchkin), and other students assist Doctor Dillamond with an experiment in which he hopes to show that humans and Talking Animals are closely related biologically. This line of research results in his murder. Galinda changes her name to Glinda in his honor because that is the way he pronounced her name. Nessarose and Nanny arrive at Shiz from Munchkinland and room with Glinda and Elphaba, forming with other friends what Maguire calls the "charmed circle," joined later by Fiyero. They learn that Dillamond's murderer was Grommetik, Morrible's mechanical servant. The headmistress offers another sequence of events that explains her robot's proximity to the goat at the time of his death, and tries to enlist Elphaba, Glinda, and Nessarose as agents for the

Wizard. Elphaba and Glinda go to the Emerald City and have a brief audience with the Wizard, who disagrees with them about the value of Talking Animals and dismisses Dillamond's importance. Glinda returns to Shiz and Elphaba remains in the Emerald City to work against the Wizard.

Five years have passed when "City of Emeralds" begins. Elphaba has been working in the resistance and reconnects with Fiyero, and they start an affair. By chance he sees Glinda, who misses Elphaba, but Fiyero tells her nothing. Before a holiday Elphaba says that she will be unavailable, so Fiyero stalks her and sees her hoping to kill Madame Morrible, but a crowd gathers and she aborts the mission. As Fiyero waits at her room the secret police arrive and kill him. Elphaba flees to a convent.

As "In the Vinkus" opens, Elphaba has been at the convent for seven years. She leaves with a boy named Liir, a possible son that she has no memory of bearing, and joins a caravan to Vinkus, where she wants to meet Fiyero's family and hopefully live the remainder of her life in seclusion. Magical events occur that she comes to realize she has caused, and she begins to dress as a witch. Elphaba, Liir, and several accompanying animals, including a monkey named Chistery, arrive at Kiamo Ko, the castle of Fiyero's family. His widow, Sarima, will not allow Elphaba to tell her story or ask for her forgiveness concerning Fiyero's death, and her children are cruel to Liir. Elphaba finds the Grimmerie, a book of spells, and kills one of Sarima's sons with a falling icicle. Elphaba's former nanny comes to Kiamo Ko and tells her that Nessarose is now leader of Munchkinland. Their father invites Elphaba to come. She flies on her broom and learns that her father wants her to help Nessarose, but her sister has become a sorceress who prays for miracles such as causing an ax to cut off limbs of the man using it, producing the Tin Woodman. Elphaba returns to Kiamo Ko; Sarima and her family have been arrested by the Wizard's soldiers. Dorothy arrives in Oz via tornado, killing Nessarose with her house. Glinda gives Dorothy the magic shoes, horrifying Elphaba. The Wizard insists on a meeting with Elphaba and pressures her to give him the Grimmerie. She meets Boq, who tells Elphaba that Dorothy is harmless. Elphaba becomes less rational and goes to Shiz to kill Madame Morrible, finding her already dead, but she still crushes her skull. A friend from Shiz introduces Elphaba to the Clock of the Time Dragon, which shows an image of her mother copulating with the Wizard. Elphaba brings Dorothy and the Lion to Kiamo Ko and attempts to get the shoes back, but she accidentally catches her skirt on fire and Dorothy melts her by throwing a bucket of water, trying to extinguish the flames. Elphaba always had a bottle of green elixir—Melena drank it before having sex with the tinker who was Elphaba's father—and Dorothy takes that to the Wizard. He realizes that Elphaba was his daughter and leaves Oz in his balloon before his ministers overthrow him.

Maguire's complex story weaves in and out of *The Wizard of Oz* with many added twists and turns. Holzman has described how they dealt with Maguire's characters and story:

> I didn't worry about the story told in the book that much. We had the rights to the book and the book became a resource. You can take whatever you need out of it. It wasn't pushing you around—you're in charge of it. . . . We were going to recreate our own story.[7]

Maguire understood the process of using another story in the creative process, describing how he used the film in his book: "I knew that people would be coming to my novel remembering the 1939 movie. I didn't even need to refer to it much. I could evoke the film with very slender, oblique comments."[8]

The musical presents Elphaba as a more appealing character than does Maguire: she is plucky and self-reliant, ambitious for a significant place in the world (as heard in her "I want" song "The Wizard and I"). She begins to learn about evil in Oz in "Something Bad," mostly sung by Doctor Dillamond, and in "Dancing through Life," when she finds herself an object of derision wearing the hat that Galinda gave her, she dances alone without music and shows her strength of character. Her rendition of "I'm Not That Girl" demonstrates her acceptance of what she believes to be her unrequited love for Fiyero. "Defying Gravity," her anthem of self-actualization that closes Act 1, confirms her willingness to become an outlaw and oppose the Wizard. Her Act 2 love duet with Fiyero, "As Long as You're Mine," is an important moment for Elphaba, when she realizes her capacity for mature love. Sometimes she is too eager to please others, especially the Wizard, as seen when she provides his monkeys with wings and then later when he starts to win her over in their second meeting. Those bitter lessons, in addition to disasters that befall her lover Fiyero and sister Nessarose, drive her to the despair heard in "No Good Deed." Elphaba can be desperate, especially when she deals with Dorothy, but she remains a sympathetic figure because the audience sees how misunderstood she is. Elphaba's essential strength, however, survives at the end, when she expresses her undying friendship for Glinda in "For Good" (Figure 10.1) and exiles herself to the Badlands with Fiyero, abandoning any hopes of rehabilitating herself in Oz and leaving Glinda to bring down the Wizard. Maguire's Elphaba is sympathetic but also more complex and malignant, a type that would not have inspired love and admiration from many young fans, like Elphaba of the musical.[9]

The musical *Wicked* benefited enormously from its two strong female characters who are also best friends; this viewpoint was made possible because Schwartz, Holzman, and Pratt realized that they were primarily telling the story

FIGURE 10.1. Kristen Chenoweth (Glinda) and Idina Menzel (Elphaba) in *Wicked* (Broadway, 2003). Credit: Photofest.

of Elphaba and Glinda. The writers have stated that Kristin Chenoweth's entry into the project in 2000 enlarged Glinda's role because the actress proved to be such a natural in it.[10] This is a major departure from Maguire's novel, where Glinda is not nearly as significant. In the musical, Glinda sings nearly as much as her green friend, and the audience follows Glinda's process of maturation. She appears first as the polished, public Glinda at the opening in "No One Mourns the Wicked," before initiating the flashback that is the show. Once the two young women learn that they will be roommates, they sing "What Is This Feeling?," an evocation of bubblegum rock where neither young woman seems especially mature, but Elphaba gets the best of Galinda by scaring her at the end. Among many plot points presented in "Dancing through Life," Galinda maliciously gives Elphaba the black, pointy hat, but she then sees the green girl's strength and finds a friend. In "Popular," Galinda shows that she is still glib and superficial. Their duet "One Short Day," as they revel in their visit to the Emerald City, confirms their friendship's depth. The dispute between them that opens "Defying Gravity" clarifies their incompatible goals, but later in the song Glinda demonstrates how much she cares about her friend. The Glinda who sings "Thank Goodness" and reprises "I'm Not That Girl" has learned that life is full of hard choices and disappointment, providing her with the depth of feeling that makes possible her reconciliation with Elphaba in "For Good" and ending the nasty careers of Madame Morrible and the Wizard. Most of Glinda's journey in the musical was the creation of Holzman and Schwartz, owing little to Maguire's novel.

The roles of other characters also changed substantially between Maguire's novel and the musical. In the show, Fiyero becomes Galinda's boyfriend but realizes that he is more attracted to the deeper Elphaba, and in the second act he gives himself up, allowing Elphaba to escape from the Wizard's men. Elphaba turns him into a scarecrow so that he will suffer less under torture. Early in the novel, Boq loves Galinda, but that ardor cools and his later appearances are less important, a far cry from the young man in the musical so consumed with Galinda that he allows himself to be tied to Nessarose, becoming the Tin Woodman for his trouble. Some actions by Madame Morrible and the Wizard are different between the novel and the musical, but their essential evil roles remain, although the Wizard is allowed a pitiable, human side at the end of the musical.

While adapting Maguire's novel into a musical, Schwartz, Holzman, Platt, Mantello, and others managed an effective collaboration and emerged with a book that provides the necessary backstory, focuses primarily on two strong characters while drawing others in sufficient detail to make them effective parts of the story, and provides impetus for the musical numbers.

Keeping an Eye on the Prized Film

There is no avoiding that the most famous version of *The Wizard of Oz* is the 1939 film; its famous images and concepts appear in both Maguire's novel and *Wicked*, the Broadway show. From the beginning of the creative process, Schwartz realized that part of the path toward finding an audience for the musical would include making rich use of the film. For example, he has reported that from the outset he wanted Elphaba to fly off on her broom at the end of Act 1, that Fiyero would become the Scarecrow, and that Boq would be transformed into the Tin Woodman.[11] Director Joe Mantello saw an early script draft where Dorothy, the Lion, Scarecrow, and Tin Woodman all came on stage together toward the beginning, which he thought exposed too much too quickly. As a hint of the disagreements known to have existed in the collaboration between Mantello and Schwartz, later the director wondered if Dorothy or the Lion should appear in the show at all "because they're so etched in our psyches."[12] In contrast, Schwartz has stated: "Part of the fun of the show for me was explaining how everything we knew from *The Wizard of Oz* happened."[13] Speaking for both of the writers, Schwartz once stated that they considered the film a "documentary," meaning that everything that would happen in *Wicked* needed to be comprehensible in that context.[14] A survey of three important documents in the musical's development demonstrates the film's consistent presence during the creation of *Wicked*.

One of the first pieces of documentary evidence from the show's creation was Schwartz's scenario from September 1998.[15] It is remarkable to see how much of the final story arc Schwartz captured in this effort; what follows is merely identification of numerous resonances from the 1939 film with bits of necessary context. Galinda tricks Elphaba into wearing the black, peaked hat to the school's orientation dance, bringing her the first part of her Wicked Witch costume. Later in Act 1, after Fiyero arrives, he starts to bond with Elphaba over rescuing a lion cub about to be experimented upon in a class, the first glimpse of what becomes the Cowardly Lion. Nessarose joins Elphaba at Shiz in her second year, but both must return to Munchkinland before their father dies. His final gift to Nessarose is a pair of silver shoes, different from the film's ruby slippers, but Baum and Maguire actually referred to silver shoes in their versions. Toward the end of Act 1, Elphaba and Glinda go to the Emerald City to meet the Wizard, who wants Elphaba to give his monkeys wings so that they might fly, which, unlike in the final version, she refuses to do—but the famous image of the winged monkeys was invoked. Elphaba flees with the Grimmerie, a book of magic, and ends up in a broom closet, where she levitates the cleaning implement and flies away. The Wicked Witch of the West has emerged!

In Act 2, Nessarose comes into possession of the Grimmerie and uses it to make herself more powerful. She enchants Boq to force him to love her instead of Glinda, but she miscasts the spell, and Elphaba turns Boq into the Tin Woodman to save his life. The remainder of the scenario is closer to the plot of the film than the musical today: Elphaba turns Fiyero into the Scarecrow to save him from harm at the hands of the Wizard's men; Elphaba flies to the site where Dorothy's house has landed on Nessarose, finding that Glinda has given Dorothy the silver shoes; Dorothy, the Tin Woodman, and Lion end up at Kiamo Ko with Elphaba and the winged monkeys, finally launching the events that seem to lead to the witch's melting; and then Dorothy and her friends return to the Wizard, where he departs with Dorothy and leaves her three friends in charge of Oz. In this scenario, the Scarecrow declines the offer and goes to the Badlands to be with Elphaba, who faked her death.

Without referencing every documentable stage of *Wicked*'s creation,[16] one can see that allusions to the film remained of primary interest in a script from March 31, 2003, marked "Rehearsal Draft," representing the show's state a few months before the San Francisco try-out run. Instead of a short scenario, this is a 147-page script, meaning that it contains quotations from the film, glosses on famous lines, and plot points and references to the film's images.

At this point in its development the musical opened with the peaked, black hat and a shriveled black garment on stage, just after Elphaba appears to have melted. Glinda enters and leads the celebration among her fellow Ozians, perhaps inspired by her film appearance in Munchkinland after Dorothy's dramatic landing. Later in this stage scene a silhouette of the Wicked Witch of the West appears in projection, keeping her image before the audience. In Act 1, Scene 2, when Madame Morrible reconsiders student room assignments after meeting the unexpected Elphaba, she states that they have a "slight gulch," part of the Ozian language that Winnie Holzman invented,[17] but also a reference to Margaret Hamilton's famous "Miss Gulch." After Elphaba demonstrates her magical powers, Morrible presents her with a crystal ball, a tool used more in the movie by Professor Marvel and the Wicked Witch of the West. This scene also includes the first time that Elphaba sings her "Unlimited" theme, the first seven notes famously based on "Over the Rainbow." Scene 5 includes Galinda presenting Elphaba with the peaked hat; her green roommate's first reaction is that she will wear it "When monkeys fly!," reminder of another image from the film. In Scene 6 the script includes a pun on a famous line from the film: Boq informs Nessarose about the contents of the punch at the party: "Lemons and melons and pears," to which, of course, she can only answer, "Oh, my." Scene 7 includes the song "Popular," nothing like the film, but we see an unknown aspect of Glinda, that famous, poised character everyone believes he or she knows from Billie Burke's portrayal. We have never seen her as a playful young woman, who knows how to project herself and is willing to help a friend, as long as that friend does not displace her social position. Our knowledge from the film of Glinda in more mature years helps this song to land with the audience. In Scene 10, Doctor Dillamond uses an iconic line to tell Elphaba why he does not wish to leave Shiz University, despite pressure: "There's no place like home!" Later in the scene, Elphaba and Fiyero look into a crystal ball and see a gray place where no animal can speak, not unlike Judy Garland's Dorothy seeing Auntie Em in the Witch's crystal ball. The monochromatic reference resembles the sepia tone used for Kansas in the film before Oz appears in Technicolor. When looking in the crystal ball at this point in the musical, Elphaba was to enunciate a gloss on a very famous line: "Fiyero, I don't think this is Oz anymore." When Glinda and Elphaba are in the Emerald City before meeting the Wizard in Scene 12, part of the song "One Short Day" is the show-within-a-show *Wizomania*, a jocular exploration of the Wizard's arrival by balloon and how his presence and leadership have so enriched the land. It is fascinating to note that the creators of *Wicked* provided their own brief piece of musical theater, also based on *The Wizard of Oz*, a moment of fetching self-reflexivity. In Scene 13 the Wizard's image in the Throne Room is the familiar enormous head, and Scene 14 includes Madame Morrible declaring Elphaba a "Wicked Witch" in a public announcement, Elphaba singing her "Unlimited" motive during "Defying Gravity," levitating the broom that she found and flying away. Toward the end of "Defying Gravity," she advises those who seek her to gaze at the sky in the west, completing her new identity.

Act 2 includes many familiar images and references. In the first scene Glinda appears as "Glinda the Good," not the "Good Witch of the North" as one keeps hearing in the film, but her association with "good" confirms her opposition to the "Wicked Witch of the West." The scene also includes a reference that water can melt Elphaba; Fiyero's response is that people are "so brainless" that they will accept anything as fact, a word later associated with him as the Scarecrow. In Scene 2, where Elphaba visits Nessarose, there is emphasis on the shoes when Elphaba puts a spell on them so that Nessarose can walk. Boq also becomes the Tin Woodman. Scene 3 takes place in the Wizard's private chamber. He almost seduces Elphaba back to his side with the song "Wonderful," and repeats a number of images from the film already mentioned. The song includes reference to the Yellow Brick Road. At the end of Scene 4, Elphaba hears the cyclone, sending her off to find Glinda at the site of the crashed house in the next scene. The good witch has just sent Dorothy down the Yellow Brick Road with the shoes. In the following confrontation, Elphaba makes fun of Glinda's bubble as a mode of travel, which her adversary answers with an insult about Elphaba's broom. At the end of the scene, after Fiyero helps Elphaba escape, the Wizard's men tie him to the poles like a scarecrow. As the witchhunters sing about their hopes to kill Elphaba in Scene 7, Boq intones the verses heard on the original cast recording about how she turned him into a Tin Woodman and that her treatment of the Lion made him a coward. Scene 8 is at Kiamo Ko; while Dorothy sobs in the locked room, Elphaba refers to her aunt and uncle. Chistery, the only flying monkey with a name, is present. When Glinda confronts Elphaba, she asks her about the poppy field from the film that she had used to put Dorothy and the Cowardly Lion to sleep. After Elphaba allows Glinda to believe that Fiyero is dead, they sing "For Good," and then, from hiding, Glinda witnesses Dorothy throw the bucket of water and apparently kill Elphaba. She finds the hat and cape on the floor. In the concluding Scene 9, objects and images from the film continue to appear but with different contexts: Madame Morrible praises the Wizard for the gifts he just gave to Dorothy's friends before they were sent on their way; Glinda appears and uses the green elixir to establish that the Wizard was Elphaba's father, and then orders him to leave in his balloon. One perhaps assumes that he leaves with Dorothy, who is not mentioned. Back at Kiamo Ko, the Scarecrow appears and collects Elphaba, in hiding after faking her death. Unlike the film, Dorothy's friends are not left in charge of Oz—apparently Glinda the Good now rules.

As I have demonstrated elsewhere, a fascinating aspect of *Wicked* was how long it took for the show to reach its final form.[18] The creative team continued to revise the script until late 2006, more than three years after it opened. A number of the changes occurred when new actors assumed roles, as when George Hearn replaced Joel Grey as the Wizard. The role then included less dancing, requiring several small changes in the song "Wonderful." Schwartz and Holzman made further adjustments when David Garrison became the Wizard on tour, and then those changes entered the Broadway show when Ben Vereen became the Wizard. Such tweaking and reconsideration resulted in a script from December 5, 2006, subtitled "Revised Performance Script." This late script demonstrates how much of the 1939 film remains in *Wicked* as it plays today in New York City. (The show also required further changes as it opened in other countries, where details of *The Wizard of Oz* are not as famous as in the United States.)[19]

As Act 1 opens, Glinda descends in her "bubble." Unlike the diaphanous creation one sees in the film, this bubble is sturdy and metal, inspired by a clock pendulum (with an added bubble machine) and derived from the Clock of Time Dragon in Maguire's novel.[20] As in the earlier script, the scene includes reports of the death of the Wicked Witch of the West, and her silhouette also appears. In Scene 2, Nessarose's father, the Governor of Munchkinland, presents her with jeweled shoes. As Madame Morrible considers her rooming problems, she again admits that there is a "slight gulch." Morrible's enthusiasm for Elphaba when she displays her magical powers causes the green girl to sing "The Wizard and I," which again includes the first statement of her "Unlimited" theme. Scene 3 sports an addition since the March 2003 script, with Elphaba cackling at Galinda at the end of "What Is This Feeling?," foreshadowing her transition to the Wicked Witch. In Scene 5, the song "Dancing through Life," Fiyero cites the benefits of being without a brain, like the scarecrow he becomes. Scene 6 continues to introduce the black, peaked hat from Galinda's collection, as she presents it to Elphaba. The evocation of the film's "Lions and tigers and bears," here referring to the punch at the party with 'lemons and melons and pears,' remains in the exchange between Boq and Nessarose in Scene 6c. The young Galinda displays her character again in the song "Popular" in Scene 7, and the lion cub that becomes the Cowardly Lion in Act 2 makes its appearance in Scenes 8–9 as Fiyero realizes that he has feelings for Elphaba. Later in Scene 9, after Elphaba sings "I'm Not That Girl," Madame Morrible informs her student that the Wizard wants to meet her and reminds Elphaba that she cannot get wet while they share an umbrella in the rain. Morrible stops the rain. As in the March 2003 script, Scene 12 is the visit to the Emerald City and includes *Wizomania*. Scenes 13–14 provide the same references and images from the film as described in the previous script.

Act 2 opens differently in the 2006 script, with the citizens of Oz looking with terror to the sky, hoping that the Witch won't appear. This is reminiscent of the film scene where the frightened people of the Emerald City run to the Wizard's palace after the Wicked Witch of the West sky-writes "Surrender,

Dorothy!" Scene 1 again includes major focus on Glinda the Good and someone in the crowd sings that water can melt the Wicked Witch. Scene 2 emphasizes the shoes and Boq's transformation into the Tin Woodman, and when Elphaba enters Nessarose's chamber she utters a version of one of the film's iconic lines: "Well, there's no place like home." Scenes 3–4 include many of the images already mentioned with one new touch in "As Long as You're Mine," where Fiyero admits that he might be missing a brain. The show then proceeds swiftly to its conclusion with continuous use of images and concepts from the film that have been identified. There are a few differences with the March 2003 script—Glinda, for example, does not mention the field of poppies in Scene 8 when she argues with Elphaba—an effort to avoid copyright infringement, as described below.

References to the film of *The Wizard of Oz* are not the only self-reflexivity of the genre found in *Wicked*. For example, when Glinda is wheeled out on a raised platform with a microphone at the beginning of Act 2, she raises her arms at the microphone, and the ghost of Evita appears. The show's final cadence is clearly based on the end of *West Side Story*, but these references are rife in the genre and not the stuff of legal action. Most references to the film *The Wizard of Oz* are similar in depth and intention, but, as described in the next section, lawyers at Universal Pictures did insist that some direct references to the MGM film be deleted.

Legal Hassles

One development in the creation of *Wicked* that Schwartz and Holzman clearly did not anticipate was the fear of their major producer, Universal Pictures, concerning possible copyright infringement claims about their use of lines and images from the 1939 film. Warner Bros. held the copyright on the film in 2003, and although there never seems to have been an intention to negotiate with them concerning these issues in the musical, lawyers at Universal had no desire to place their employer in jeopardy. Winnie Holzman found herself summoned to Los Angeles for a meeting with Universal lawyers the week that previews began in San Francisco in spring 2003. Designers on the creative team for *Wicked* had already been given instructions concerning things they needed to do to avoid copyright infringement, and their work had gone in a different direction; but that was not the case with the script. The lawyers told Holzman what cuts needed to be made or the show simply would not be produced.[21] For Schwartz and Holzman this smacked of censorship, and the composer/lyricist was especially irate. The blade fell late in the creative process. One wonders why Universal's legal department did not have this discussion with the writers earlier, as they did with the designers. Schwartz has spoken about how he and Holzman stood together as an "authorial unit" when under pressure from other forces in the collaboration,[22] and that solidarity surely occurred here, but Universal was adamant and a number of lines had to be removed. Schwartz reports that these were lines that earned big laughs, and, indeed, some of these deletions can be viewed in scripts prepared at various moments in the collaboration.[23] In the rehearsal script from March 31, 2003, completed shortly before this battle occurred, in Act 2, Scene 5, Glinda said "Goodbye, Dorothy—!" (p. 125) while standing in front of the wrecked house in Munchkinland just before Elphaba arrives, a line that does not appear in the "PRE-New York Rehearsal Script," dated July 28, 2003. Later, Glinda confronts Elphaba at Kiamo Ko in Act 2, Scene 8, shortly before they sing "For Good." She tries to convince her friend that she is out of control, and, as reported above, asked her the following in the March 31 script: "Making poppy fields for people to fall asleep in; what was *that* about?" (Act 2, Scene 8, p. 136). This line also fails to appear in the New York rehearsal script.

One has to admit that these legal decisions seem arbitrary. Glinda stood in front of the wrecked house in Act 2, Scene 5, when she said farewell to Dorothy, a strong evocation of the film, but apparently mentioning the girl's name in that context was too much. This is proven by the fact that the name "Dorothy" does not appear in the scripts from July 28, 2003, and December 5, 2006. The name "Glinda" was acceptable, and in the final script Elphaba screams at Dorothy, threatening that she will never see "your Aunt Em and your Uncle What's-his-name again" (Act 2, Scene 8, p. 112), but the name "Dorothy" perhaps was judged to have placed Universal in too much legal danger. The dog's name, "Toto," apparently also became a point of contention: it appears in Act 2, Scene 8, in the July 28, 2003, script (p. 114) but not in the December 5, 2006 script. Also, the line from March 31, 2003 about the poppies appeared early in a scene where Glinda watches her friend apparently melting, viewed by the audience in shadows behind a curtain—a clear reference to the film, but without seeing Dorothy's famous blue and white checked gingham dress. For some reason, however, even mentioning a poppy field was *verboten*. The Universal lawyers also demanded that Nessarose's shoes not be ruby colored, but the compromise came when they allowed the production to light the shoes with a red follow spot.[24] Another concession they managed to achieve was keeping the funny line about contents of the punch at the dance in Act 1.

Schwartz and Holzman lost the battle concerning a number of lines, and then they had to change the scenes and maintain the quality of the script. Schwartz reports that the character most affected by the deleted lines was Glinda, who lost six to ten funny lines, a problem because that was a major part of the role's appeal. Glinda sings a lot in *Wicked*, but Elphaba's role has more songs of dramatic importance, and Kristin Chenoweth had worked very hard on the comic aspect of her role. Schwartz notes that she was disappointed but cooperative as they rewrote the scenes, choosing not to play the diva who might have called her agent or tried to pull out of the production. The composer/lyricist was impressed with the way that Winnie Holzman recrafted the scenes so that Glinda still could get some laughs.[25] For example, in the two later scripts cited above, Glinda pleads with Elphaba to release the "little girl" and "that poor little dog," which she calls "Dodo" (December 5, 2006, Act 2, Scene 8, p. 112). Such efforts helped mitigate the situation and also remind us how much of *The Wizard of Oz* remains in *Wicked*, even after legal scrutiny.

"Over the Rainbow" versus "Unlimited"

While working on *Wicked*, Schwartz finished his score for *Geppetto* for the Disney Channel. Unlike the animated film *Pinocchio*, in this version the camera stays on the father as he hunts for his son. In addition to his own songs, Schwartz wanted permission to use "When You Wish upon a Star" and "I've Got No Strings" from the film, and this was arranged.[26] In *Wicked*, no similar attempt was made to gain the rights to use elements of the score from the film *The Wizard of Oz*, but that did not stop Schwartz from making a playful musical reference. As noted above, the first seven notes in Elphaba's "Unlimited" *Leitmotiv* are the same as the notes that set the first four words to "Over the Rainbow" by Harold Arlen and Yip Harburg. Schwartz profoundly changed the rhythm and harmonic background; if one were not listening for the reference, it might not be heard.[27] By using such a small snippet, Schwartz avoided copyright issues, but he has made no secret of the quotation, and its significance would seem to go beyond superficial delight for musical theater geeks. "Over the Rainbow," after all, is one of the most famous songs from the entire century. Judy Garland singing the song with her improbably mature voice next to the wagon with Toto looking on is an indelible Hollywood image. In 2001, an MTV poll named "Over the Rainbow" the "Century's Best Song"[28] and in 2011 critics from *Time* magazine placed it atop a list of "ALL-TIME 100 Songs."[29] Why wouldn't Schwartz wish to associate his own score with this monument of American popular music? However, beyond working part of "Over the Rainbow" into his own score without having to pay a cent for the royalties, what does this quotation mean?

A possible association between the meaning of "Over the Rainbow" and Elphaba's "Unlimited" theme seems plain. Dorothy seeks a place outside of her current circumstances, a youthful dream that she discovers is excessive during her trek through Oz. There is, after all, no place like home. Elphaba's personal journey to the point where she arrives at Shiz University has been bleaker than Dorothy's, with a difficult family life and constant derision because of her coloring. She dreams of fame and popularity. In the end, she cannot achieve her dreams and she turns her quest over to Glinda. Through this musical choice, Schwartz associated the Wicked Witch of the West, the protagonist in his story, with Dorothy. It is the musical equivalent of Maguire's inversion of the story.

Schwartz reaches into the American musical past more than once in his score, most extensively in the songs that he wrote for the Wizard: "Sentimental Man" and "Wonderful." Schwartz has called the latter a "deliberate pastiche" and Joel Grey, who premiered the number on Broadway, has spoken of it as a "soft-shoe."[30] Both songs include stylistic markers of ragtime and vaudeville music from the early twentieth century (Baum's time, when the author also pursued stage versions of his *Oz* stories), a goal assisted greatly by William David Brohn with his orchestrations.[31] The Wizard thus takes on the role of the song and dance man pulling off his con, convincing Elphaba to put a spell on the monkeys to give them wings and in Act 2 nearly bringing her into his fold. He performs in a similar style in the first scene when he seduces Elphaba's mother with the green elixir. Schwartz also makes use of other musical styles for dramatic reasons, helping Elphaba to emerge as a diva with such numbers as "The Wizard and I," which goes down a stylistic path toward rhythm and blues, the rock tune "Defying Gravity," and the power ballad "As Long as You're Mine" sung after she has consummated her relationship with Fiyero. Schwartz's mining of the musical past in this score is not as impressive as what he did in *The Baker's Wife* with its witty use of sounds redolent of Debussy, Ravel, French cabaret songs, and French film scores,[32] but he does place his score to *Wicked* within a recognizable musical past. He offers the exclamation point on this effort at the conclusion of "No One Mourns the Wicked" with the tritone motion in the bass between E and A sharp, an unmistakable reference to Bernstein's *West Side Story*, reaching back to one of the iconic shows in the genre and paying homage to a master he actually worked with on *Mass* in 1971.[33]

Wicked as Part of the Oz Universe

Even with the numerous resonances that the musical *Wicked* includes from the film *The Wizard of Oz*, the many differences between the two properties have changed how we view *Oz*. To begin with, despite Schwartz's declaration that the writers thought of the film as a "documentary" and that everything they included in the show needed to be explainable in the film's context (cited above), this was not the case. Many details from the film disappear in the show, such as how Dorothy was rescued by her three famous friends from the Wicked Witch of the

West, or any mention of Dorothy or the "little girl" (as she is known in *Wicked*) when the Wizard heads to his balloon at the end. Fans must choose between competing *Oz* stories in the musical and the film, let alone differences between the film's and Baum's original plots, or the competing rendition that Maguire told when compared with any of these versions. Second, *Wicked* provided *Oz* with another soundtrack, songs that might not become quite as ubiquitous as "Over the Rainbow" or "Ding-Dong! The Witch Is Dead," but a Broadway musical that runs for more than a decade with successful versions elsewhere in the world and a popular original cast album makes a strong mark in popular culture, and Universal has scheduled the release of a movie version for 2019. Songs like "The Wizard and I" and "Defying Gravity" will remain with us for generations, and they will always be understood in an Ozian context.

Perhaps the largest effect that *Wicked* has on the Oz Universe, however, is how much it has complicated our understanding of the Wicked Witch of the West. For some of us, Margaret Hamilton's version of the character was one of the ultimate representations of evil of our early years, malevolent and supremely frightening. Elphaba, however, is good, caused to appear evil by forces beyond her control, a far more complicated figure. With Elphaba, the Oz Universe grows up, with the many shades of gray (or green!) that one must regard to make mature sense of the world around us. This was the main triumph of the likes of Maguire, Schwartz, and Holzman, and our understanding of Oz, and our relation to it, will never be the same.

Notes

1. Personal interview by the author with Stephen Schwartz, New York, March 22, 2005, reported in "The Creation of a Broadway Musical: Stephen Schwartz, Winnie Holzman, and *Wicked*," in *The Cambridge Companion to the Musical*, 2nd ed., William A. Everett and Paul R. Laird, 340–352 (Cambridge: Cambridge University Press, 2008), 340.

2. For more on Schwartz's discussions with Platt, see Carol de Giere, *Defying Gravity: The Creative Career of Stephen Schwartz from* Godspell *to* Wicked (New York: Applause Theatre and Cinema Books, 2008), 287–289, and Paul R. Laird, *Wicked: A Musical Biography* (Lanham, MD: Scarecrow Press, 2011), 30–31.

3. David Cote, Wicked: *The Grimmerie: A Behind-the-Scenes Look at the Hit Broadway Musical* (New York: Hyperion, 2005), 22.

4. Personal interview by the author with Stephen Schwartz, New York, March 22, 2005.

5. Gregory Maguire, *Wicked: The Life and Times of the Wicked Witch of the West* (New York: ReganBooks, 1995).

6. In reference to both the novel and show, this character is referred to by the correct name for that moment: "Galinda" or "Glinda." She changes her name in both in tribute to Doctor Dillamond, who is unable to pronounce her given name of "Galinda."

7. Personal telephone interview by the author with Winnie Holzman, March 29, 2005.

8. Cote, Wicked: *The Grimmerie*, 35.

9. Stacy Wolf has described the world of *Wicked* fandom among young women in her "*Wicked* Divas, Musical Theatre, and Internet Girl Fans," *Camera Obscura* 65 (2007): 39–71.

10. Laird, Wicked: *A Musical Biography*, 33, 53.

11. Cote, Wicked: *The Grimmerie*, 38.

12. Cote, Wicked: *The Grimmerie*, 26.

13. De Giere, *Defying Gravity*, 279.

14. De Giere, *Defying Gravity*, 316.

15. Published in de Giere, *Defying Gravity*, 503–509.

16. My book on the show, Wicked: *A Musical Biography*, benefited from access to a scenario and a number of scripts made available by Schwartz's office and other sources: Scenario (entitled *Wicked* Outline 11/21/99); *Wicked*: A New Musical, First Complete Draft, March 12, 2001; *Wicked*: A New Musical, First Complete Draft [*sic*], November 21, 2001; *Wicked* Script—workshop draft, October 2002; *Wicked* Rehearsal Script, March 31, 2003; *Wicked*, Pre-New York Rehearsal, July 28, 2003; *Wicked*, Pre-New York Rehearsal Script, August 25, 2003; *Wicked*, New York Rehearsal Script, September 16, 2003; *Wicked*, New York Rehearsal Script, October 5, 2003; and *Wicked Broadway*, Revised Performance Script, December 5, 2006. For simplicity's sake in this essay, I describe the influence of the 1939 film in the scripts dated March 31, 2003, July 28, 2003, and December 5, 2006.

17. The Ozian language that Winnie Holzman developed for the show mostly includes recognizable English words with nonstandard endings and new conceptions of nouns and verbs. For a glossary intended for fans of the show, see Cote, Wicked: *The Grimmerie*, 190–191.

18. See my Wicked: *A Musical Biography*, 53–87.

19. See, for example, Laird, Wicked: *A Musical Biography*, 265, for material on how they adapted the show for the London audience.

20. Cote, Wicked: *The Grimmerie*, 103.

21. The writer who has covered this process between the Universal lawyers and those writing the show is de Giere, *Defying Gravity*, 382–385.

22. See my "The Creation of a Broadway Musical: Stephen Schwartz, Winnie Holzman, and *Wicked*," in *The Cambridge Companion to the Musical*, 342.

23. Schwartz reported three lines that the lawyers cut in de Giere, *Defying Gravity*, 383.

24. De Giere, *Defying Gravity*, 385.

25. De Giere, *Defying Gravity*, 384.

26. Paul R. Laird, *The Musical Theater of Stephen Schwartz: From* Godspell *to* Wicked *and Beyond* (Lanham, MD: Rowman and Littlefield, 2014), 259.

27. Schwartz does comment on this in de Giere, *Defying Gravity*, 305.

28. http://www.mtv.com/news/1441426/over-the-rainbow-voted-20th-centurys-best-song/, accessed July 25, 2017.

29. http://entertainment.time.com/2011/10/24/the-all-time-100-songs/slide/over-the-rainbow-judy-garland/, accessed July 25, 2017.

30. Cote, Wicked: *The Grimmerie*, 85, 44.

31. See my Wicked: *A Musical Biography*, 236–237, 241–242.

32. See my *The Musical Theater of Stephen Schwartz*, 120–131.

33. See my Wicked: *A Musical Biography*, 166–167. For Schwartz's work on Leonard Bernstein's *Mass*, see my *The Musical Theater of Stephen Schwartz*, 45–54.

"BEYOND THE RAINBOW"

AFTERLIVES OF THE SONGS FROM *THE WIZARD OF OZ*

Walter Frisch

Two recent events involved Harold Arlen and E. Y. ("Yip") Harburg's songs from *The Wizard of Oz*. In the spring of 2013, in the days immediately following the death of Margaret Thatcher on April 8, opponents of the former British prime minister mounted a campaign that helped push the song "Ding-Dong! The Witch Is Dead" near the top of the UK charts. Even though the director-general of the BBC1 found the campaign "distasteful and inappropriate," the television station played a five-second excerpt of the song, while a reporter explained its significance to listeners. Keeping a stiff upper lip, Lord Parkinson, a former member of Thatcher's Cabinet, said that this way of celebrating the Iron Lady's death would not have upset her because "she was convinced that what she was doing was the right thing for Britain."[1]

Earlier in 2013, just weeks after the massacre at the Sandy Hook Elementary School in Newtown, Connecticut, singer-songwriter Ingrid Michaelson assembled a group of children from the town to sing and record "Over the Rainbow." The song was made available on Amazon and iTunes; the profits would go to those in the local community most affected by the tragedy. A video was posted on YouTube with the message, "The hope of this video is to convey the beautiful, resilient spirit that members of this community demonstrated during those sessions. This is a testament to a community whose determined process of recovery, founded on goodwill, hope and love, can serve as an inspiration to us all."[2]

These events, taking place within a few weeks of each other, reveal clearly how the songs of *The Wizard of Oz* have continued to resonate well beyond the 1939 MGM film, extending deep into the political, cultural, and social contexts of the early twenty-first century. Obviously, to para-phrase one of the most famous lines in movie history, we are not in Kansas—or in Oz—any more. This chapter explores something of the afterlives of the songs, with a special focus on the most popular one, "Over the Rainbow," which has achieved iconic status over the past eighty years.[3]

The Songs Go Public

The story of the songs' journeys out of Kansas and Oz, and into the ears and hearts of a public worldwide, begins in the late fall of 1938, when *The Wizard of Oz* was still in production. MGM was keeping a tight lid on the music, which had been prerecorded for the soundtrack. At this point, copyists' piano-vocal scores and the orchestral scores and parts were circulating only in-house. Yet an East Coast bandleader named Larry Clinton managed to get two numbers, "Over the Rainbow" and "The Jitterbug," which he recorded in December for RCA Victor, with two leading vocalists (Bea Wain and Ford Leary, respec-tively). Despite strong protests from the film's producers, who demanded that no recordings of the film's songs be made or issued until authorization was given by MGM, RCA released the Clinton disk in February 1939.[4] This re-cording would allow the public to hear music from *The Wizard of Oz* for the first time. At this point, Clinton and his singers had no direct acquaintance with the soundtrack recordings. On the RCA disk, sung by Wain up-tempo and in a syncopated style, "Over the Rainbow" becomes a typical smooth fox-trot song of the period, far from the ballad of longing Judy Garland had re-corded for her Kansas scene.

The next time the public would hear music from *The Wizard of Oz* was on a June 29 broadcast of the radio show *Good News*, as part of MGM's official rollout for the film in the early summer of 1939. *Good News*, produced between 1937 and 1940 by MGM, and sponsored by Maxwell House Coffee, showcased the studio's stars and films by giving listeners an audible peek behind the scenes.[5] The June 29 show was devoted entirely to *The Wizard of Oz*. One amusing segment with Judy Garland, Harold Arlen, and Yip Harburg supposedly recreates the moment when the creators introduced Garland to "Over the Rainbow" and taught her to sing it. In other segments, musical numbers from the film are sung complete with a full orchestra and choir led by the regular music director of *Good News*, Meredith Willson (later to become the composer and lyricist of *The Music Man*).

As part of the publicity campaign for the film, Leo Feist, Inc., the music publishing arm of MGM, issued piano-vocal scores for six numbers from the film: "Over the Rainbow," "If I Only Had a Brain," "Ding-Dong! The Witch Is Dead," "The Merry Old Land of Oz," "We're Off to See the Wizard," and "The

Jitterbug." The sheet music covers had headshots of the main characters and elegantly whimsical illustrations by Al Hirschfeld (Figure 11.1). Even before the official release, Feist had sent "advanced artist" copies of the sheet music to prominent bandleaders and singers.

By the summer of 1939, other big band recordings quickly joined those of Larry Clinton, who had jumped the gun. Among these were records by Del

FIGURE 11.1. Sheet music for *The Wizard of Oz* with illustrations by Al Hirschfield.

Courtney and vocalist Sherman Hayes (recorded July 7, 1939), Glenn Miller and Ray Eberle (July 12), and Bob Crosby and Teddy Grace (July 24). Miller's disk also included "Ding-Dong! The Witch Is Dead."[6]

Decca Records, a label with which Judy Garland had worked since 1935, initiated the largest project involving the *Wizard of Oz* songs. On July 28 and 29, 1939, Garland, the Ken Darby Singers, and Victor Young and his orchestra recorded eight sides of music from the film. One disk, with "Over the Rainbow" on one side and "Jitterbug" on the other, was released in September 1939. The others would be issued as part of a four-disk set in March 1940.[7] They included one with the Munchkinland sequence on two sides; another with "If I Only Had a Brain" on one side and "If I Only Had a Heart" on the other; and a fourth with "The Merry Old Land of Oz" and "We're Off to See the Wizard." It is important to note that these were not soundtrack recordings. Garland and the Darby Singers were the only actual cast members of *The Wizard of Oz* to participate in the Decca set. (Harold Arlen speaks the part of the Scarecrow in the introduction to "The Jitterbug.") A soundtrack recording of the film would become available only in the 1950s.

The Miller-Eberle, Crosby-Grace, and Young-Garland recordings of "Over the Rainbow" all sat at the top of the charts (numbers 1, 2, and 5, respectively) for many weeks in the fall of 1939. The Clinton-Wain recording, which had not garnered much attention on its initial appearance, rose with this tide, cresting at number 10.[8]

The "Lemon-Drop" Songs

Harold Arlen referred to the lighter numbers in *The Wizard of Oz* score—those that are sung within the Land of Oz—as the "lemon-drop" songs.[9] Perhaps inevitably, because they are so closely linked to the specific characters and situations in Oz, these songs have had a more limited post-film life than "Over the Rainbow." The two most frequently recorded lemon-drop songs are "Ding-Dong! The Witch Is Dead" and "If I Only Had a Brain" (and its contrafacta "If I Only Had a Heart" and "If I Only Had the Nerve"). "Ding-Dong" has been recorded by a number of major artists, including Bing Crosby, Sammy Davis Jr. (with Buddy Rich), Rosemary Clooney, and Harry Connick Jr. It was also featured in an episode of the television show *Glee* (2011), when Chris Colfer and Lea Michele sing (and dance) a cover of the arrangement Peter Matz had made for Barbra Streisand and Arlen on the 1966 album *Harold Sings Arlen (With Friend)* (Columbia OS 2920). "If I Only Had a Brain" was recorded by vocalists as diverse as jazz great Abbey Lincoln and the actor-singer Mandy Patinkin.[10]

As we saw above with "Ding-Dong! The Witch Is Dead" being used to celebrate the death of Margaret Thatcher, the lemon-drop songs also turn up in contexts that play on, or sometimes against, their original meanings. Since at least the appearance of the film *The Wizard of Oz*, residents of Australia have referred to themselves as "Aussies" (often pronounced as "Ozzies"). Hence the long-standing link between Australia and Oz, and the reference to Sydney as the Emerald City (as in the 1988 film *Emerald City*).

In November 1939, very soon after the release of the film, the Australian bandleader Jim Davidson and his ABC Dance Orchestra recorded "We're Off to See the Wizard" (Regal Zonophone G 23890). When World War II broke out, "We're Off to Meet the Wizard," which is essentially a march, became a rallying song for Australian troops. It played a prominent role during the Battle of Bardia in Libya in north Africa in early January 1941, when Australian soldiers confronted and defeated Italian forces. Sir Winston Churchill told the story dramatically in his history of the war:

> The attack opened early on January 3. One Australian battalion, covered by a strong artillery concentration, seized and held a lodgment in the western perimeter. Behind them engineers filled in the anti-tank ditch. Two Australian brigades carried on the attack and swept east and southeastwards. They sang at that time a song from an American film, which soon became popular also in Britain:
>
> > "We're off to see the Wizard,
> > The wonderful Wizard of Oz.
> > We hear he is a Whiz of a Wiz,
> > If ever a Wiz there was."
>
> This tune always reminds me of those buoyant days.[11]

Harold Arlen was pleased at the use of his song by Australian soldiers. In November 1943 he appeared on a broadcast of the wartime radio show, *America Talks to Australia and New Zealand*. The host asked him, "Harold, being able to talk to our friends Down Under has a special significance, doesn't it?" Arlen replied that indeed it did: Australian troops "used my song 'We're Off to See the Wizard' as a marching song when they stormed the heights of Bardia, and that is an honor I'll cherish as one of the high points in my life." Arlen went on to sing and accompany himself in the song, prefacing his performance with these comments: "When I wrote, 'We're Off to See the Wizard,' I didn't dream it would ever be used as a battle song. But since it is, I can't help but be proud to know that you fellows Down Under think enough of it to sing it as you go into a scrap. I want to say Happy New Year to you grand guys. And now, 'We're Off to See the Wizard.'"[12]

In recent years another of the lemon-drop songs, "If I Only Had a Brain" / "If I Only Had a Heart," has been featured in television commercials when a company seeks to attract customers possibly wary of its reputation or image. The University of Phoenix is perhaps the best known and most notorious of for-profit universities in the United States; it has been the subject of many investigations, lawsuits, and controversies. The university's reputation suffered especially in the years after 2010, when enrollment dropped by almost 70 percent. In 2016 it aired a number of ads seeking to restore its image. In one, "If I Only Had a Brain" is sung off-screen by a young woman with a reedy and seemingly untrained voice, against a minimalist drone-like background. Harburg's lyrics are recast to reflect a strong work ethic and the idea that someone from the singer's social stratum (likely lower middle class) can have a worthy brain. She performs the last line of each verse in a speech-song style:

> So my kids don't have to forage,
> Got two jobs to pay a mortgage,
> And I've also got a brain.
> Life's short, talk is cheap,
> I'll be workin' while you sleep,
> Still don't think I've got a brain?
>
> You can try, I'll do it faster,
> I was born a multi-tasker,
> I was raised against the grain.
> I took two bullets in the chest,
> Got three kids, I never rest,
> And I've also got a brain.
>
> You think a resume's enough,
> We'll step up when things get tough,
> Don't you want that kind of brain?
> A degree is a degree,
> You're gonna want someone like me,
> But only if *you* have a brain.[13]

In a similar vein—here seeking to break a stereotype of the hard-hearted banker—the NEFCU (Nassau Educators Federal Credit Union), a financial institution based on Long Island in New York featured "If I Only Had a Heart" in a 2015 commercial.

We see several men in business suits dancing and singing lines (with original lyrics) to the bemused surprise of their tellers and customers. On a voice-over an announcer says, "If banks did have a heart, then instead of charging all sorts of fees, they'd offer free checking with up to 3 percent interest, like NECFU does."[14]

"Over the Rainbow"

It will be no surprise to readers of this chapter, or to those familiar with *The Wizard of Oz,* that "Over the Rainbow," which won the Oscar for Best Song in 1940, has transcended its original context far more widely and frequently than other numbers in the film. "Over the Rainbow" is one of the most beloved songs of all time. In a survey conducted in 2000, the National Endowment for the Arts and the Recording Industry Association of America asked elected officials, people in the music industry and media, and teachers and students what they felt was the greatest song of the twentieth century. "Over the Rainbow" won handily, beating out such titles as "White Christmas," "This Land Is Your Land," and "Respect."[15] In 2004, the American Film Institute put "Over the Rainbow" at the head of a list of the top one hundred songs in American cinema.[16]

"Over the Rainbow" is such a cultural fixture, at least in the Anglo-American world, that it turns up in versions that range from the sublime to the ridiculous. We saw above how it served as a gesture of solace and solidarity in the aftermath of a mass shooting. In a similar gesture, but taking place on a much larger scale, the pop star Ariana Grande sang "Over the Rainbow" as the encore at her One Love Manchester concert in England on June 4, 2017. A benefit for victims of the recent suicide bombing at that city's arena, the event was attended by 50,000, and broadcast and live-streamed to millions more worldwide. Members of the mostly young audience wept during the number, and Grande herself almost broke down in the coda.[17]

"Over the Rainbow" has also had its share of purely silly incarnations. In one YouTube video, a man plays the tune on an "organ" comprised of differently pitched stuffed cats. In a different video, Judy Garland's original scene from *The Wizard of Oz* is given a death metal voice over.[18] Here we can only explore some of the incarnations of the most famous song from the film.

Judy Garland and "Over the Rainbow"

For generations, "Over the Rainbow" was most closely associated with Judy Garland, who created it as a sixteen-year-old playing Dorothy and would continue to sing the song until her tragic death at the age of forty-seven. "Over the Rainbow" became Garland's theme song, reflecting the tumult of her adulthood, which was marked by substance abuse, depression, weight problems, hospitalizations, failed marriages, custody battles, and financial difficulties.

Garland acknowledged, and mostly embraced, this association with "Over the Rainbow." But she also stressed the universality of the song's message. In 1961 she told Arlen's biographer Edward Jablonski:

> [As for] my feeling toward "Over the Rainbow" now, it has become a part of my life. It is so symbolic of everybody's dream and wish that I am sure that's why people sometimes get tears in their eyes when they hear it. I have sung it dozens of times and it's still the song that is closest to my heart. It is very gratifying to have a song that is more or less known as my song, or my theme song, and to have had it written by the fantastic Harold Arlen.[19]

Garland made a number of studio recordings of "Over the Rainbow" and also sang it frequently in concert, where it usually was one of the last numbers—and one for which the audience had been waiting all evening. Over the course of her career, as her voice darkened, the song morphed from innocent optimism to heart-wrenching despair. The coda, "If happy little bluebirds fly / Beyond the rainbow, Why oh why can't I ?" which is a gentle plea in the earliest performances, became a passionate *cri de coeur* in which Garland emphasizes each word. We can hear this approach in her version of "Over the Rainbow" sung as the figure of the Tramp in a television broadcast of 1955 (see Figure 11.2), and in her two late recordings for Capitol Records, in 1955 and 1960.[20]

During the latter part of her career, Judy Garland became a gay icon; her persona and her songs appealed strongly to an ever more visible and liberated male homosexual community. "Over the Rainbow" was closely linked with this identity. As Steven Frank wrote in 2007: "When Judy Garland sang 'Over the Rainbow,' the sadness in her voice . . . was, in effect, the sound of the closet, and it spoke to gay men's consciousness that the image they presented in their own public lives was often at odds with a truer sense of self that mainstream society would not condone."[21] Gay men flocked to Garland's concerts, where she warmly acknowledged their presence and their support. At one concert in Philadelphia in 1968, she said, "I finally made it over the rainbow thanks to you all." She began "Over the Rainbow," then interrupted it by yelling, "We can all do it, you know."[22]

Other "Rainbows"

"Over the Rainbow" has of course had a life outside of the career and legacy of Judy Garland. It has been recorded or covered thousands of times. As of July

FIGURE 11.2. Judy Garland performing "Over the Rainbow" as the figure of the Tramp in a 1955 television broadcast.

2017, one comprehensive database, the Jazz Discography Online, listed 1,054 recordings. Another, SecondHand Songs, which overlaps only partially with the jazz one, lists 692 versions.[23]

Yet, perhaps fearing comparison with Garland, many vocalists have steered clear of "Over the Rainbow." In a spoken introduction to a live recording of 1987, Barbra Streisand calls "Over the Rainbow" "one of the finest songs ever written" but says she resisted singing it "because it's identified with one of the greatest singers who ever lived."[24] In addition to Streisand, singers who overcame hesitation and made notable recordings of "Over the Rainbow" include Frank Sinatra (1945), Rosemary Clooney (1952), Harold Arlen himself (1955), Sarah Vaughan (1956), Diahann Carroll (1957), Aretha Franklin (1960), Ella Fitzgerald (1961), Tony Bennett (1961), Patti LaBelle (1981), Eva Cassidy (1992), Jane Monheit (2004), Judy Collins (2010), and Josh Groban (2015). The wide range of traditions and styles represented by these artists—from pop to folk to jazz to soul—indicate how wide is the appeal of "Over the Rainbow." Each of the singers mentioned here captures in his or her own way the blend of concern and hope that lies at the core of this song.

When the lyrics of "Over the Rainbow" are translated into other languages, at least in Europe, the song has often become a rather different kind of number. In

1941, the French chanteuse Léo Marjane recorded a version in which the rainbow becomes a symbol of romantic love, "passionate and almost unreal." This is clearly not Dorothy's rainbow:

> *Verse* [sung after chorus on Marjane's recording]
> Au même endroit peut-être un jour
> J'attendrais ton retour,
> Guettant malgré moi
> L'accent familier de ta voix.
> Bientôt plus loin iront tes pas.
> Tu ne reviendras pas.
> On peut désormais
> Rester seul à tout jamais.
>
> *Chorus*
> Là-bas renaît lentement l'arc-en-ciel.
> Pareil à notre amour ardent et presque irréel.
> Vers lui je voudrais partir avec vous.
> Car tout y parait plus charmant, plus clair, et plus doux.
>
> Adieu chagrin, tristesse adieu,
> C'est comme un nouveau paradis de rêve.
> Et ses couleurs ont à mes yeux
> L'éclat d'un bonheur merveilleux
> Changeant sans trêve.
>
> Après l'orage viennent les beaux jours.
> Après les larmes d'un instant reviendra l'amour.[25]

[In the same place perhaps one day I will await your return, anticipating despite myself the familiar tone of your voice. But soon your steps will lead you away; you will not return. And I might from then on remain alone forever.

Over there the rainbow is slowly reappearing, like our love that is passionate and almost unreal. I'd like to go to it with you because everything there appears more charming, clearer, and more gentle.

Farewell sorrow, farewell sadness. It's like a new dream-like paradise. And its colors strike my eyes with a wonderful happiness that constantly changes.

After the storm come beautiful days; after the tears love will quickly return.]

An Italian version by Piero Michetti has a similar romantic tinge. In the second verse of the song's chorus ("Somewhere over the rainbow, / Skies are blue"), the rainbow emits scents that remind the singer of kisses:

> Il profumo del cielo
> Che manda giù
> È il profumo dei baci
> Che io non sento piu.[26]
> [The perfume that the heavens send down is the perfume of kisses that
> I no longer smell.]

Jazz "Rainbows"

"Over the Rainbow" quickly became a standard among jazz instrumentalists, especially solo pianists, many of whom, even in the absence of the lyrics, "paint" the rainbow with as much feeling and imagination as the great vocalists. Distinguished recordings of the song include those by Art Tatum (1939, c. 1948, 1953, 1956), Bud Powell (1951, 1956), George Shearing (1951, 1963), Dave Brubeck (1952), Ellis Larkins (1952), Oscar Peterson (1954, 1959), Erroll Garner (1955), Dick Marx (1955), André Previn (1960), Mary Lou Williams (1978), and Keith Jarrett (1982, 1984, 1991, 1995, 2009).

Chronological priority alone would make Tatum's first version, created in the summer of the song's release, worthy of attention.[27] But more significant is its musical inventiveness, conveyed with the technically dazzling, stride-inflected swing of which Tatum was the undisputed master. Tatum introduces the chorus of "Over the Rainbow" with two statements of a pungent, upward rolled dominant chord with a flatted ninth (that is, lowered by a half step) and a raised eleventh and thirteenth. Tatum then plays three full choruses of "Over the Rainbow," each becoming progressively more virtuosic. He tends to perform Arlen's melody mostly straight, but underpins it with a wide array of substitutions for the original harmonies. In between phrases of "Over the Rainbow" he intersperses his trademark lightning-fast scales (sometimes impressionistic whole-tone ones) and arpeggios running up and down almost the entire length of the keyboard.

If Tatum is the virtuoso's rainbow that spreads its colors fast and wide, then Keith Jarrett's is the poet's rainbow, painted in delicate, understated strokes. "Over the Rainbow" appears to be one of the first numbers to which Keith Jarrett turned when he began doing more classic jazz improvisation on standard tunes in the later 1970s. He has played it many times in concert, often as an encore. Five different Jarrett versions of "Over the Rainbow" exist on recording or video, among them his renowned La Scala version of 1995.[28] Although not straying far from Arlen's original harmonies, Jarrett enhances them by adding tones and unusual voicings, and he animates the texture with inner parts and rich counterpoint. The melody, always identifiable, is refracted through a variety of rhythmic figures, which are often suspended across beats or bar lines. All these features give Jarrett's playing a unique blend of fluidity and hesitation. What Jarrett's "Rainbow" retains above all—and in this he is distinctive among pianists—is something of the child's perspective, Dorothy's perspective. The sophisticated transparency at certain moments rivals another great musical portrait of youthful imagination, Robert Schumann's *Scenes from Childhood*.

"Over the Rainbow" in Film

Less than a year after the release of *The Wizard of Oz*, "Over the Rainbow" turned up in another MGM film, *The Philadelphia Story*. This would be only the first of many appearances of the song in movies and on television. In *The Philadelphia Story*, Katharine Hepburn, playing a wealthy socialite on the eve of her wedding, and James Stewart, a tabloid reporter sent to get a scoop on the event, share a drunken (but innocent) midnight swim at her family estate. As he carries her back from the pool in his arms, Mike sings a somewhat garbled "Over the Rainbow" ("*Someday* over the rainbow"). "Don't stop, Mikey," says Tracy groggily. "Keep crooning."

At the time of *The Philadelphia Story*, "Over the Rainbow" was a recent song. By including "Over the Rainbow" as a prominent part of the film's narrative, sung by one character to another, MGM was perhaps offering a tongue-in-cheek salute to a song they had almost cut from *The Wizard of Oz* because it was felt to slow up the action. The transformation of Dorothy's wistful ballad into a drunken serenade in a sophisticated romantic comedy set on Philadelphia's Main Line also makes clear how far and how quickly "Over the Rainbow" had traveled from the world of the original film.

That journey continued when two years later, in 1941, "Over the Rainbow" appeared in the soundtrack of a film noir from 20th Century Fox, *I Wake Up Screaming*. In the movie, a sports promoter (played by Victor Mature) is falsely accused of murdering a young actress. Pursued ruthlessly by a detective who is trying to frame him, he falls in love with the actress's sister (Betty Grable). In a score that is often dissonant, "Over the Rainbow" provides the expressive contrast, appearing frequently at moments that trace the flowering romance between Mature and Grable.

MGM inserted a brief reference to "Over the Rainbow" in one of their best-known animated series, *Tom and Jerry*. In Episode 23, "Springtime for Thomas" from 1946, Tom, who has become besotted with a beautiful, flirtatious she-cat, sings the opening of "Over the Rainbow" wordlessly to himself from inside a trash can.[29]

The closing moments of the 1998 film *You've Got Mail* capture something of what the song has conveyed for much of its later history. Kathleen (Meg Ryan) and Joe (Tom Hanks) meet in Riverside Park in New York, and she realizes tearfully that the man she loves and her email pen pal are one and the same. Harry Nilsson's smooth version of "Over the Rainbow" wafts over the soundtrack as Joe tells Kathleen, "Don't cry, Shopgirl." "I wanted it to be you," she sobs. "I wanted it to be you so badly." Here "Over the Rainbow" expresses hope for fulfillment after struggle, or for the triumph of love over strife. *Per aspera ad astra*—through hardships we reach the stars (or go over the rainbow).

IZ's "Rainbow"

At 3:00 AM one day in 1988, so the story goes, a recording engineer working late in his Honolulu studio received a call from a manager whose client, a singer named Israel Kamakawiwo'ole, wanted to come in right away to record a demo. The engineer was not familiar with Kamakawiwo'ole but reluctantly agreed to make the tape. The recording session was casual, completed in less than twenty minutes. In a high, light tenor voice, accompanying himself on the ukulele, Kamakawiwo'ole sang—and perhaps largely improvised—a medley of "Over the Rainbow" and "What a Wonderful World," a song composed by Bob Thiele and George David Weiss and made popular by Louis Armstrong.[30] The medley, which freely alters the lyrics of both songs, moves over five minutes from "Rainbow" (about two and a half minutes) to "World" (one and a half), and then back to "Rainbow."

The "Rainbow"/"World" medley was released on IZ's 1993 album *Facing Future,* whose cover shows the singer from the back, contemplating a large rainbow (Figure 11.3). "Rainbow"/ "World" became a worldwide hit, the most familiar version of the Arlen-Harburg ballad, and the biggest-selling recording by the Hawaiian artist known as "Bruddah Iz" or simply "IZ" (a nickname we will use here). It has by now sold millions of digital copies. It has spent a record-breaking 392 weeks at or near the top of the *Billboard* World Digital Songs chart.[31] So ubiquitous is it, and so complete is the association between the song and the artist, that today many (perhaps most) people around the world believe that IZ composed the song himself. He did not, of course, though arguably more than anyone who has recorded the song since Garland, IZ has given it a new identity.

IZ's recording of "Over the Rainbow" formed a part of his advocacy for Hawaiian sovereignty. The rainbow is a frequent symbol for Hawaii, found on logos, license plates, and in many advertisements. As the critic Nate Chinen notes,

FIGURE 11.3. Cover for IZ's album *Facing Future* (Mountain Apple Records, 1993).

"Kamakawiwo'ole was someone who had actually resided in a land of rainbows. With his version he managed to make the song both sweeter and sadder, using it not to express longing for a paradise unseen but for a paradise lost, or more precisely, occupied and annexed: an Oz becoming Kansas, right before his eyes."[32]

Over the past decades IZ's "Rainbow" has transcended its Hawaiian roots in ways that he and his producers could scarcely have imagined at the beginning, and it has brought enormous revenue to the producer John de Mello's Mountain Apple Company. IZ's "Over the Rainbow" has been widely licensed for television commercials, where it is used (sometimes with, sometimes without "World") to promote the Norwegian lottery, Dutch health insurance, Austrian sugar, Korean cosmetics, American and Hungarian banks, AT&T cellular services, Rice Krispies, Fiat Croma cars (endorsed by Jeremy Irons), Lynx body spray, and eToys. Although the contexts and intended markets differ widely among these commercials, none references the Hawaiianness of IZ's "Over the Rainbow."

Instead, the song provides an optimistic, feel-good, and occasionally tongue-in-cheek sonic backdrop for the sales pitch.

When IZ's "Rainbow" has appeared in film or on television, it frequently communicates an optimism tinged with sorrow, much like Arlen and Harburg's original song. In the final episode of the first season of *Glee* (2010), Matthew Morrison, playing the glee club director Will Schuester, and Mark Salling, playing the student Puck, sing a cover of IZ's "Rainbow" to console the group after they have lost a regional competition, but also to celebrate their reprieve from having to give up their rehearsal space at the high school.

In the films *Meet Joe Black* (1998) and *Finding Forrester* (2000) IZ's "Rainbow" is associated with death, but also with rebirth or hope. Both are movies with bittersweet endings involving the loss of an older male character (played by Anthony Hopkins and Sean Connery, respectively), but also promising a bright future for younger people they have loved or mentored (the couple Claire Forlani and Brad Pitt, the high school student Rob Brown). In both films, IZ's song appears on the soundtrack at the very end, clearly intended to convey something of this muted optimism.

Perhaps the most powerfully affecting appearance of IZ's "Rainbow," because it fits both the geographic and narrative dimensions of the plot, occurs at the death of the main character Dr. Mark Greene in the long-running television series *ER* (season 8, episode 21, broadcast May 9, 2002). Greene, suffering from an inoperable brain tumor, moves from Chicago to Hawaii, where he had spent happy times in his childhood. As he lies dying on his bed, we hear the ocean waves in the background. His formerly estranged teenage daughter Rachel tells him how she remembers a lullaby that Greene used to sing her. She puts a pair of headphones over his ears. As he smiles and closes his eyes for the last time, IZ's version of "Rainbow" replaces the ocean on the soundtrack. As the song continues for about two minutes, a series of flashbacks alternates with images of Greene lying on his deathbed: Rachel, his current wife Elizabeth and their small baby, and the Chicago hospital where Greene worked. As in the films discussed above, IZ's "Rainbow" carries a double-edged affect in the *ER* segment: sadness and poignancy at Greene's death, but also reassurance that life carries on.

Epilogue: Goodbye, Yellow Brick Road

What the lemon-drop songs and "Over the Rainbow" share is a vision of Oz (or "somewhere") as a place of fulfillment, a place where wishes can be granted and dreams can come true. But as Dorothy and her companions learn, Oz is not utopia. The Scarecrow, Tin Man, and Cowardly Lion learn from the humbugged

Wizard that all along they had the brains, heart, and courage, respectively, that they needed. They demonstrated such virtues when rescuing Dorothy from the Wicked Witch. For her part, Dorothy wants to leave Oz to return home to Kansas. Glinda assures her that she had the power to do so all along.

Oz is a foil to, but not a replacement for, the real world. And if there is any overarching legacy of the songs stretching over eighty years, it is perhaps the idea that however much we dream and hope, we should not give up our home, our roots. This sentiment was expressed most directly some years ago by Bernie Taupin in the lyrics for one of the best-known songs he wrote with Elton John, "Goodbye, Yellow Brick Road" of 1973:

> So goodbye yellow brick road
> Where the dogs of society howl.
> You can't plant me in your penthouse
> I'm going back to my plough.

The yellow brick road has led the protagonist to superficial fulfillment in the "penthouse," among the "dogs of society." But he wants out; he wishes to return to his "plough," to nature, "beyond" the yellow brick road, as he says in the next stanza. We might think of these lyrics, and John's powerful performance, as bitter and pessimistic. But for Taupin and John, as for Dorothy, going "beyond" can also mean a return. The journey on the yellow brick road has changed us; we do not return home the same as we were.

Notes

1. http://www.telegraph.co.uk/news/politics/margaret-thatcher/9993713/Anti-Margaret-Thatcher-song-Ding-Dong-The-Witch-is-Dead-fails-to-reach-number-one.html, accessed July 16, 2017.
2. https://youtu.be/t1RwCTNdX78, accessed July 16, 2017.
3. Material in this chapter has been adapted from parts of Walter Frisch, *Arlen and Harburg's Over the Rainbow* (Oxford: Oxford University Press, 2017).
4. Disk number: RCA 26174.
5. Jazz Records released the complete *Good News* broadcast on CD in 1991 as *Behind the Scenes at the Making of The Wizard of Oz,* J-CD-629.
6. Recording dates are taken from Tom Lord, *The Jazz Discography*, accessed December 31, 2016, http://www.lordisco.com.
7. Decca A[lbum]-74.
8. Joel Whitburn, *Pop Memories 1890–1954* (Menomonee Falls, WI: Record Research, 1986), 85, 114, 170, and 309.

9. Edward Jablonski, *Happy with the Blues* (1961: New York: Da Capo, 1986), 120.

10. https://youtu.be/WI3fVgcumx4, accessed July16, 2017. For data on the recordings of the songs from *The Wizard of Oz* I rely mainly on two comprehensive (but not always overlapping) databases: Tom Lord, *The Jazz Discography,* http://www.lordisco.com, which focuses mainly on jazz instrumentalists and vocalists who perform with them; and SecondHandSongs, https://secondhandsongs.com/, which has a range of mainly pop vocal recordings.

11. Winston S. Churchill, *The Second World War: Abridged Edition with an Epilogue on the Years 1945 to 1957* (1959; London: Bloomsbury, 2013), 386.

12. A recording of this broadcast is held in the Recorded Sound Research Center at the Library of Congress (RGA 3637, track 2). I am grateful to Erica Fedor for her assistance in transcribing the recording.

13. https://youtu.be/v2IkZZmd6RA, accessed July 16, 2017.

14. https://youtu.be/zptYRqFfghU, accessed July 16, 2017.

15. "New Song List Puts 'Rainbow' Way Up High," *CNN Entertainment*, March 7, 2001, http://www.cnn.com/2001/SHOWBIZ/Music/03/07/365.songs/, accessed July 16, 2017.

16. "AFI's 100 Greatest American Movie Music [*sic*]," http://www.afi.com/100Years/songs.aspx, accessed July 16, 2017.

17. https://www.youtube.com/watch?v=iMNtiSvQWyg, accessed July 16, 2017.

18. https://youtu.be/U9u1V2MUUak and https://youtu.be/QcBYpmD29ik, accessed July 16, 2017.

19. Edward Jablonski, *Happy with the Blues*, 121.

20. The television performance, from a Ford Star Jubilee Show, can be seen at https://youtu.be/ss49euDqwHA, accessed July 16, 2017. The Capitol recordings, as well as five other Garland versions of "Over the Rainbow," can be heard on the superb CD set *Judy Garland Sings Harold Arlen,* JSP 4246 (2016).

21. Steven Frank, "What Does It Take to Be a Gay Icon Today?," accessed November 1 2015, http://www.newnownext.com/what-does-it-take-to-be-a-gay-icon-today/09/2007/3/.

22. Richard Dyer, "Judy Garland and Gay Men," in *Heavenly Bodies: Film Stars and Society*, 2nd ed. (London: Routledge, 2004), 148.

23. See http://www.lordisco.com/tjd/TuneDetail?tid=2192 and https://second-handsongs.com/performance/5316, accessed July 16, 20177.

24. Streisand, *One Voice* (Columbia, CK 40788).

25. https://youtu.be/rO-cBiZbTzc, accessed July 16, 2017.

26. https://youtu.be/UIKU3UrDcmI, accessed July 16, 2017.

27. Originally released on Black Lion (E) BLP 30194. See https://youtu.be/tuc3MYjBm2U, accessed July 16, 2017.

28. On CD as Keith Jarrett, *La Scala,* ECM 1640, track 3.

29. See http://www.dailymotion.com/video/x3imrsz at 2:42, accessed July 21, 2017.

30. ABC Records 45-10982 (released October 1967).
31. Billboard, "World Digital Song Sales," accessed July 16, 20177, http://www.billboard.com/biz/charts/world-digital-songs.
32. Nate Chinen, "(Over the) Rainbow Warrior: Israel Kamakawiwo'ole and Another Kind of Somewhere," in *Pop When the World Falls Apart: Music in the Shadow of Doubt*, edited by Eric Weisbard (Durham, NC: Duke University Press, 2012), 178.

ALL THINGS OZ

1900	Publication of the novel *The Wonderful Wizard of Oz* by L. Frank Baum
1902	The first stage musical adaptation of *The Wonderful Wizard of Oz* opens in Chicago, with music by Paul Tietjens
1904	Baum's second novel, *The Marvellous Land of Oz,* is published
1907	Baum publishes another sequel novel entitled *Ozma of Oz*
1908	The fourth novel in the Oz stories appears: *Dorothy and the Wizard of Oz*
1908	Selig Polyscope Company produces a multimedia show, *Fairylogue and Radio-Plays*, based on Baum's original novel
1909	Baum publishes the fifth book in the series: *The Road to Oz*
1910	Another Oz story, *The Emerald City of Oz*, is published by Baum
1910	Selig Polyscope Company produces a short motion picture based on Baum's first novel
1913	Baum's seventh Oz story appears, *The Patchwork Girl of Oz*, with a live-action film adaptation released the following year
1914–1920	Over the next seven years, Baum publishes a further seven novels: *Tik-Tok of Oz; The Scarecrow of Oz; Rinkitink in Oz; The Lost Process of Oz; The Tin Woodman of Oz; The Magic of Oz; Glinda of Oz*
1925	Feature-length silent film of *The Wonderful Wizard of Oz* is produced by Chadwick Pictures, directed by Larry Semon
1928	A theatrical adaptation of *The Wonderful Wizard of Oz* is produced by playwright Elizabeth Fuller Goodspeed
1933	The first animated motion-picture version of the story is produced, directed by Ted Eshbaugh (however, legal problems prevented the film's release)
1939	Metro-Goldwyn-Mayer releases a musical film version of *The Wizard of Oz*, directed by Victor Fleming and starring Judy Garland, Ray Bolger, Jack Haley, Bert Lahr, and Frank Morgan

1942   A stage musical that uses songs from the 1939 film is adapted for the St. Louis Municipal Opera

1960   *The Shirley Temple Show* premieres *The Land of Oz* TV episode, which is based on the second Baum novel

1962   An animated series of short TV episodes (*Tales of the Wizard of Oz*) appears, based on characters from Baum's novels

1964   An animated remodeling of the 1939 film, *Return to Oz*, appears on television

1969   A low-budget children's movie adaptation of *The Marvellous Land of Oz* is released

1974   With music and lyrics by Charlie Smalls, *The Wiz: The Super Soul Musical "Wonderful Wizard of Oz,"* opens in Baltimore, transferring to Broadway the following year

1976   An Australian rock musical film, *Oz: A Rock 'n' Roll Road Movie*, is released

1978   Universal Pictures and Motown Productions release a film adaptation of *The Wiz*, directed by Sidney Lumet and starring Diana Ross and Michael Jackson

1981   A stage musical adaptation of *The Marvelous Land of Oz* opens in Minneapolis and was later filmed for television

1982   Another feature-length anime adaptation of *The Wizard of Oz* is produced for television

1985   Walt Disney Pictures releases *Return to Oz*, an unofficial sequel to the 1939 MGM film that is loosely based on Baum's other novels

1986   A fifty-two-episode anime adaptation commences on television, based on Baum's Oz books

1987   The Royal Shakespeare Company stages a production of *The Wizard of Oz* based on the novel and 1939 film

1990   Another animated series based on the 1939 film is broadcast on ABC and features Dorothy returning to Oz and reuniting with her friends

1995   Gregory Maguire publishes *Wicked: The Life and Times of the Wicked Witch of the West*. Written for adults, the book takes a revisionist look at the land and characters of Oz

2000   A musical stage version of *The Wonderful Wizard of Oz* premieres in Toronto and has had two further revivals in 2002 and 2010

2003   Maguire's 1995 novel is transformed into a stage musical and opens on Broadway: *Wicked: The Untold Story of the Witches in Oz*

2003   A charity special of *EastEnders, OzEnders*, is broadcast on television as a spoof remake of *The Wizard of Oz*

2005   *The Muppets' Wizard of Oz* appears on television

2011   *Tom and Jerry and the Wizard of Oz* is released on Cartoon Network

2011	Andrew Lloyd Webber and Jeremy Sams stage a new musical adaptation of *The Wizard of Oz*, incorporating some new songs
2012	*After the Wizard*, an independently produced film, premieres as a semi-sequel to *The Wizard of Oz*
2013	Walt Disney Pictures releases *Oz the Great and Powerful*, directed by Sam Raimi
2014	An independent fantasy/sci-fi drama film, *OzLand*, inspired by characters and events from Baum's books, appears
2016	The Royal New Zealand Ballet premieres a *Wizard of Oz* ballet using a score created by Francis Poulenc

SELECTED BIBLIOGRAPHY

Alexander, Elizabeth. *The Black Interior*. St. Paul, MN: Graywolf, 2004.

Altman, Rick. *Silent Film Sound*. New York: Columbia University Press, 2004.

Anobile, Richard J. *The Wiz Scrapbook*. New York: Berkley Windhover, 1978.

Askari, Kaveh, Scott Curtis, Frank Gray, Louis Pelletier, Tami Williams, and Joshua Yumibe, eds. *Performing New Media*. New Barnet, UK: John Libbey, 2015.

Auxier, Randall and Phillip Seng. *The Wizard of Oz and Philosophy: Wicked Wisdom of the West*. Chicago, IL: Open Court, 2008.

Baum, Frank Joslyn and Russell P. MacFall. *To Please a Child: A Biography of L. Frank Baum*, Chicago, IL: Reilly & Lee, 1961.

Baum, L. Frank. *The Annotated Wizard of Oz*. Edited by Michael Hearn. New York: W. W. Norton, 1973, 2000.

Baum, L. Frank. *The Wonderful Wizard of Oz*. Burbank, CA: Disney Press, 2013.

Barnes, Clive. "Stage: The Wiz (of Oz): Black Musical Shows Vitality and Style." *New York Times*, January 6, 1975.

Belton, John. "Technology and Aesthetics of Film Sound." In *Film Sound: Theory and Practice*, edited by Elisabeth Weis and John Belton, 63–72. New York: Columbia University Press, 1985.

Brown, William F. and Charlie Smalls. *The Wiz*. Libretto. 1974. Revised and rewritten. New York: Samuel French, 1979.

Bukatman, Scott. *Matters of Gravity: Special Effects and Supermen in the 20th Century*. Durham, NC: Duke University Press, 2003.

Bunch, Ryan. "Oz and the Musical: The American Art Form and the Reinvention of the American Fairy Tale." *Studies in Musical Theatre* 9 (2015): 53–69.

Bunch, Ryan. "You Can't Stop the Tweet: Social Media and Networks of Participation in the Live Television Musical." In *iBroadway: Musical Theatre in the Digital Age*, edited by Jessica Hillman. New York: Palgrave Macmillan, forthcoming.

Burger, Alissa. The Wizard of Oz *as American Myth: A Critical Study of Six Versions of the Story, 1900–2007*. Jefferson, NC: McFarland, 2012.

Caponi, Gena Dagel, ed. *Signifyin(g), Sanctifyin', and Slam Dunking: A Reader in African American Expressive Culture*. Amherst: University of Massachusetts Press, 1999.

Carpenter, Angelica Shirley and Jean Shirley. *L. Frank Baum: Royal Historian of Oz*. Minneapolis, MN: Lerner, 1992.

Clarke, Roger. "Story of the Scene: The Wizard of Oz; Victor Fleming (1939)." *Independent*, June 19, 2008.

Cooke, Mervyn and Fiona Ford, eds. *The Cambridge Companion to Film Music*. Cambridge: Cambridge University Press, 2016.

Crease, Robert. "Divine Frivolity: Hollywood Representations of the Lindy Hop, 1937–1942." In *Representing Jazz*, edited by Gabbard Krin, 207–228. Durham, NC: Duke University Press, 1995.

Curry, Tommy J. "When *The Wiz* Goes Black, Does It Ever Go Back?" In *The Wizard of Oz and Philosophy: Wicked Wisdom of the West*, edited by Randall E. Auxier and Phillip S. Seng, 63–78. Chicago, IL: Open Court, 2008.

Dighe, Ranjit S. *The Historian's Wizard of Oz: Reading L. Frank Baum's Classic as a Political and Monetary Allegory*. Santa Barbara, CA: Praeger, 2002.

Donnelly, K. J. *Occult Aesthetics: Synchronization in Sound Film*. New York: Oxford University Press, 2014.

Donnelly, K. J. *The Spectre of Sound: Music in Film and Television*. London: BFI, 2005.

Du Bois, W. E. B. *The Souls of Black Folk*. 1903; New York: Dover, 1994.

Durand, Kevin K. and Mary K. Leigh. *The Universe of Oz: Essays on Baum's Series and Its Progeny*. Jefferson, NC: McFarland, 2010.

Earle, Neil. The Wonderful Wizard of Oz *in American Popular Culture: Uneasy in Eden*. Lewiston, NY: Edwin Mellen Press, 1993.

Erenberg, Lewis A. *Swinging the Dream: Big Band Jazz and the Rebirth of American Culture*. Chicago, IL: University of Chicago Press, 1998.

Floyd, Samuel A. Jr. *The Power of Black Music: Interpreting Its History from Africa to the United States*. New York: Oxford University Press, 1995.

Ford, Fiona. "Be it [N]ever so Humble? The Narrating Voice in the Underscore to The Wizard of Oz (MGM, 1939)." In *Melodramatic Voices: Understanding Music Drama*, edited by Sarah Hibberd, 197–214. Burlington, VT: Ashgate, 2011.

Fordin, Hugh. *M-G-M's Greatest Musicals: The Arthur Freed Unit*. 1975; New York: Da Capo Press, 1996.

Fordin, Hugh. *The World of Entertainment! Hollywood's Greatest Musicals*. New York: Doubleday, 1975.

Fricke, John. *Judy: A Legendary Film Career*. Philadelphia, PA: Running Press, 2011.

Fricke, John, Jay Scarfone, and William Stillman. "*The Wizard of Oz*": *The Official 50th Anniversary Pictorial History*. New York: Warner Books, 1989.

Fricke, John and Jonathan Shirshekan. *The Wizard of Oz: An Illustrated Companion to the Timeless Movie Classic*. New York: Sterling, 2009.

Gates, Henry Louis Jr. *The Signifying Monkey: A Theory of African-American Literary Criticism*. New York: Oxford University Press, 1988.

Gilroy, Paul. *The Black Atlantic: Modernity and Double Consciousness*. Cambridge, MA: Harvard University Press, 1993.

Green, Stanley. *The World of Musical Comedy*. 4th ed. New York: Da Capo Press, 1980.

Greene, David L. and Dick Martin. *The Oz Scrapbook*. New York: Random House, 1967.

Griswold, Jerry. "There's No Place but Home: The Wizard of Oz." *Antioch Review* 45, no. 4 (1987): 462–475.

Gunning, Tom. "The Cinema of Attraction: Early Film, Its Spectator, and the Avant-Garde." In *The Cinema of Attractions Reloaded*, edited by Wanda Strauven, 381–388. Amsterdam: Amsterdam University Press, 2006.

Hansen, Bradley A. "The Fable of the Allegory: The Wizard of Oz in Economics." *Journal of Economic Education* 33, no. 3 (2002): 254–264.

Hansen, Linda. "Experiencing the World as Home: Reflections on Dorothy's Quest in 'The Wizard of Oz.'" *Soundings: An Interdisciplinary Journal* 67, no. 1 (1984): 91–102.

Harburg, Ernie and Harold Meyerson. *Who Put the Rainbow in the Wizard of Oz?* Ann Arbor: University of Michigan Press, 1993.

Harmetz, Aljean. *The Making of The Wizard of Oz*. Chicago, IL: Chicago Review Press, 1977.

Harper, Ken. Papers. Billy Rose Theatre Division, New York Public Library for the Performing Arts.

Hazzard-Gordon, Katrina. *Jookin': The Rise of Social Dance Formations in African American Culture*. Philadelphia: Temple Press, 1990.

Hearn, Michael Patrick. *The Annotated* The Wonderful Wizard of Oz. New York: W. W. Norton, 1973.

Hearn, Michael Patrick. "Discovering Oz (the Great and Terrible) at the Library of Congress." *Quarterly Journal of the Library of Congress* 39, no. 2 (1982): 70–79.

Hearn, Michael Patrick. *Introduction to* The Wizard of Oz: *The Screenplay*. New York: Delta, 1989.

Hearn, Michael Patrick and L. Frank Baum. *The Annotated Wizard of Oz*. Centennial Edition. New York: W. W. Norton, 2000.

hooks, bell. "Postmodern Blackness." *Postmodern Culture* 1, no. 1 (1990): 1–7.

Horrigan, Patrick E. *Widescreen Dreams: Growing Up Gay at the Movies*. Madison: University of Wisconsin Press, 1999.

Hubbard, Karen. "Social Dancing at the Savoy." In *Ballroom, Boogie, Shimmy Sham Shake: A Social and Popular Dance Reader*. Chicago: University of Illinois Press, 2009.

Hunter, Tera W. *Joy My Freedom: Southern Black Women's Lives and Labors after the Civil War*. Cambridge, MA: Harvard University Press, 1997.

Jablonski, Edward. *Harold Arlen: Happy with the Blues*. Boston, MA: Da Capo Press, 1986.

Jablonski, Edward. *Harold Arlen: Rhythm, Rainbows, and Blues*. Boston: Northeastern University Press, 1996.

Jones, Barbara. "The Wizard of Oz," *The Enchanted Manor*, blog. August 25, 2015. http://theenchantedmanor.com/tag/over-the-rainbow-song/.

Kael, Pauline. "Saint Dorothy." *New Yorker*, September 30, 1978.

Kalem, T. E. "The Theatre: Jumping Jivernacular." *Time*, January 20, 1975.

King, Susan. "How Did 'Wizard of Oz' Fare on Its 1939 Release?' *Los Angeles Times*, March 11, 2013.

Kmi, Helen M. "Strategic Credulity: Oz as Mass Cultural Parable." *Cultural Critique* 33 (1996): 213–233.

Knapp, Raymond. *The American Musical and the Performance of Personal Identity*. Princeton, NJ: Princeton University Press, 2006.

Koblin, John. "*The Wiz Live!* Scores Strong Ratings," *New York Times*, December 4, 2015.

Kroll, Jack. "*Oz* with Soul." *Newsweek*, January 20, 1975, 55.

Kroll, Jack. "Under the Rainbow." *Newsweek*, October 30, 1978.

Langley, Noel, Florence Ryerson, and Edgar Allan Woolf. *The Wizard of Oz: The Screenplay*. Edited by Michael Patrick Hearn. New York: Delta, 1989.

Laird, Paul. *Wicked: A Musical Biography*. Lanham, MD: Scarecrow Press, 2011.

Leach, William. *Land of Desire: Merchants, Power, and the Rise of a New American Culture*. New York: Vintage Books, 1993.

Littlefield, Henry. "The Wizard of Ox: Parable on Populism." *American Quarterly* 16, no. 1 (1964): 27–58.

Loncraine, Rebecca. *The Real Wizard of Oz: The Life and Times of L. Frank Baum*. New York: Gotham Books, 2009.

London, Justin. "Leitmotifs and Musical Reference in the Classical Score." In *Music and Cinema*, edited by James Buhler, Caryl Flinn, and David Neumeyer, 85–98. Hanover, NH: Wesleyan University Press, 2000.

MacDonell, Francis, "'The Emerald City was the New Deal': E. Y. Harburg and *The Wonderful Wizard of Oz*." *Journal of American Culture* 13, no. 4 (1990): 71–75.

MacKenzie, Annah E. "From Screen to Shining Screen: *The Wizard of Oz* in the Age of Mechanical Reproduction." In *The Fantastic Made Visible*, edited by Matthew William Kapell and Ace G. Pilkington, 175–191. Jefferson, NC: McFarland, 2015.

Malone, Jacqui. *Steppin' on the Blues: The Visible Rhythms of African American Dance*. Chicago: University of Illinois, 1996.

Manning, Frankie and Cynthia R. Millman. *Frankie Manning: Ambassador of Lindy Hop*. Philadelphia: Temple University Press, 2007.

Maultsby, Portia K. "Soul." In *African American Music: An Introduction*, edited by Mellonee V. Burnim and Portia K. Maultsby, 271–289. New York: Routledge, 2006.

McClelland, Doug. *Down the Yellow Brick Road: The Making of "The Wizard of Oz."* New York: Pyramid, 1976.

McCurdy, Michael, Ray Bradbury, and L. Frank Baum. *The Wonderful Wizard of Oz: The Kansas Centennial Edition.* Lawrence: University Press of Kansas, 1999.

Menten, Theodore. *The Wizard of Oz: Postcard Book.* New York: Courier Dover, 1986.

Mercer, Kobena. *Welcome to the Jungle: New Positions in Black Cultural Studies.* New York: Routledge, 1994.

Miller, Norma and Evette Jensen. *Swingin' at the Savoy: A Memoir of a Jazz Dancer.* Philadelphia: Temple University Press, 1996.

Mitchell-Kernan, Claudia. "Signifying, Loud-Talking, and Marking." In *Signifyin(g), Sanctifyin', and Slam Dunking: A Reader in African American Expressive Culture*, edited by Gena Degal Caponi, 309–330. Amherst: University of Massachusetts Press, 1999.

Mordden, Ethan. "I Got a Song." *New Yorker*, October 22, 1990.

Mueller, John. *Astaire Dancing—The Musical Films of Fred Astaire.* New York: Alfred A. Knopf, 1985.

Nathanson, Paul. *Over the Rainbow: "The Wizard of Oz" as a Secular Myth of America.* Albany: State University of New York Press, 1991.

Neal, Mark Anthony. *Soul Babies: Black Popular Culture and the Post-Soul Aesthetic.* New York: Routledge, 2002.

Pacheco, Patrick. "The Wiz." *After Dark*, March 1975.

Paulin, Scott. "'Cinematic' Music: Analogies, Fallacies, and the Case of Debussy." *Music and the Moving Image* 3, no. 1 (2010): 1–21.

Platte, Nathan. "Nostalgia, the Silent Cinema, and the Art of Quotation in Herbert Stothart's Score for *The Wizard of Oz* (1939)." *Journal of Film Music* 4, no. 1 (2011): 45–64.

Powell, Martin and Jorge Break. *The Wizard of Oz: Graphic Novel.* London: Stone Arch Books, 2010.

Ramsey, Guthrie. *Race Music: Black Cultures from Bebop to Hip-Hop.* Berkeley: University of California Press, 2003.

Rogers, Katherine M. *L. Frank Baum: Creator of Oz.* Boston, MA: Da Capo Press, 2003.

Rollins, Bryant. "Does 'The Wiz' Say Something Extra to Blacks?" *New York Times*, December 28, 1975.

Reed, Rex. "The Wiz." *New York Sunday News*, January 12, 1975, 6.

Richards, Stanley, ed. *Great Rock Musicals.* New York: Stein and Day, 1979.

Ritter, Gretchen. "Silver Slippers and a Golden Cap: L. Frank Baum's 'The Wonderful Wizard of Oz' and Historical Memory in American Politics." *Journal of American Studies* 31, no. 2 (1997): 171–202.

Rockoff, Hugh. "'The "Wizard of Oz" as a Monetary Allegory." *Journal of Political Economy* 98, no. 4 (1990): 739–760.

Rodman, Ronald. "'There's No Place Like Home': Tonal Closure and Design in The Wizard of Oz." *Indiana Theory Review* 19 (Spring/Fall 1998): 125–144.

Rogers, Katherine. *L. Frank Baum: Creator of Oz.* New York: St. Martin's Press, 2002.

Rosar, William. "Stravinsky and MGM." In *Film Music 1*, edited by Clifford McCarty, 109–121. New York: Garland, 1989.

Rozenkrantz, Timme. *Harlem Jazz Adventures: A European Baron's Memoir 1934–1969.* Lanham, MD: Scarecrow Press, 2012.

Rushdie, Salman. *The Wizard of Oz.* London: British Film Institute, 2012.

Saunders, Vicci Lovette. "Dorothy and the Boyz: Race Education of the American Movie Ticket Buyer." *Journal of Black Studies* 38, no. 4 (2008): 622–649.

Scarfone, Jay and William Stillman. *The Wizard of Oz Collector's Treasury.* Atglen, PA: Schiffer, 1992.

Scarfone, Jay and William Stillman. *The Wizard of Oz: The Official 75th Anniversary Companion.* London: HarperCollins, 2013.

Scarfone, Jay and William Stillman. *The Wizardry of Oz: The Artistry and Magic of the 1939 MGM Classic.* New York: Applause Theatre and Cinema Books, 2004.

Schatz, Thomas. *The Genius of the System: Hollywood Filmmaking in the Studio Era.* 1989; New York: Henry Holt, 1996.

Scheuer, Timothy E. *Music and Mythmaking in Film: Genre and the Role of the Composer.* Jefferson, NC: McFarland, 2005.

Scott, Jesse. "The Black Interior, Reparations and African American Masculinity in *The Wiz.*" In *Pimps, Wimps, Studs, Thugs and Gentlemen*, edited by Elwood Watson. Jefferson, NC: McFarland, 2009.

Sherman, Fraser A. *The Wizard of Oz Catalogue.* Jefferson, NC: McFarland, 2005.

Singalong Version of *The Wizard of Oz*, 2 disk special edition DVD, Turner Entertainment, 2009.

Smith, Sid. "'The Wiz' Works Wonders to Put Its Controversy Aside." *Chicago Tribune*, January 29, 1987.

"Some Like It Lukewarm." Episode No. 56 of *The Monkees*. NBC, March 4, 1968.

"Special Editorial Part II: Now, It's the Drama Critics." *New Amsterdam News*, January 11, 1975.

Sragow, Michael *Victor Fleming: An American Movie Master.* New York: Pantheon Books 2008.

Stasio, Marilyn. "Witty Wiz." *Cue Magazine*, 1975.

Stearns, Marshall and Jean Stearns. *Jazz Dance.* New York: Macmillan, 1994.

Stevens, Tamara and Erin Stevens. *Swing Dancing.* Santa Barbara, CA: Greenwood, 2011.

Stothart, Herbert. "Film Music." In *Behind the Screen: How Films Are Made*, edited by Stephen Watts, 139–146. London: Arthur Barker, 1938.

Swartz, Mark Evan. *Oz before the Rainbow: L. Frank Baum's the Wonderful Wizard of Oz on Stage and Screen to 1939.* Baltimore, MD: Johns Hopkins University Press, 2000.

Taraborrelli, J. Randy. *Diana Ross: A Biography.* New York: Citadel Press, 2007.

Thomas, Bob and Fred Astaire. *Astaire the Man, the Dancer.* Sydney: Collins, 1985.

Tuerk, Richard. *Oz in Perspective: Magic and Myth in the L. Frank Baum Books.* Jefferson, NC: McFarland, 2007.

Turnock, Julie A. *Plastic Reality: Special Effects, Technology, and the Emergence of 1970s Blockbuster Aesthetics.* New York: Columbia University Press, 2015.

Verini, Bob. "Review: 'The Wiz.'" *Variety,* October 12, 2006.

Warwick, Jacqueline. "You Can't Win Child, but You Can't Get Out of the Game: Michael Jackson's Transition from Child Star to Superstar." *Popular Music and Society* 35, no. 2 (2012): 241–259.

Watson, Sonny. "Streetswings Dance History Archives: Jitterbug." *Sonny Watson's Streetswing.com.* http://www.streetswing.com/histmain/z3jtrbg.htm.

Watt, Douglas. "Fine Cast and Splendid Look in 'Wiz.'" *New York Daily News,* January 6, 1975.

White, Robert. "RIP Ray Hirsch, Great So-Cal 'Swing' Dancer." *Swungover* blog, September 1, 2015. https://swungover.wordpress.com/2015/09/01/r-i-p-ray-hirsch-great-so-cal-swing-dancer/, accessed November 15, 2016.

Williams, Mance. *Black Theatre in the 1960s and 1970s: A Historical-Critical Analysis of the Movement.* Westport, CT: Greenwood Press, 1985.

Williams, Rhonda. "*The Wiz*: American Culture at Its Best." In *The Universe of Oz: Essays on Baum's Series and Its Progeny,* edited by Kevin K. Durand and Lary K. Leigh, 191–199. Jefferson, NC: McFarland, 2010.

Willis, Artemis. "'Marvelous and Fascinating': L. Frank Baum's *Fairylogue and Radio-Plays* (1908)." In *Performing New Media,* edited by Kaveh Askari et al. Indianapolis: Indiana University Press, 2014.

The Wiz. On Blu-ray. Directed by Sydney Lumet. 1978; Universal City: Universal Studios Home Entertainment, 2010.

The Wiz Collection, Manuscripts, Archives, and Rare Books Division, Schomburg Center for Research in Black Culture, New York Public Library.

Wolf, Stacy. *Changed for Good: A Feminist History of the Broadway Musical.* New York: Oxford University Press, 2011.

Wolf, Stacy. "'Defying Gravity': Queer Conventions in the Musical 'Wicked.'" *Theatre Journal* 60, no. 1 (2008): 1–21.

Woll, Allen. *Black Musical Theatre: From Coontown to Dreamgirls.* 1989; New York: Da Capo Press, 1991.

Zank, Ronald. "'Come Out, Come Out, Wherever You Are': How Tina Landau's *1969* Stages a Queer Reading of *The Wizard of Oz*." In *The Universe of Oz: Essays on Baum's Series and Its Progeny,* edited by Kevin K. Durand and Mary K. Leigh, 61–76. Jefferson, NC: McFarland, 2010.

Zipes, Jack. *Fairy Tale as Myth/Myth as Fairy Tale.* Lexington: University Press of Kentucky, 1994.

INDEX